AF247469

The Creation of the
Local Authority Sector
of Higher Education

The Creation of the Local Authority Sector of Higher Education

P R Sharp

The Falmer Press

(A member of the Taylor and Francis Group)
London and Philadelphia

UK   The Falmer Press, Falmer House, Barcombe, Lewes, East Sussex, BN8 5DL

USA   The Falmer Press, Taylor & Francis Inc., 242 Cherry Street, Philadelphia, PA 19106-1906

First published 1987

Library of Congress Cataloging in Publication Data

Library of Congress Catalog Number: 86-83076

ISBN 1-85000-176-6
ISBN 1-85000-183-9 (pbk.)

Jacket design by Caroline Archer

Typeset in 11/13 Bembo by
Imago Publishing Ltd, Thame, Oxon

Printed in Great Britain by Taylor & Francis (Printers) Ltd, Basingstoke

Contents

List of Abbreviations

AFE	Advanced Further Education
AFEC	Advanced Further Education Committee
ACSTT	Advisory Council on the Supply and Training of Teachers
ATO	Area Training Organization
ACFHE	Association of Colleges of Further and Higher Education
ACC	Association of County Councils
AEC	Association of Education Committees
AMA	Association of Metropolitan Authorities
AMC	Association of Municipal Corporations
APC	Association of Principals of Colleges
APT	Association of Polytechnic Teachers
ATCDE	Association of Teachers in Colleges and Departments of Education
ATTI	Association of Teachers in Technical Institutions
AUT	Association of University Teachers
CEO	Chief/County Education Officer
CAT	College of Advanced Technology
CEGC	College of Education Grants Committee
CDP	Committee of Directors of Polytechnics
CVCP	Committee of Vice-Chancellors and Principals
CID	Conference of Institute of Directors
CLEA	Council for Local Education Authorities
CNAA	Council for National Academic Awards
CCA	County Councils Association
DES	Department of Education and Science
LAHEC	Local Authority Higher Education Committee
LEA	Local Education Authority
LUCFO	Leeds University Central Filing Office
LUIE	Leeds University Institute of Education

NAB	National Advisory Body
NACTST	National Advisory Council on the Training and Supply of Teachers
NATFHE	National Association of Teachers in Further and Higher Education
NUS	National Union of Students
NUT	National Union of Teachers
PGC	Polytechnics Grant Committee
RAC	Regional Advisory Council
SPERTT	Society for the Promotion of Educational Reform through Teacher Training
SCRAC	Standing Conference of Regional Advisory Councils
TES	Times Educational Supplement
THES	Times Higher Education Supplement
UCET	Universities Council for the Education of Teachers
UGC	University Grants Committee
WUMRC	Warwick University Modern Record Centre

Chronology of Events in the Evolution of the Local Authority Sector of Higher Education*

October 1963   Robbins Report on Higher Education.

February 1964   Creation of CNAA.

December 1964   Government announcement on the future of Colleges of Education.

April 1965   Crosland's Woolwich speech on binary policy.

March 1966   Weaver Study Group Report on College Governing Bodies.

May 1966   Government White Paper: A Plan for Polytechnics and Other Colleges.

January 1967   Crosland's Lancaster speech on binary policy.

May 1968   Creation of the Pooling Committee.

August 1968   Education (No. 2) Act. Legislation on College Governing Bodies.

January 1972   James Report on Teacher Training.

July 1972   Creation of the Local Authority Higher Education Committee.

December 1972   Government White Paper: *Education: A Framework for Expansion*.

March 1973   DES Circular 7/73 *Development of Higher Education in Non-University Sector*.

April 1974   Local Government Reorganization.

March 1978   Oakes Report on *The Management of Higher Education in the Maintained Sector*.

July 1980   Education Act including provisions to 'cap' the AFE Pool.

---

* This table includes the formal events normally regarded as landmarks in the development of local authority higher education. The text argues that rather lesser known happenings and considerations were often as important as these prominent milestones.

October 1980	Select Committee Report on the Funding and Organization of Courses in Higher Education.
July 1981	DES: *Higher Education in England outside the Universities: Policy, Funding and Management.*
January 1982	Creation of the National Advisory Body (NAB).

Introduction

This study is an analysis of the creation and development of the local authority sector of higher education from the early 1960s to the 1980s. It is essentially a survey of educational policy-making and decision-making in England at the national level. It assesses the relative importance and influence on policy of key interest groups and of individual personalities. The roles of the Department of Education and Science, the major political parties, the local authority associations and the college teachers' unions are all considered. Well-known ministers such as Edward Boyle, Anthony Crosland, Shirley Williams and Margaret Thatcher figure prominently as do senior civil servants including Herbert Andrew, William Pile and Toby Weaver. Before 1974 and the demise of the AEC, William Alexander played a key part in the leadership of the local authority associations on these issues, and college teachers' union leaders such as Edward Britton, Eric Robinson and Stanley Hewett, were all involved.

It is hoped that this book will shed new light in two main areas. Firstly, the study attempts to identify those really responsible for creating the local authority sector of higher education and reconsiders how and why it was done. Secondly, it attempts to place the problems facing contemporary local authority higher education into their recent historical perspective. In many respects the most basic, and perhaps most intractable, issues still facing the sector are those which have dogged it since its creation.

It should be remembered that local authorities have been involved with higher education over a remarkably long period. Very soon after the county and county borough councils were created in 1888, they were granted permissive powers to aid technical education under the Technical Instruction Act of 1889 and the following year the Local Taxation (Customs and Excise) Act provided them with central government funds to carry out this task. In practice the term technical instruction was interpreted widely, and several local authorities began to give grants to the developing university colleges. During the 1890s some of these colleges became heavily dependent on local authority support, for example, the Yorkshire College, Leeds and Firth College, Sheffield, both received over one-quarter of their annual recurrent income in grants from their neighbouring local authorities.[1] In the same period municipal technical colleges (sometimes the successors of earlier initiatives taken by mechanics' institutes) were built up with the newly-available funds, and by the end of the century a number of these institutions were providing at least some advanced instruction in scientific and technical subjects usually on a part-time basis. In Manchester, for example, the technical school passed from private to municipal ownership in 1892.[2] Large new premises with the very latest equipment were opened in 1902 when the institution was renamed the Manchester Municipal School of Technology. This was short-lived, for in 1904 it became the Faculty of Technology of Manchester University. Although there were a number of full-time students following degree courses in this Faculty, for some years it was dominated by part-time non-advanced students and retained strong links with local industries. The local authorities' contribution (particularly their financial aid) to the development of the civic universities should not be underestimated, and this contribution continued well into the twentieth century. In the 1920s Leeds and Sheffield universities were still receiving over one-quarter of their recurrent income from local authority grants, and, excluding Oxford and Cambridge, at a national level the local authorities' contributions consistently amounted to over 10 per cent of recurrent costs.[3] These proportions declined slightly in the 1930s and the 1940s, but it was not until the 1950s and 1960s that local authority grants to English universities lost their importance. Although the local authorities exercised comparatively little influence over university policy in the first half of the twentieth century, their financial contribution was, more often than is normally recognized, crucial to the development of some of the institutions concerned.

The Education Act of 1902 gave the local authorities further duties in the field of post-elementary education. From this time they were empowered to establish their own teacher training colleges. A few progressive local education authorities moved quickly into this field although the majority did not take steps to set up their own colleges. By the early 1920s twenty-two local education authority colleges had been established, but the relatively low demand for teachers in the inter-war years prevented further growth. The voluntary bodies still provided more than twice as many colleges as this (approximately fifty), and the relative importance of the churches and the LEAs in the supply of trained teachers remained comparatively constant from the early 1920s until the end of the Second World War.

From the mid-1940s, with the post-war teacher shortage, the situation changed dramatically. The local authorities bore the brunt of the expansion of teacher training, and by 1962 they provided ninety-eight (including many of the largest) of the 146 colleges. In 1960 the length of the training course was extended from two to three years and a projected fall in the demand for teachers did not materialize. Thus, through their teacher training colleges, the local authorities were making an important and increasingly large contribution to national provisions for higher education.

During the same period, local authority commitments in advanced further education grew by similar proportions. It has been estimated that about 6000 full-time students attended advanced courses in the further education sector in 1938–39,[4] and although there were, without doubt, considerably more taking such courses on a part-time basis, it is clear that advanced further education remained a very small part of the local education service. The considerably increased provision for advanced further education in the post-war years is shown in table 1.

Table 1: Students on advanced courses in the local authority sector in England and Wales

	Full-time	*Part-time*
1951–2*	13,000	28,000
1962–3†	27,000	94,000
1962–3‡	37,000	103,000

* Excluding art colleges.
† Excluding CATs.
‡ Including CATs. By 1962–3 the CATs were direct grant institutions recently removed from the local authority sector.

The expansion of advanced work had transformed some of the further education institutions. Their pre-war municipal technical college roots were increasingly remote from their current concerns. In 1956 the Ministry of Education institutionalized the differences between colleges when it introduced four categories 'to facilitate a national distribution of resources'.[5] These categories were: colleges of advanced technology (CATs), regional colleges, area colleges and local colleges. All except the local colleges were involved with advanced courses to some extent. The ten CATs and the twenty-five regional colleges were heavily committed to this work, and, although the CATs had more postgraduate courses and research, it was not possible to draw a sharp dividing line between the two categories in educational terms. There were 160 area colleges where lower level work predominated, but they made a very substantial contribution to the part-time advanced work of the sector. Not long after the designation of the

CATs, pressure mounted, not least because of the cost of providing these major institutions, to remove them from local authority control and give them direct grant status. This was implemented in 1962, but it proved to be only an interim arrangement as the colleges were granted university status, with almost universal approval, soon after the Robbins Committee reported. Although there was little concerted or overt local authority opposition to their loss of the CATs, it made local authority leaders reflect upon the future role of their sector in the provision of higher education generally. During the 1940s and 1950s 'university' was still commonly used as a synonym for higher education, and, if considered at all, further education and teacher training colleges were regarded as overspill institutions. These colleges had just expanded to meet the increased demand for places. There were no notions of a binary structure for higher education with the local authority institutions providing an alternative to the universities. The LEAs themselves did not see potential unity in their institutions regarding advanced courses in technical colleges and teacher training as two distinct and disparate activities. In the 1940s and 1950s successive governments were dominated in the higher education field by the need to increase the supply of places. Industry, teaching and the people themselves demanded expansion. From the early 1960s powerful leaders in the educational system began to stress that the supply of places could not be divorced from questions of structure, control, organization and funding. In many ways it has been these latter issues, along with student numbers, which have dominated higher education from the 1960s to the 1980s.

Notes

1 Sharp P R, 'Finance', in Taylor A J and Gosden P H J H, *Studies in the History of a University*, (1975), p. 93.
2 Short P J, 'The municipal school of technology and the university', in Cardwell D S L, *From Artisan to Graduate*, (1974), pp. 157–64.
3 Sharp P R, (1975), *op. cit.*, p. 121.
4 Robbins Report, p. 15.
5 *Ibid.*, p. 30.

Chapter 1

The Nadir of Local Authority Influence: The Robbins Report

In November 1960 the Conservative Government announced its intention to set up an enquiry into the development of higher education. The Ministry of Education soon made it clear that this Committee of Enquiry, to be chaired by Professor L C Robbins, was not to be directly representative of interested bodies but would be composed of 'knowledgeable people appointed as individuals'.[1] Although the local authority associations did not dissent from these arrangements,[2] several LEAs were clearly displeased when the composition of the Robbins Committee was announced. They were particularly aggrieved that only one of the twelve members, Harold Shearman, Chairman of the London County Council Education Committee, was a 'local authority' person. The Yorkshire Association of Education Committees protested to the Minister about the lack of local authority association representation, and Alec Clegg of the West Riding wrote privately to William Alexander, Secretary of the AEC, thus,

> The constitution of the Committee would tend to make one believe that it is already accepted that not only the CATs and the training colleges but some of the lesser colleges of technology are going to be handed over lock stock and barrel to a body or authority which is going to administer higher education as such and nobody is going to raise any objections.[3]

Alexander assured Clegg that he shared his concern that the liaison between the schools and the establishments of further and higher education should be strengthened rather than weakened[4], and added that this would be kept in mind when the AEC prepared its evidence for Robbins.

In their evidence to Robbins the AMC and the CCA maintained that local authorities should continue to control their training colleges and higher education courses in technical colleges, but Alexander of the AEC, preferring attack to defence, proposed the development of a much more clearly defined local authority sector of higher education.[5] Alexander suggested that institutions of higher education should be divided into two sectors. The first would concentrate on honours degree teaching, postgraduate work and research, whereas the second would be largely concerned with teaching at pass or ordinary degree level. Alexander expected the first sector to be based on the existing universities and the promoted CATs, and it was to be administered through the UGC or a similar body. The second sector, which was to include former teacher training and further education colleges, was to be administered by regional councils. Alexander maintained that there would be difficulties if this sector was directly controlled by 146 different LEAs. He proposed that the regional councils should be constituted from 'representatives of local education authorities in the region, together with other persons representative of appropriate industrial, commercial and educational interests'. The regional councils were to receive grants from the Ministry of Education and would also obtain money by precepting on local education authorities, or, if it were felt necessary, by raising a direct levy on the people in the area in the form of a higher education rate or tax. Alexander stressed that he saw this proposal as a means of keeping local government in higher education despite the fact that individual LEAs would no longer participate directly. In the same memorandum radical proposals were also put forward for the future of teacher training. According to Alexander's scheme intending teachers were to receive education and training lasting for four years. Initially students were to follow three-year degree courses (honours or pass) in one of the two sectors of higher education. All intending teachers would then go on to one-year professional training courses in special centres. These professional training centres were to be established and administered by the regional councils, and they were to replace the existing area training organizations (the university institutes of education).

In January 1962 Alexander put these ideas to the Sub-committee on the Pattern of Training of the National Advisory Council on the Training and Supply of Teachers (NACTST).[6] He stressed that there was a need for new degree courses, but doubted whether it would be in the best interests of these courses or the institutions which provided them if the academic approach characteristic of the universities was adopted. He maintained that in the future the training colleges' affinity should lie with institutions of higher education in the maintained sector rather than with the universities. Alexander also mentioned that the institutes of education lacked influence in their dealings with the universities and argued that they should be replaced by stronger institutions of professional training.

Other local authority representatives on the Sub-committee, especially Sir Lionel Russell[7], gave Alexander some support. W F Houghton[8] made it clear, however, that he did not wish to be committed to the concept of regional organization or to the creation of a clear-cut hierarchy of institutions.[9] For the Ministry, P R Odgers said he had always thought that the institutes might provide a basis for future development and wondered whether it would be sensible to adopt a rigid policy which made it necessary to break the link between the training colleges and the universities.[10] Later Russell contended that an administrative separation of the colleges from the universities did not imply that the former could no longer benefit from close academic contact with the latter.[11]

The main opposition to Alexander came, predictably, from the representatives of the institutes of education. Professor W R Niblett of Leeds University thought that it would be disastrous if teachers, in contrast with members of other professions, found themselves divorced from the influence of the universities[12], but the intensity of this opposition was not revealed until the Sub-committee's report was considered by the full Council. At this juncture Professor B S Morris of Bristol University wrote a note of dissent which questioned the whole basis of Alexander's scheme. Morris argued that the new institutions proposed would be inferior to the universities, and he did not believe that 'degree-giving institutions which are neither universities nor institutions (however named) of university standing'[13] should be created. He mentioned that the Sub-committee had proposed a dual system of higher education which would 'create the same types of problem as the dual system of secondary education does now'.[14] He asked members of the Council to consider 'Do we, in fact, want to perpetuate at a higher level a situation analagous to that which obtains between grammar and secondary modern schools within the secondary system?'[15] Russell and Houghton responded that Morris had misunderstood the proposals. They did not envisage a rigid structure in which institutions other than universities were regarded as inferior, but a multiple rather than a dual system which gave maximum flexibility.[16] These assurances did not allay the fears of the representatives of the institutes. According to Morris, Alexander's supporters learned too much from his first note of dissent and they consequently toned down some of their memorandum.[17] He alleged that 'their mouths are now full of pious words' and 'the redrafting has served further to conceal the main intentions . . . . Nevertheless, sufficient of the cloven hoof appears for us to call their bluff'.[18] The representatives of the institutes sent a further note of dissent[19] to the Council, and sought to organize continued opposition through their national association, the Conference of Institute Directors (CID). The majority of the members of NACTST, however, were not convinced, and Alexander's ideas were incorporated into the Council's Eighth Report.

At its meeting on 16 March 1962 CID considered a forthright paper from Professor M V C Jeffreys of Birmingham University. This claimed:

> The memorandum submitted to the Robbins Committee by the AEC makes it quite clear that the local authority interests are making a bid for a predominant control of a large sector of higher education. What seems to be happening is that LEAs, realizing that they can no longer keep their *individual* control of institutions of higher education (for example, the development of the CATs) will make great efforts to secure for the LEAs acting in regional groups, plus the Ministry of Education, the major control of as much of higher education as possible. Thus the LEAs *appear* to be giving something away (the CATs) in order to get more back.
>
> I doubt whether the Vice-Chancellors have really seen this situation, and I think we ought to draw their attention to the AEC's proposal for regional councils, with degree-granting powers, and to the proposals for regional ATOs detached from universities. If a large sector of higher education were to pass into the control of LEAs and the Ministry, the universities would find themselves out on a limb, and might in the end have to go the same way. (There is evidence that *both* the main political parties might favour such a development.)
>
> Do the universities really want to see this happen? If not, what is the alternative? Only a much bolder and more progressive policy on the part of the universities, affirming their readiness to take ultimate responsibility for the work of a whole range of institutions of higher education. In the long run there is probably a clear choice for the universities — to go forward or to go back.[20]

CID accepted Jeffreys' diagnosis, but there were doubts expressed about how these ideas could be presented to the educational world generally and to the Vice-Chancellors in particular. Professor Niblett reported that

> Sir Charles Morris had given some indication that the Vice-Chancellors disliked the idea of universities becoming responsible, even academically, for a whole range of institutions in higher education on the grounds that, inevitably, the government of a country had to control the supply of technically-trained people and it would not, therefore, be easy for universities to maintain their academic freedom.[21]

Several members felt that the universities would be very reluctant to take on any additional financial responsibility, and others that, although Vice-Chancellors might feel some concern for their institutes of education, there was great danger in suggesting that they should assume wider educational responsibilities. In essence members of CID feared that the Vice-Chancellors might have sympathy for the view expressed by Sir Lionel Russell[22] that it would not be in the interests of the universities themselves to assume responsibility for the whole field of higher education at a time of rapid expansion. It was clear, for example, that J S Fulton, Chairman of NACTST and a Vice-Chancellor himself, attached importance to this consideration and argued in favour of the majority view in NACTST before the Robbins Committee a little later in the year. He predicted that the new higher educational institutions in the maintained sector might produce 'some remarkable people for the service of the country' and felt that the end result could be 'very exciting'.[23]

One group from which CID might have expected strong support was the Association of Teachers in Colleges and Departments of Education (ATCDE). There can be no doubt that in general ATCDE supported the development of the association between the colleges and the universities in the institutes of education.[24] ATCDE, however, was very disappointed by the universities' attitude to the provision of degree courses for training college students. In 1961 ATCDE suggested to the Committee of Vice-Chancellors and Principals (CVCP) that a new kind of university degree obtainable in two years by students who had completed a three-year training college course should be introduced, but this was given a cool reception. Some universities expressed a willingness to exempt ex-training college students from part of the requirements of an existing degree course, but in the early 1960s the universities clearly lacked enthusiasm for developments in this field. Indeed, CVCP witnesses before the Robbins Committee were told that their proposals on this matter were the most modest which had been received.[25] In these circumstances ATCDE was frustrated by the universities and felt that it had a better chance of obtaining degree facilities for its students in the proposed local authority sector of higher education. Consequently, the representatives of ATCDE on NACTST did not join those of CID in their note of dissent. According to J D Browne, ATCDE did not object to experiments with a federal system in the maintained sector as long as these did not interfere with the development of the institutes.[26] She explained the crux of the matter on a subsequent occasion when she said that she was a little nervous of what the universities would or would not give the colleges as far as degrees were concerned and of the price they might exact.[27] H L Elvin,

Director of the London Institute, and a member of the Robbins Committee, summed up the situation accurately,

> the training colleges want to keep close contact with the universities but see the National Advisory Council's document at its face value. If the university institutes cannot offer them anything then they will support the alternative scheme for awarding degrees.[28]

CID eventually sent comments on NACTST's Eighth Report to the Robbins Committee and to individual Vice-Chancellors claiming that the Report offered the teaching profession and the teacher training world 'a route to fuller recognition and to apparently higher social status at a price. The price is the creation of a second system of higher education and the gradual eroding of the concern and interest of universities as we know them in the education and training of teachers.'[29] On a more positive note it continued that it believed that both teachers and the colleges would prefer that developments towards degree work should take place within the university framework and suggested that consideration should be given to a new university degree course of four years duration involving both academic and professional studies.[30] CID thus took the lead in opposing NACTST's Eighth Report which was indirectly based on Alexander's scheme for a local government sector of higher education. This was a predictable move as the institutes were under threat, but CID was a small body with an extremely limited power-base and as such did not pose a really serious challenge to Alexander's scheme.

Alexander soon had to face opposition to aspects of his scheme from a more unexpected and potentially more threatening source — rank and file members of the AEC. When Alexander explained his ideas to the 1961 annual meeting of the Association very little dissent was expressed.[31] Once the AEC's evidence to Robbins was published, however, the Yorkshire Association of Education Committees, prompted by the West Riding representatives, passed a resolution condemning the proposals for the regional administration of higher education and teacher training.[32] Walter Hyman, Chairman of the West Riding Education Committee, continued this attack in 1962[33], and at the annual meeting in June opposed the endorsement of the AEC's evidence to Robbins. Hyman maintained that 'once a process of regionalization was started, they could say goodbye to the control of education by LEAs',[34] and claimed that the real basis for the evidence was financial. These views were shared by the spokesmen for the Association of Chief Education Officers in their evidence to Robbins. G Sylvester felt, 'some of those who advocate change do so because they see it as an easier way of raising the money. They see the possibility of an "ad hoc" body precepting upon local authorities as an easier way of raising money than at present'.[35] At the AEC conference a substantial body of opinion favoured individual LEAs retaining direct responsibility for institutions of higher education, and on a card vote Hyman won the day by 124 votes to 121.[36] Alexander thus had the embarrassing task of informing the Robbins Committee of this reversal, but the LEAs had shown clearly that they were unwilling to make any concessions in this field.

It is difficult to give a full assessment of the Ministry of Education's attitude to Alexander's scheme as the Ministry's records are not yet available to researchers. The Ministry was not in a position to react publicly to these proposals in the early 1960s, but its evidence to Robbins shows that in certain respects there were important similarities between Alexander's proposals and its own thinking on higher education. Like Alexander, the Ministry opposed the concept of 'the comprehensive university'.[37] It predicted that the universities would be preoccupied for many years with major problems arising from their own rapid growth. The universities, moreover, lacked experience of the wide range of further education colleges which would be providing degree courses in future. In these circumstances the Ministry saw little prospect of administrative unity for these two sectors. The assimilation of a college into an existing university was not ruled out when it seemed the most appropriate step[38], but the Ministry doubted 'whether the development of the large number of institutions of higher education now outside the university ambit would be best served, at any rate during the next twenty-five years, by bringing them *all* administratively within it'.[39] The Ministry also believed that, 'with their own distinctive traditions and experience, the technical and other colleges of further education already engaged on advanced work, and the teacher training colleges, have an essential contribution to make to the future pattern of higher education'.[40] In much the same way as Alexander, the Ministry saw an important distinction between (i) institutions which would concentrate on honours degrees, postgraduate work and research; and (ii) institutions which would normally provide only first degree (and often only pass degree) courses.[41] It was expected that initially the institutions in (i) would be the universities and the promoted CATs and the institutions in (ii) would be built up from some of the existing further education and training colleges. It was suggested that 'there might be fruitful amalgamations between some technical and teacher training colleges which between them cover a wide span of work'.[42] The Ministry predicted that many of the regional technical colleges would continue to develop their degree courses and increasingly shed their lower level work.[43] The future role of the 160 area colleges which were already partially engaged in advanced work was also considered. The Ministry proposed that advanced work, especially for part-time students, should continue in these colleges, but thought that much of it would be at sub-degree level and would take place alongside non-advanced work. It is clear, however, that attempts to categorize the work and the administrative future of the regional and area colleges were posing senior civil servants with some intractable problems.[44] The Ministry had no doubt that 'comparable awards should be available for comparable achievement, whether the course is provided at a university or another suitable institution of higher education, and whether or not it is primarily vocational'.[45] The universities had considerable experience of monitoring the standards of their awards, but it was felt that other institutions would need external checks until they had shown themselves capable of becoming autonomous. The Ministry suggested such checks could be provided in one or both of two ways. Firstly, institutions could be associated with universities and enabled to enter students for internal or external degrees. Secondly (and not mutually exclusively), a national body could be set up with the power to award its own degrees to students taking approved courses in approved institutions. This body could work through committees controlling particular fields and subjects of study. The Ministry also put forward alternative ways of administering public aid to higher education.[46] The first involved the extension of the grants committee principle to a wide range of institutions including the regional and the training colleges. The second restricted this principle to the universities and the CATs, leaving the regional and probably most of the training colleges[47], at least initially, under the jurisdiction of the LEAs. Dame Mary Smieton, the Permanent Secretary, told Robbins that the Ministry felt that the second alternative was more practicable.[48] It certainly implied less radical change which was seen by the Ministry as a virtue.[49] If the second and preferred solution was adopted, it preserved the LEAs' stake in higher education, and in this respect the Ministry and Alexander were working towards a common aim. The AEC's scheme was, of course, more clear cut, but it was to be expected that the Ministry would be somewhat circumspect and leave many doors open in the context of providing evidence to a committee of enquiry.

Those who favoured the development of a local authority sector of higher education did not expect the Robbins Committee to produce recommendations which would please them and their fears were fully justified. The Robbins Report, published in October 1963, proposed radical changes for teacher training which were later described by Lord Robbins himself as 'the most far-reaching of anything we had to say'.[50] The influence of Lionel Elvin, Director of the London Institute of Education, was particularly apparent in this section of the Report. It was suggested that in the future some college students should be eligible for four-year BEd degrees. The Report argued that 'the status of the colleges would be best assured and the problem of degrees satisfactorily solved by a closer association with the universities',[51] and recommended that university schools of education should be developed from the existing institutes. All the colleges were to become members of the new schools of education which were to be financed through the grants committee system. This implied, of course, that the LEAs would lose jurisdiction over colleges which they had established.

Robbins' recommendations for the further education colleges were much less radical. Predictably it was suggested that the CATs should be given charters as technological universities which was by 1963 almost universally accepted in the educational world. The regional and area colleges were to be left much as they were. The Committee hoped that there would be 'much experiment' and believed that there was 'room for much variety'. Of the regional colleges it was said, 'some may be best suited by their present system of government. Others may profit from federation with another technical college or with a college of education, or both. Others again may become constituent parts of universities new or old. Some may follow the colleges of advanced technology and attain university status'.[52] It was fairly clear that Robbins did not know what to do about the regional colleges. On the other hand, the area colleges were warned that 'for reasons of economy of staff and equipment, the work of university level will be concentrated as far as possible in selected centres',[53] but it was added, softening the blow, that the Committee attached great value to the continued provision of facilities for part-time work of university level over a wide area. In a potentially more radical vein, the Report suggested that students taking advanced courses in regional and area colleges should have the same opportunity for degrees as those in universities, and recommended the creation of a Council for National Academic Awards (CNAA) to control and award these degrees. Lord Robbins, however, later maintained that his Committee did not foresee that this body would be used as a key piece of machinery in the development of the local authority sector of higher education.[54] The Committee expected the CNAA to be employed in a relatively modest and restricted sphere. It was also suggested in the Report that ten regional colleges and colleges of education in Great Britain could expect to be promoted to university status by 1980.[55] With regard to ministerial responsibility, it was proposed that a new ministry should be created to look after the autonomous institutions in higher education (the universities, the promoted CATs and the colleges of education administered through the new university schools of education) and the research councils.[56] The Ministry of Education was to continue to have responsibility for the schools and the further education colleges.

In an important note of reservation[57] Harold Shearman, the only 'local authority' person on the Committee, made it clear that he did not agree with the division of central control between two ministries. He also argued that local authorities should retain their training colleges, maintaining that these colleges could be associated with universities for the provision of degree courses without disrupting the existing administrative structure.

The Report of the Robbins Committee indicated quite clearly how it saw the future for the universities and the training colleges, but its recommendations concerning higher education in the regional and area colleges were both vague and non-committal. It was not surprising that many of those working in these colleges felt that their institutions had been left in limbo. There was no suggestion in the Report that the advanced courses in the regional and area colleges should be transferred to, or in any way come under, the jurisdiction of the universities. Thus, in no sense did Robbins propose a unitary system of higher education. As Pratt and Burgess have pointed out,[58] both its composition and its terms of reference made it difficult for the Robbins Committee to see that the advanced courses in the further education sector could be more than an appendage to the system of higher education in this country. Very few members[59] of the Committee had experience or direct knowledge of technical colleges, and Robbins' terms of reference were confined to full-time higher education which meant that little attention was paid to part-time students who were particularly important to the advanced work of the technical colleges. It must be stressed, in addition, that the evidence submitted to the Committee by the technical education interest groups such as the ATTI had not been particularly helpful. The ATTI's evidence was fragmentary, no doubt reflecting the different groups of teachers represented in the Association, and in many respects the ATTI failed to indicate clearly how it wanted the technical colleges' contribution to higher education to be developed. The evidence from the AEC which set out a clear case for building up a local authority sector of higher education was hardly discussed in the Report, and it was assumed, as Pratt and Burgess have mentioned,[60] that historical trends would continue. There can be little doubt that in drafting its section on technological and further education the Committee relied heavily on the evidence submitted by the Ministry of Education. The Ministry had predicted that 'the need for students to obtain degree level qualifications by part-time study will diminish',[61] and this statement must have encouraged the Committee to give even less thought to a subject already outside its terms of reference. The

Committee certainly took up the one major innovation proposed by the Ministry in this field — the creation of the CNAA. Like the Ministry, Robbins expected that advanced courses would continue to be provided in the regional and area colleges, and it was also prepared, again like the Ministry, to recommend that in the long run a few regional colleges should attain university status. In many ways Robbins was as committed to the preservation of the local authority stake in providing higher education in the technical colleges as the Ministry of Education and the AEC. Unlike the AEC, it had few ideas about how this sector of higher education could be developed. Alexander saw the future in terms of a united local authority sector incorporating both technical and teacher training colleges, Robbins wanted teacher training to go in another direction. For the moment the Ministry kept its own counsel.

Notes

1   AEC, File A278, Notes of meeting at Ministry of Education, 8 December 1960.
2   *Ibid.*
3   *Ibid.*, Clegg to Alexander, 30 March 1961.
4   *Ibid.*, Alexander to Clegg, 7 April 1961.
5   ROBBINS COMMITTEE, Evidence, pp. 758–78.
6   NACTST, Sub-committee on the Pattern of Training, Minutes, 11, 17 and 23 January 1962.
7   Chief Education Officer for Birmingham.
8   Chief Education Officer for London County Council.
9   NACTST, Sub-committee on the pattern of Training, Minutes, 11 and 17 January 1962.
10 *Ibid.*
11 *Ibid.*, 23 January 1962.
12 *Ibid.*
13 NACTST, Paper 289, February 1962.
14 *Ibid.*
15 *Ibid.*
16 NACTST, Minutes, 1 March 1962.
17 LUIE, File 1806, Morris to Fletcher, 9 March 1962.
18 *Ibid.*
19 NACTST, Eighth Report, *The Future Pattern of the Education and Training of Teachers*, (1962) Annexe B, pp. 31–4.
20 LUIE, File 1806, Memo by Jeffreys, 10 March 1962.
21 *Ibid.*, CID, Minutes, 16 March 1962.
22 NACTST, Sub-committee on the Pattern of Training, Minutes, 11 and 23 January 1962.
23 ROBBINS COMMITTEE, Evidence, p. 1827.
24 *Ibid.*, pp. 185–208.

25 *Ibid.*, p. 1158.
26 NACTST, Sub-committee on the Pattern of Training, Minutes, 23 January 1962.
27 ROBBINS COMMITTEE, Evidence, p. 1828.
28 LUIE, File 1806, CID Minutes, 24 May 1962.
29 ROBBINS COMMITTEE, Evidence, p. 1613.
30 *Ibid.*, p. 1614.
31 *Education*, 30 June 1961.
32 AEC, File A278, Oldman to Alexander, 14 November 1961.
33 *Education*, 15 June 1962.
34 *Ibid.*, 29 June 1962.
35 ROBBINS COMMITTEE, Evidence, p. 1295.
36 *Education*, 29 June 1962.
37 ROBBINS COMMITTEE, Evidence, p. 1905.
38 *Ibid.*, p. 1901.
39 *Ibid.*, p. 1905.
40 *Ibid.*, p. 1901.
41 *Ibid.*
42 *Ibid.*, p. 1903.
43 *Ibid.*, p. 1904.
44 *Ibid.*, pp. 1943–4.
45 *Ibid.*, p. 1899.
46 *Ibid.*, pp. 1908–10.
47 The Ministry explained in a footnote that it was not essential under the second alternative that local authority training colleges should remain in that status. It pointed out that various other proposals had been canvassed but added that none was free from difficulty.
48 ROBBINS COMMITTEE, Evidence, p. 1936.
49 *Ibid.*
50 LORD ROBBINS and B FORD, 'Report on Robbins', *Universities Quarterly*, December 1965, p. 5.
51 ROBBINS REPORT, p. 270.
52 *Ibid.*, p. 138.
53 *Ibid.*, p. 271.
54 LORD ROBBINS and B FORD, (1965), *op. cit.*, p. 7.
55 ROBBINS REPORT, p. 272.
56 *Ibid.*, p. 276.
57 *Ibid.*, pp. 293–6.
58 J PRATT and T BURGESS, *Polytechnics: A Report* (1974).
59 SIR DAVID ANDERSON had considerable experience in the technical education field. He had been the Director of the Royal College of Science and Technology, Glasgow, for many years, but this institution was about to be granted university status. HAROLD SHEARMAN, the 'local authority' person, was also familiar with the work of the technical colleges.
60 J PRATT and T BURGESS, (1974), *op. cit.*, p. 36.
61 ROBBINS COMMITTEE, Evidence, p. 1900.

Chapter 2

The Struggle for the Control of the Colleges of Education

Soon after the publication of the Robbins Report the struggle for the control of the training colleges resumed. Initially Alexander concentrated on opposing Robbins' proposals for two ministries in the field of education, but several members of the AEC[1] objected that he had conveyed the false impression that the Association had accepted the Robbins' solution for teacher training in a published letter to the Prime Minister.[2] Alexander denied this and maintained that he had reserved this item for later discussion.[3] He argued that it would have been tactically a great mistake at that stage to fight the teacher training issue, for he was anxious not to 'alienate the whole training college world and drive them into the university camp on the ministerial issue'.[4] Nonetheless, several education committees interpreted Alexander's silence on this issue as weakness and attacked him for it. The most vociferous committee in this respect was the West Riding and an acrimonious private correspondence between Alexander and Hyman ensued.[5] Alexander, however, was now completely sure that he would receive strong support from most of his members when he continued to fight the teacher training battle. Although there was always a minority view in the AEC in favour of the Robbins' solution, it never gained the support of more than a handful of members.[6]

The Government intimated that it did not intend to make speedy decisions concerning the future of teacher training, and at the end of November 1963 asked interested groups to forward their views on the arrangements recommended by Robbins. About this time the AMC took the initiative amongst the local authority associations and organized a joint conference to discuss the future administration of the colleges.[7] It was decided that the associations should write jointly to the Prime Minister setting out their views. This letter[8] welcomed closer academic contacts between the universities and the colleges but deplored Robbins' administrative proposals. The associations doubted whether the proposed university schools of education would be able to respond quickly enough to the changing needs of teacher supply and felt that the smaller colleges and the specialist colleges for housecraft, physical education and technical subjects, where no degree work was envisaged, would be put into a difficult position. The associations argued that the transfer of about 100 LEA colleges would involve a great deal of complex legal work and pointed out how burdensome the transfer of the ten CATs had been. Reference was also made to the rapid growth of the colleges under the LEAs, and it was claimed that this had been made possible partly by the wide range of resources and skills at the disposal of local authorities. The associations wondered whether the present rate of growth would be sustained and the same value for money obtained if the colleges were removed from their present owners. The letter concluded by suggesting that the administrative responsibility for the colleges should not be changed, but action should be taken to increase the independence of the colleges. In this connection the associations proposed to examine the existing arrangements for the freedom and responsibility of the governing bodies of LEA colleges and to invite the ATCDE to join them in this examination.

There was at least one other reason why local authorities did not wish the colleges to come further into the orbit of the universities — this was their lack of respect for the institutes of education on which the proposed schools of education were to be based. It was, of course, difficult to state this publicly, but a number of 'local authority' people were quite prepared to express themselves forcefully in private. John Haynes, Education Officer for Kent, for example, wrote:

> I have been a member of three institutes of education and have been concerned with two others and have never been able to feel that they confer much real benefit upon the training colleges, except of course for formal examinations and matters of that kind. You will probably also agree that the professors and staffs of education departments at many universities do not receive the same respect from their academic colleagues as all the other professors and departments get and you may feel that this is not an unfair estimation of their quality ... I think that this (the attempt to bring the colleges within the orbit of the universities) is rather a piece of empire building on the part of the universities and that the lack of interest which most of them have shown in their institutes of education in the past does not really give them a very strong case now.[9]

In contrast to the LEAs, the ATCDE gave the Robbins' proposals an extremely warm reception and wished to see them implemented *in toto*.[10] It refused to join the local authority associations in their examination of the arrangements for governing bodies and preferred to wait for the Government's decision concerning the whole future of the colleges. This did not surprise Alexander who felt that the ATCDE had nothing to lose by taking this course of action.[11] Alexander admitted privately that the LEAs should have tried to find ways of giving the colleges more status several years earlier.[12] W L Dacey of the CCA agreed with this view, but felt that the associations' letter to the Prime Minister now put them into a better position on this issue.[13] Early in 1964 Alexander tried to persuade Helen Simpson, Secretary of ATCDE, that the institutes of education did not have the administrative capacity and competence to secure the expansion in teacher supply envisaged.[14] He further warned her that the colleges might be regarded by the universities as second-rate citizens, but Simpson was not convinced.

The universities welcomed the Robbins' recommendations concerning the future of the training colleges. The CVCP was united on this issue, but advised the UGC to ask individual universities for their views.[15] In November 1963 the CVCP met Government ministers, John Boyd-Carpenter and Quintin Hogg to discuss the Robbins Report. Hogg was outspoken about the future of the colleges. He is reported to have said:

> The difficulty is that you (the CVCP) will find almost hysterical opposition from the local authorities to the transfer and quite strong opposition from the Ministry itself. I think that the local authorities having lost the CATs will bitterly resent the loss of their teacher training colleges. I also think that the Ministry will be very sorry to lose them ... You expressed support for the Robbins' proposals for ministerial responsibility. Talking as a politician, I am quiet sure that this is rendered more difficult by pressing the transfer of the teacher training colleges. It may be that the Government, if it came down on the Robbins' side on ministerial responsibility, would have to sacrifice the transfer of responsibility for the teacher train- ing colleges at least for a time. These may by the facts of life.[16]

Led by Sir Philip Morris, the CVCP representatives at this meeting continued to stress that it would be intolerable for the universities to be responsible for the colleges academically but not financially and administratively.

CID was predictably enthusiastic about the Robbins proposals, and it felt that there would be considerable tactical advantage if one or two universities could move quickly to set up schools of education.[17] On 18

December 1963 CID met permanent officials of the Ministry at the latters' request to discuss difficulties connected with the implementation of Robbins.[18] The problems raised were very similar to those highlighted in the local authority associations' letter to the Prime Minister. It is reported that a 'no holds barred' discussion took place, and that, 'although some air was cleared, not as much as was darkened by the smoke of battle; some views were very opposed'.[19] Thus, by the end of 1963 the universities knew that they were up against very considerable opponents. Lionel Elvin maintained that the LEAs should be told that they would have to recognize the climate of opinion. In his view the LEAs had made their stand purely in terms of power, and had consulted neither the governing bodies of their colleges nor their principals and staffs.[20] At this stage Elvin did not want CID to discuss whether it would be possible to devise ways of introducing degrees for some college students without the organizational changes, but some directors pressed this issue feeling that, if from their point of view the worst came to the worst, they should try to find means of implementing the academic side only.[21] There can be little doubt that some directors feared that universities might even be prevented from developing their academic connections with the colleges. The CNAA was being created, and the possibility of using this body to award degrees to teachers had already been mentioned in local authority circles.[22] Early in 1964 Elvin reported to CID that he understood that Hogg favoured BEd degrees in the colleges to be awarded by CNAA.[23] According to Edward Boyle, the Government had decided by the summer of 1964 to reject the Robbins' recommendation for teacher training[24], and had the support of the UGC 'who were understandably worried about the implications for university autonomy if there were to be wholesale transfer of expenditure on the colleges to the UGC vote'.[25]

No decision was announced before the general election of 1964 and in the campaign both major parties reserved their positions on the future of the colleges.[26] With the Labour victory in the election Michael Stewart became Secretary of State for Education. Previously in 1963 a Labour Party Study Group chaired by Lord Taylor had come to the conclusion that the training colleges should be incorporated into universities[27], and Michael Stewart himself had given evidence to Robbins on behalf of the Fabian Society much on these lines.[28] There was, however, no immediate announcement of policy. During November 1964 Stewart met deputations from most of the interested parties. At this juncture the AEC, led by Alexander, returned to the theme that CNAA would be an appropriate body to award degrees for teachers.[29] It was suggested that CNAA was likely to produce more flexible BEd schemes than universities. In the same month Eric Robinson of ATTI presented a paper to the Long Term Forecasting Sub-committee of

NACTST proposing that technical colleges might begin to offer teacher training courses[30], and his union was already urging that CNAA should set up recognized awards for teachers outside the machinery of the institutes of education. ATCDE did not oppose investigating possibilities of the former at a time of teacher shortage, but found the proposal about CNAA validation completely unacceptable as it was likely to disrupt the close and continuous collaboration[31] which had developed between the colleges and the universities. CID took much the same line.

The local authority associations met the Secretary of State on 30 November. Alexander told Stewart that the colleges could only achieve their aspirations through independence, and a system of higher education independent of the universities was needed.[32] He maintained that the ultimate aim must be an all-graduate teaching profession, but suggested that this could only happen if degrees, which were quite different from university degrees, became available. In Alexander's view the Robbins' solution would bring disunity to the teaching profession as university degrees were to be made available for only a minority of students. He asked whether, if the supply of teachers from a university controlled system proved inadequate, local authorities would have the right to establish their own colleges. Alec Clegg added that university-orientated training courses would be disastrous for the low ability streams in the schools, and predicted that if the CATs and the training colleges were transferred to the university sector, it would not be long before the tenth of higher education remaining with the local authorities went the same way. Stewart replied that although illiberal government of colleges was not a problem everywhere there were serious deficiencies to be remedied in some areas. He stressed that if the decision was favourable to the local authorities the colleges would have to be reassured that this was not against their best interests. Alexander concluded the meeting by saying that any disappointment on the part of the colleges should be rapidly assuaged by early action on making degrees available and re-organizing governing bodies. Afterwards Alexander told A C Hetherington of the CCA that he thought the meeting had gone well and that he had reason to believe their representations would prove successful.[33] A few days later the AEC was making plans on the assumption that local authorities would retain their colleges.[34]

The Secretary of State also met representatives of the UGC which had consulted individual universities about their views on the Robbins' proposals. The UGC admitted that nearly all the universities had declared in favour, and some felt that the academic side could only be accepted alongside the financial and administrative provision.[35] The Committee, however, stressed that 'many universities did not share the latter view or did not feel so strongly about it'.[36] This latter position was supported strongly by the UGC which argued that the academic and the administrative proposals could be separated. It concluded that at a time of expansion 'it would be unwise to introduce comprehensive changes which were bound to result in prolonged local argument and upheaval'.[37] Its Chairman, Sir John Wolfenden, also feared that financing the colleges through the university grants system might lead to greater government control of university expenditure.

On 11 December Stewart announced in the Commons that there were not to be fundamental changes in the administrative and financial arrangements for training colleges.[38] He mentioned that he had been influenced by the UGC's advice that the academic and administrative aspects of the question were separable. The arrangements for the internal government of colleges were to be reviewed. For the Conservatives, Hogg acknowledged that he would have come to the same conclusion as Stewart.[39] It is interesting that Stewart eventually decided that the colleges should stay with the local authorities despite the Labour Party's Study Group's rather different solution. According to Richard Crossman, Stewart 'quietly accepted the departmental line',[40] and the AEC also mentioned that there were 'those in the DES who strove as hard as anyone to keep the training colleges within the scope of the authorities who run the schools'.[41] The evidence, thus, strongly suggests that the civil servants at the DES had more sympathy for the views of the local authorities than for those of ATCDE, CID and CVCP. Quintin Hogg had, indeed, hinted that this was the case as early as November 1963[42], and Edward Boyle has indicated that the Schools Branch and those responsible for teacher supply at the Ministry opposed the transfer to the universities whereas the branch in charge of teacher training favoured it.[43] It is likely that the political changes of 1964 altered little in this respect.

Lord Robbins reacted sharply to Stewart's announcement. He wrote,

> It must be a matter of profound regret that a Government which claims to be progressive, aided and abetted apparently by a UGC which has certainly not yet risen to the level of the new opportunities with which it is confronted, should have chosen this poor-spirited solution to this very important educational problem.[44]

Elvin took the same view, and was particularly annoyed by the UGC's claim that the academic and administrative aspects of the question were separable. He commented,

> This is very odd: the UGC exists, and the Government agrees that it should exist, precisely because we know that in higher education these two things are not separable ... And why should the Secretary of State consult the UGC, whether it denies the reasons for its own

existence or not? This is not a question of size of grant, but a question of national policy. The appropriate bodies to listen to were the universities and, to the extent to which they were able to speak for them, the Vice-chancellors and Principals. Their Committee has already indicated its views, and in a somewhat different sense.[45]

Robbins and Elvin knew that the important battle had been lost. The institutes of education could not go forward now. For the time being they were to remain in the rather anomalous half-way position which they had occupied since the 1940s, but in the long-term it looked likely that they would be under threat.

The ATCDE realized that it could do little but accept Stewart's decision. Simpson accordingly wrote to the local authority associations offering ATCDE's cooperation in implementing the Government's proposals.[46] Alexander replied that the associations were in favour of 'strengthening academic relations between the colleges and the universities',[47] but added, perhaps somewhat ominously,

> though I think you appreciate that we are much concerned with the many students in colleges for whom internal degrees of universities may not be available or indeed appropriate, but who should also have the fullest opportunities which may be available through the National Council for Academic Awards.[48]

This point was developed further in *Education*. Alexander maintained that it was CNAA, rather than the universities, which opened up the possibility of an all-graduate teaching profession. He argued that Stewart's decision had wide significance for higher education as a whole. He wrote:

> The alternatives are clear: the steady movement towards one system of higher education under the general control of the universities or, on the other hand, the recognition of the need for two alternative systems. That is, the universities on the one hand, and the colleges, under the general administrative control of local education authorities on the other, providing courses in higher education of degree standard over a much wider range of subjects of study. The decision now made makes available the alternative system of higher education which clearly not only includes colleges of education, as they will be called, concerned with training teachers, it also includes the wide range of technical, commercial, art and other colleges which are offering opportunities of higher education over a very wide range of subjects.[49]

In many ways this statement was reminiscent of the AEC's evidence to

Robbins, and at the same time it set out a very clear notion of a binary system of higher education.

During the first few months of 1965 the main bone of contention between the university institutes of education and ATCDE, on the one hand, and the DES and local authorities, on the other, was the promised group to examine the government of colleges of education. The local authority associations never doubted that concessions would have to be made in this area[50], and agreed that 'time was ripe for a review of the constitution and powers of governing bodies'.[51] They told the Prime Minister that 'action should be taken to increase the independence and academic status of the colleges'.[52] When ATCDE refused the associations' initial invitation to join them in their investigation[53], a local authority working party was set up. It was admitted privately that this group made little progress during 1964[54], but the DES stressed the paramount importance of changes in this area[55] and soon set up a national study group. The DES offered to provide a chairman and a secretariat and proposed that membership should consist of ten representatives of the local authority associations, four from the voluntary bodies and four from the ATCDE.[56] The DES added, 'it would be best for the study group to decide whether, and if so how, they could best bring university or other experience to throw light on the subect of their discussions'.[57] Eventually it was agreed to increase ATCDE representation to six.

ATCDE and CID had assumed from the moment that the examination had been announced that the universities, and probably the institutes in their own right, would be represented.[58] They were completely dismayed when they heard about its proposed composition, and ATCDE, CID and the voluntary bodies all protested strongly to the DES.[59] CVCP was similarly disappointed, and agreed to write to the Chairman of the UGC pointing out that 'the universities' long-standing relationships with the colleges were being adversely affected'.[60] The AUT approached Alexander and asked whether the AEC Executive Committee would meet AUT officers to discuss this question, but Alexander replied that he could see no purpose in this.[61]

The DES made no concessions, and at one stage it looked as if ATCDE might refuse to take part in the whole exercise.[62] The newly-appointed Secretary of State, Anthony Crosland, took the view that the internal government of the colleges was an administrative issue, and therefore in line with Stewart's decision of December, it was first and foremost a question for the providing authorities and their employees. He reminded ATCDE that it was the local authority associations, not the Government, which had taken the initiative and set up a working party on the subject.[63] He agreed that the universities and their institutes had an interest in these matters because of their academic relationships with the colleges, but he did not offer to amend the composition of the group.[64] Eventually, after informal consultations with the universities, ATCDE came to an uneasy compromise with the DES.[65] ATCDE agreed to take part as long as it was understood that the main item on the agenda of the first meeting of the group was the participation of the universities. Even at this late stage bitter exchanges were still taking place between Crosland on the one hand and Simpson of ATCDE and W A C Stewart, Chairman of CID, on the other. Stewart concluded that, 'The Department's handling of the composition of the working party has been calculated to destroy the idea of partnership between the LEAs, the colleges, the institutes and through them the universities'.[66] Eventually the first meeting of the study group was held on 17 May 1965 with Toby Weaver of the DES in the chair and with Crosland present.[67] It was agreed that 'the universities would be invited to take part in the deliberations at the earliest appropriate moment'.[68]

In many ways this protracted and bitter dispute did more to sour the relations between ATCDE, supported by CID and the universities, and the DES than the decision of December 1964 itself. The institutes of education and ATCDE were clearly on the defensive after they had lost the post-Robbins battle, but the DES and the local authorities did little to reassure them. In many ways during the first few months of 1965 the rift widened further. During this difficult period Simpson of ATCDE was convinced that Weaver, Deputy Secretary at the DES and Alexander of the AEC were 'using all their joint power and determination to ensure that the influence of the universities in the present university training college discussion (was) reduced to a minimum'.[69] In a letter to Harold Wilson, Robin Pedley, the Director of the Exeter Institute of Education, mentioned Alexander's influence on policy concerning higher education and teacher training.[70] He claimed that Alexander had been a bitter opponent of comprehensive schools and held that his views on post-school education were no more reliable. Pedley also alleged that the Government's teacher training policy was being determined by civil servants.[71] He mentioned that the universities felt that they were persistently provoked in the first four months of 1965, and claimed that the institutes' enemies deliberately exacerbated the situation in the hope that the universities would become so disenchanted that they would opt out of the BEd field altogether, leaving it to be taken over by those on the other side of the binary line.[72] It is not possible to substantiate this claim, but it is clear that Weaver had very strong views on the future of teacher training. In a private conversation he maintained that it would be fatal for the universities to take over the colleges.[73] To support this he relied on two main arguments: firstly, there was a great deal of low quality teaching in the colleges and there were staff there with whom universities should not be saddled; secondly a take-over of the colleges implied such large increases in student members and financial liabilities for the universities that greater Government interference, which might impinge on academic freedom, would inevitably follow.[74] Weaver's listener in this conversation was convinced that the civil servant's attitude was coloured by the experience of his own daughter who had 'attended a "posh" training college and emerged with a lot of useless information and without the foggiest idea of how to teach the young'.[75] The listener concluded that Weaver believed that the qualities needed for university work and school teaching were of an entirely different order and that universities would give school teachers grand ideas which would cut them off from their pupils. Beliefs such as these were commonly attributed to Alexander and Weaver by their opponents in this period. The events of the first four months of 1965 only seemed to confirm the worst fears of the ATCDE, the institutes and their allies.

By the end of April the university interest and the ATCDE feared that there was a distinct possibility that some colleges of education would be taken out of the hands of their institutes and be put under the academic jurisdiction of CNAA. This was surprising as the Government's December decision had clearly indicated that the academic associations between the colleges and the universities were to be strengthened. Nonetheless, during March and April it became clear that there were influential people who were intent on reopening the whole question of the academic future of the colleges. For some time Alexander had stressed that schools were not restricted to academic studies, and contended that students of physical education, domestic science, arts and crafts should have the same opportunity to obtain graduate status as their colleagues who were learning to teach the more traditional university subjects. He proposed that CNAA was available to solve any problems which arose in these subject areas. In March the Chairman of the UGC asked individual universities whether they thought that CNAA had a part to play in validating degree courses for colleges.[76] The very fact that this question had been asked by the Chairman of the UGC caused consternation in both CID and CVCP.[77] The universities replied in clear terms that they did not expect CNAA involvement, and later Wolfenden, Chairman of the UGC, told the CVCP that he had fully expected them to adopt this line.[78] This, however, was certainly not clear from Wolfenden's original letter, and many doubts were raised about where the UGC stood on this issue especially in the light of the line it had taken over the administrative future of the colleges. At about this time CNAA put out an important statement that, although it expected many colleges to establish links with nearby universities, it would be interested to hear from any colleges which might wish it to consider proposals for teacher training courses leading to degrees.[79] Sir James Cook, Vice-Chancellor of Exeter University and a member of CNAA, told the CVCP that this statement had been issued over his objection.[80] Soon afterwards the Secretary of State announced at the NUT Conference in Douglas that the Government intended to prepare plans to train some teachers in technical colleges. Eric Robinson of the ATTI had pushed this idea in NACTST for some time, and it was prominent in his 'note of dissent' to NACTST's Ninth Report which Crosland had recently received. This notion was repeated about a week later in Crosland's Woolwich speech which put the universities firmly on one side of the proposed binary line and the technical colleges and colleges of education together on the other. This suggestion was, of course, by no means original, but it was the first time that it had been announced as official Government policy. What the universities, CID and the ATCDE wanted to know was whether Woolwich implied a direct reversal of Michael Stewart's December decision. Was the academic future of the colleges to be with the universities or elsewhere? The whole matter now appeared to be in some doubt.

W A C Stewart, Chairman of CID, was so concerned about these developments that he telephoned Herbert Andrew, Permanent Secretary at the DES.[81] Andrew said that he had heard that there was a good deal of anxiety in the institutes, but denied that he was working with Weaver, Odgers and the Secretary of State against the universities in these matters. He assured Stewart that the main purpose of the Woolwich speech was to make more definite the arrangements for the regional technical colleges, and claimed that references to the colleges of education were not intended to be more than marginal. He expected these colleges to retain their present academic links with the institutes of education. On the other hand, he maintained that the DES wanted some technical colleges to develop education departments and train teachers. He felt that the academic arrangements for these departments could well follow the pattern being developed for the regional technical colleges, and this implied that they would look to the CNAA rather than to the institutes for validation of their courses. Although Stewart was wary of this last point, generally he was somewhat reassured by this conversation. Nonetheless, he urged members of CID to put pressure on their universities to proceed with their BEd schemes as quickly as possible.[82] Stewart argued that if a number of universities and their associated colleges were committed to BEd degrees Crosland and the DES could be presented with a *fait accompli*. The existence of university BEd schemes would make it difficult to insist that all colleges should prepare CNAA courses. Stewart concluded that it was his impression that the

Government favoured a 'mixed economy' in teacher training. This view was confirmed a few weeks later when Stewart and Niblett from CID and Andrew and Weaver from the DES met for lunch.[83] The civil servants insisted that there was no reason why education departments set up in technical colleges should come under institutes of education. CNAA could validate their courses and recommendations for qualified teacher status could come direct to the DES. Andrew and Weaver maintained that colleges should be allowed to develop with the maximum degree of freedom. If a college did not like the BEd scheme offered by its local university, it ought to have the right to look elsewhere to CNAA. In essence, the DES officials wanted the monopoly control of institutes of education broken. They preferred a binary system for the training of teachers as well as for the award of degrees.[84] It was now clear to the institutes that, although all was not lost, another important and difficult battle had to be fought.

The question of training teachers in technical colleges had been raised by the DES in 1963. At this juncture ATCDE told the Teachers' Branch that, although it did not regard technical colleges as inherently suitable for teacher training, it would not oppose this suggestion because of the urgency of increasing teacher supply and because there was available space in these colleges.[85] ATCDE stressed that its collaboration was dependent on plans being made in conjunction with the institutes of education. During November 1965 DES officials put more specific proposals to both ATCDE and CID. It was suggested that education departments should be established in about five regional technical colleges. These departments would offer four-year BEd, three-year certificate and one-year postgraduate certificate in education courses.[86] It was expected that these departments would concentrate mainly on preparing students to teach the secondary school age range, but primary courses were also to be included. The DES made it clear that it wanted CNAA to act as the validating body for the courses provided by these departments. It claimed that it would be 'dangerous' to have two validating authorities for one institution as this would make transfer from one course to another difficult. It added that as technical colleges looked to CNAA to validate their degree courses, they might be expected to look in the same direction for their teacher training courses.[87] Nonetheless, at a meeting with CID, DES officials were prepared to concede that the new departments should be allowed to choose their validating authorities.[88] ATCDE condemned several aspects of this scheme. It argued that there would be inequity between the technical colleges and the colleges of education if the former could offer BA, BSc and BEd degrees and the latter only the BEd. It commented that it was strange that the main emphasis was to be put on secondary training when there was a much greater shortage of primary teachers. Finally, the proposal that CNAA should be used as the validating body was roundly condemned by both ATCDE and CID as completely unnecessary and an undesirable breach of the institute principle. The CVCP had similar views and expressed its concerned to Weaver at the DES. The NUT took the same line, and only the ATTI, amongst the interest groups involved, strongly supported the DES scheme. After a meeting between ATCDE, CID, Crosland and Reg Prentice, Minister of State, in December, W A C Stewart concluded that the DES was strongly committed to education departments in technical colleges but rather less certain about CNAA validation.[89] The scheme was eventually made public in an amended form in April 1966.[90] Education departments were to be established in five technical colleges and initially they were to offer only three-year certificate courses. There was consequently much greater emphasis on primary training than had been originally envisaged. The colleges were to be permitted to choose between CNAA and their local institutes for validation. Eventually all five collegesopted for their institutes to the obvious dismay of the ATTI and to the delight of ATCDE, CID and CVCP.

CNAA, meanwhile, had begun to consider setting up machinery to validate courses in education. Early in February 1966 Alexander approached F R Hornby, the Chief Administrative Officer at CNAA, about this subject. He wrote, 'we (the AEC) are most anxious that you will take a sympathetic line with such applications when they are made to you and will handle them with as much encouragement to the colleges as is consistent with the application of your normal procedure'.[91] Hornby replied that CNAA was moving rather delicately on this matter as it did not wish 'to appear to be poaching on what the institutes looked upon as their own preserves'.[92] He told Alexander that, although no formal proposals had been received from colleges of education, there had been one or two 'nibbles'.[93] He acknowledged that the line that he was taking in informal discussions was that if the Council was asked to deal with courses in education it would be certainly be very willing to do so[94], and he hoped that the subject would be discussed further at the Council's May meeting. From the outset, Hornby ensured that ATCDE and CID were fully informed of developments and he was clearly anxious to avoid conflict. Although some members of the ATCDE Executive initially urged a boycott of CNAA validation machinery for education courses, eventually it was agreed to adopt a less extreme policy.[95] According to J D Browne, 'it seemed illogical to express concern about standards and refuse the assistance of the experience of members'.[96] In July W A C Stewart told CID that the unified teacher training principle had not yet been breached but warned members to expect a split in the near future.[97] Stewart asked CID if it wished to boycott CNAA validation machinery for education courses, but mentioned that this might be seen as unfair in two contexts. These were: (i) the situation in the Cambridge Institute where the University refused to implement a BEd scheme; and (ii) a situation in which a college found the BEd scheme offered by its local university unsatisfactory. Eventually CID agreed that it would be wrong to refuse to cooperate with CNAA if it wished to meet needs such as these, and in such circumstances would offer official CID representation on a CNAA educational panel. CID, however, maintained that an entirely different principle arose if a college sought validation of its certificate course through CNAA. In such cases it was felt that the local institute could justifiably sever all links with the college concerned. In September members of ATCDE and CID attended a CNAA working party on arrangements for education courses, and Lionel Elvin reported back to CID that the feeling in the working party was that CNAA was prepared to enter the BEd field but had serious doubts about involving itself in certificate work.[98] This was confirmed a few weeks later in an official CNAA policy statement.[99] Hornby told CID that he thought it was for the best that all five technical colleges had opted to go into their local institute for their education courses as most of them had little or no experience of CNAA validation outside of engineering. He felt that the colleges concerned would need considerable help in developing their courses.[100] During 1966 Hornby worked hard to ensure that ATCDE and CID did not become alienated from CNAA. Throughout he encouraged a spirit of cooperation and in January 1967 he was able to tell Alexander that 'the Council will be starting off its work in education with a fair amount of goodwill'.[101] ATCDE and CID were certainly pleased that the institute monopoly control of certificate work had been preserved at least for the moment, and agreed to nominate representatives on to CNAA's newly created Education Committee.

Meanwhile, the Study Group on the Government of the Colleges was doing its work. With hindsight it may seem strange that technical questions of college government aroused so much passion, but contemporaries never doubted their paramount importance. In practice both sides recognized that the real issues were about status, prestige, power and influence, and that these matters could be most conveniently settled in the context of college government. In the Group the local authority associations adopted a relatively conciliatory attitude towards the ATCDE. This was hardly surprising. From December 1963 the associations had, in effect, offered to give more independence and academic freedom to the colleges in return for continued ownership. When Michael Stewart gave the local authorities what they wanted in December 1964, the associations knew that they would have to keep their side of the bargain and, between themselves, they discussed the concessions which would have to be made.[102] At this stage the associations recognized that the governing bodies of the colleges would have to be taken out of the committee structure of local authorities and put outside the standing orders of councils.[103] This certainly met one of the colleges' main grievances, and the authorities knew that new legislation would be necessary to implement this change. It was also agreed that there was no need for local education authority representatives to be in the majority on governing bodies nor for chairmen to be local education authority representatives. Moreover, they did not want changes in the party political control of councils to be reflected in changes in personnel on governing bodies. The associations were prepared to see the teaching staffs of colleges play a greater part in their government, and they expected that the position and responsibilities of academic boards would be strengthened. It was also felt that governing bodies could be given more control over day-to-day maintenance, spending of approved estimates and the appointment of teaching staff. On the other hand, the associations did not want the liberalization of the government of colleges carried too far. They stressed that the local authorities must retain sufficient controls to preserve economy and efficiency and to ensure that the colleges responded rapidly to national needs. It was not forgotten that the local authorities maintained technical as well as teacher training colleges, and it was felt that 'there should not be undue differences in the arrangements for their government and maintenance'.[104] There were however, disagreements between the local authorities on two important but related issues. These were (i) the position of senior administrative officers in a college; and (ii) chief education officers' relationships with the colleges and their governing bodies. These matters were still unresolved when the Study Group first met.

Throughout the proceedings of the Weaver Group the ATCDE formed a united group which was able to rely on the regular support of the representatives of the voluntary bodies and the universities.[105] The local authority associations, on the other hand, found it much more difficult to preserve unity. At the first meeting, Lionel Russell, CEO for Birmingham, expressed the view that there was no need for local education authority nominees to form a majority on governing bodies[106], but later the 'considered view' of the local authority people was that the report 'would be much less well received if they directly recommended that local authority representatives on a governing body should be in a minority'.[107] They proposed that there should be 'suggested limits of representation which allowed representatives of authorities to be either in a majority or in a minority',[108] and this proposal was included in the Study Group's Report.[109] It was agreed early on that colleges should not be governed by sub-committees of education committees, although, interestingly, Weaver told Alexander privately that he thought a governing body ought to remain a sub-committee of the appropriate committee of the local education authority[110] on the grounds that the authority should keep the administration of colleges in line with that of its other institutions. Weaver did not put this to the Study Group, and eventually it was recommended that legislation should be passed to make colleges' articles of government subject to the approval of the Secretary of State. This enabled the Secretary of State to ensure that governing bodies were independent of the local authority committee structure and free from council standing orders, but, of course, it in no way removed them from the general fabric of local government. According to Weaver (and the DES legal adviser) this put the colleges on exactly the same footing as maintained secondary schools.[111]

After several meetings of the Group, Percy Lord, CEO for Lancashire, felt strongly that the local authorities were giving too much away. He wrote to Hetherington of the CCA:

> The universities have been brought into the Study Group without any consultation, and it is clear that they, allied as it were to the college people, are out to produce a final solution which will be far more in keeping with the Robbins' recommendations than it will be with the Government's decision on the future of the colleges. I have noted that whereas we, from the Authorities' side, talk freely and sometimes appear to hold different views, those who represent the 'other' side are, far more careful to present a united front.[112]

Lord proposed that the local authority association members should in future come together prior to Study Group meetings to decide common strategies and this was arranged. The issue which led to the greatest contention was who should act as clerk to a governing body. The local authorities argued that the CEO should hold this position, but ATCDE felt that this was inconsistent with removing governing bodies from the local authority committee structure. The ATCDE representatives insisted (with strong support from the universities) that this job should be done by the college's own senior administrative officer. They remained adamant that the clerk to the governors should be the college's 'own person', and they collected a long list[113] of examples of petty restrictions, delays and illiberal handling of colleges by local authorities which they wanted to circulate to the Study Group.[114] Weaver resisted this, and tried to persuade the local authorities that, if the appointment of a college's senior administrative officer was approved by the local authority this provided sufficient safeguard that the administration of the college was in good hands.[115] At this stage the local authorities remained unconvinced[116], although Russell was slightly more amenable, suggesting that the vital point was that the CEO should be able to advise the governing body and attend its meetings.[117] Weaver had to work hard to avoid a complete rift, and even when a definitive version of the Report was drafted he was still not sure that there would be final agreement on this issue.[118] He was determined that divisive notes of dissent should be avoided at all costs, and eventually all members of the Group were persuaded to accept a carefully worded compromise. Both sides of the argument were recorded in some detail in the Report, but the recommendation made was that the senior administrative officer of the college should act as clerk to the governing body on the understanding that his appointment was subject to confirmation by the authority.[119] Some of the Group's members, especially Lord and L W K Brown of the CCA, were still far from happy, and Brown was particularly annoyed by the tone of Weaver's covering letter to Crosland. This mentioned that the disappointment felt by the college staffs at the Government's December decision had not prevented them from entering into the work of the Group wholeheartedly. Brown told the Secretary to the Group:

> If this gratuitous puff to the self-sacrificing nobility of the training college representatives has to be made, why shouldn't one go on to say, in polite terms, that the LEA representatives didn't let the sulky resentment of the training college staffs prevent them from being cooperative also?[120]

Clearly the strong feelings had not subsided, but in the Study Group it was largely the college members and the university representatives who held firmly to their ground and the local authority associations which made concessions. This was not surprising as in this particular exercise the local authorities were on the defensive from the outset, and ATCDE (and CID) knew that they could not afford to lose another battle.

In 1966 ATCDE and CID consoled themselves with the thought that they had gained some concessions in the Study Group. A A Evans, General Secretary of ATCDE, acknowledged that the Weaver Report was a compromise, but expected that 'many of the petty restrictions and the interference with the academic side' would go.[121] The preservation of the institute monopoly in three-year certificate courses also encouraged college and institute staffs. In many ways, however, these were minor achievements compared with the major defeat of December 1964. By 1965 and 1966 ATCDE and CID realized that they were really involved in a rearguard action, and that even the academic side of the Robbins' solution was vulnerable.

Notes

1   AEC, File A1132.
2   *Ibid.*, Alexander to Douglas-Home, 25 October 1963.
3   *Ibid.*, Alexander to Stone, 4 November 1963.
4   *Ibid.*
5   AEC, File A1132, November 1963.
6   AEC, File A1133.
7   AEC, File A1132, Swaffield to Alexander, 26 November 1963.
8   *Ibid.*, local authority associations to Douglas-Home, 23 December 1963.
9   *Ibid.*, Haynes to Alexander, 3 December 1963.
10 *Ibid.*, ATCDE Press Report, 21 November 1963.
11 AEC, File A1133, Alexander to Dacey, 8 January 1964.
12 *Ibid.*
13 *Ibid.*, Dacey to Alexander, 9 January 1964.
14 AEC, File A1133.
15 LUIE, File 2389, Stevens to Fletcher, 26 November 1963.
16 LUCFO, CVCP papers, Account of meeting with ministers, 22 November 1963.
17 LUIE, File 1973, CID Minutes, 29 November 1963.
18 LUIE, File 2388, CID Minutes, 18 December 1963.
19 LUIE, File 2389, Fletcher to Stevens, 19 December 1963.
20 LUIE, File 2388, CID Minutes, 31 January 1964.
21 *Ibid.*
22 AEC, File A1133, Note of meeting at CCA offices, 12 December 1963.
23 LUIE, File 2388, CID Minutes, 23 March 1964.
24 E BOYLE, *Government, Parliament and the Robbins Report*, Joseph Payne Memorial Lecture, (1979), p. 15.
25 *Ibid.*, pp. 15–16.
26 E ROBINSON, *The New Polytechnics*, (1968), p. 32.
27 Labour Party, Study Group on Higher Education, *The Years of Crisis*, (1963), pp. 30–1.
28 E ROBINSON, (1968), *op. cit.*, p. 33.
29 *Education*, 11 November 1964.
30 NACTST, Long Term Forecasting Sub-committee, Memorandum by E ROBINSON, November 1964.
31 ATCDE, Letter to correspondents and principals, 18 November 1964.
32 AEC, File A1133, DES note of meeting with representatives of local authority associations, 30 November 1964.
33 *Ibid.*, Alexander to Hetherington, 4 December 1964.
34 *Ibid.*, Advisory sub-committee note, 8 December 1964.
35 UGC, *University Development, 1962–67*, (1968), p. 74.
36 *Ibid.*
37 *Ibid.*
38 *The Times*, 12 December 1964.
39 *Ibid.*
40 R H CROSSMAN, *The Diaries of a Cabinet Minister*, Volume I, (1975), p. 326.
41 *Education*, 1 January 1965.

42 LUCFO, CVCP papers, meeting with ministers at the Treasury, 22 November 1963.
43 E BOYLE, (1979), *op. cit.*
44 *The Times*, 15 December 1964.
45 *Education*, 18 December 1964.
46 AEC, File A1133, Simpson to Alexander, 14 December 1964.
47 *Ibid.*, Alexander to Simpson, 16 December 1964.
48 Alexander explained in *Education* that he included in this category students following courses in physical education, domestic science, arts, crafts, infant teaching.
49 *Education*, 18 December 1964.
50 AEC, File A1133, Note of meeting, 12 December 1963.
51 *Ibid.*
52 *Ibid.*, File A1132, local authority associations to Douglas-Home, 23 December 1963.
53 *Supra.*
54 AEC, File A1133, Joint meeting, 30 November 1964.
55 *Ibid.*, DES note of meeting with local authority associations, 30 November 1964.
56 *Ibid.*, Odgers to Alexander, 12 January 1965.
57 *Ibid.*
58 LUIE, File 2426, CID/CHUDE meeting, 7 January 1965.
59 LUIE, Files 2426–8.
60 LUIE, File 2428, Note of CVCP meeting, 2 March 1965.
61 AEC, File A1133, Alexander to Urwin, 3 March 1965.
62 WUMRC, ATCDE, 176/CD/AT/3/T2, ATCDE to Crosland, 25 February 1965.
63 *Ibid.*, Crosland to Simpson, 6 April 1965.
64 LUIE, File 2426, Crosland to Stewart, 8 March 1965.
65 WUMRC, ATCDE, *op. cit.*, Simpson to Odgers, 16 March 1965, and Simpson to Crosland, 30 March 1965.
66 LUIE, File 2426, Stewart to Crosland, 1 April 1965.
67 AEC, File A713, Study Group on the Government of Colleges of Education, Minutes, 17 May 1965.
68 LUIE, File 2428, Simpson to Fletcher, 19 May 1965.
69 LUIE, File 2428, Fletcher to Stevens, 12 March 1965.
70 *Ibid.*, File 2426, Pedley to Wilson, 29 April 1965.
71 *Ibid.*
72 *Ibid.*
73 This information is taken from a written source dated April 1965. The author does not wish to cite full details.
74 *Ibid.*
75 *Ibid.*
76 *Ibid.*, Wolfenden to Stevens, 25 March 1965.
77 *Ibid.*, *passim.*
78 *Ibid.*, note of CVCP meeting, 21 May 1965.
79 CNAA, Statement 2 April 1965.
80 LUIE, File 2428, note of CVCP meeting 23 April 1965.

81 LUIE, File 2426, Stewart to Fletcher, 3 May 1965.
82 *Ibid.*, Stewart to CID members, 7 March 1965.
83 LUIE, File 2428, Niblett to Fletcher, 28 May 1965.
84 *Ibid.*
85 *Ibid.*, File 2798, ATCDE, Note on Training for Teaching in Technical Colleges, 24 November 1965.
86 *Ibid.*, and File 2800, CID, conference, 26–28 November 1965.
87 *Ibid.*
88 *Ibid.*
89 *Ibid.*, CID, Report of consultation with DES, 17 December 1965.
90 *Ibid.*, DES, Departments of Education in Technical Colleges, April 1966.
91 AEC, File A887, Alexander to Hornby, 1 February 1966.
92 *Ibid.*, Hornby to Alexander, 2 February 1966.
93 *Ibid.*
94 *Ibid.*
95 J D Browne, *Teachers of Teachers*, (1979), p. 187.
96 *Ibid.*
97 LUIE, File 2800, CID Minutes, 21 July 1966.
98 *Ibid.*, File 3028, CID Minutes, 14 October 1966.
99 AEC, File A420, CNAA, Degrees in Education.
100 LUIE, File 3028, CID, conference, 18–20 November 1966.
101 AEC, File A420, Hornby to Alexander, 12 January 1967.
102 AEC, File A1133, Note of meeting of local authority associations, 20 January 1965.
103 *Ibid.*
104 *Ibid.*
105 ATCDE, *The Government of Colleges of Education*, (nd), p. 7.
106 AEC, File A713, Study Group on Government of Colleges of Education, Minutes, 17 May 1965.
107 *Ibid.*, Minutes, 15 September 1965.
108 *Ibid.*
109 DES, *Report of the Study Group on the Government of Colleges of Education* (1966), Paragraph 92.
110 AEC, File A713, Weaver to Alexander, September 1965.
111 *Ibid.*, Weaver to Alexander, 17 January 1966.
112 *Ibid.*, Lord to Hetherington, 11 October 1965.
113 LUIE, File 2428, ATCDE, *The Government of Colleges of Education Administered by the Local Education Authorities* (nd).
114 AEC, File A713, Weaver to Alexander, September 1965.
115 *Ibid.*
116 *Ibid.*, SGGCE, Minutes, 7 October 1965.
117 *Ibid.*
118 *Ibid.* Weaver to Alexander, 19 January 1966.
119 DES, *Report of SGGCE* (1966), Paragraph 123.
120 AEC, File A713, Brown to Walker, 10 February 1966.
121 WUMRC, ATCDE, *op. cit.*, Evans to Friend, 13 April 1966.

Chapter 3

The Emergence of the Polytechnics

The Ministry of Education acted immediately on the Robbins' proposal that CNAA should be created. Interested parties, including the universities and the local authority associations, were informed early in November 1963 that the Ministry wanted to set up this body with the least possible delay.[1] The Ministry stressed that it wanted to move swiftly on this issue to enable the regional and other colleges to make their maximum contribution to the demand for courses of degree level in the years immediately ahead. Alexander was pleased by this development and congratulated the Ministry on its prompt action.[2] The universities also responded swiftly and positively. The CVCP considered the matter on 22 November and later that day its Chairman, Sir William Mansfield Cooper, told senior ministers at a meeting at the Treasury that his Committee felt that the creation of CNAA was 'extremely desirable'.[3] Later, representatives of the CVCP and the UGC met officials at the Ministry to consider the matter in more detail. In this cordial meeting the only serious difference of opinion was over the Council's power to introduce higher degrees. The CVCP felt that 'on both academic and financial grounds it was important to keep within reasonable limits the number of institutions providing courses and facilities for higher degrees'.[4] Herbert Andrew, the new Permanent Secretary at the Ministry, argued that it would seriously detract from the Council's status if it were laid down that it could not award higher degrees. Andrew stressed that the intention was only to give permissive powers, and he thought that it might be possible to make the introduction of higher degrees dependent on a two-thirds majority of the Council voting for it.[5] At its next meeting the CVCP relented and did not insist on a restrictive clause in the Council's Charter, and the UGC and the Ministry were informed accordingly.[6] The universities were, therefore, most cooperative in the establishment of CNAA, but they did not foresee how it would be developed in the future.

Although the Government moved quickly over the establishment of CNAA, it dealt much more slowly with the question of the future of the regional colleges. In this connection Robbins had merely proposed that some ten regional colleges and colleges of education should be given university status by 1980. During the 1964 election campaign both major parties were largely silent about the future of the regional colleges, and no public indication of DES policy was given at this juncture. A related issue on which senior Labour leaders were prepared to express an opinion was the question of integration between certain universities and neighbouring regional colleges. In particular, suggestions had been made that closer connections should be made between Sussex University and the then Brighton College of Technology and that Lanchester College of Technology, Coventry, should be merged with the new University of Warwick. The latter proposal proved particularly interesting. Richard Crossman, who was the Labour spokesman on education in 1964 and represented a Coventry constituency in Parliament, had considerable detailed knowledge of the situation. He was very much in favour of the merger, and during the election campaign persuaded Harold Wilson to visit Lanchester College[7] where he condemned 'futile and senseless divisions between the various branches of higher education'.[8] Wilson went on to say that he supported the principle of integration of colleges such as Lanchester with universities and that he thought the Coventry and Brighton institutions provided very good test cases.[9] Such notions clearly worried William Alexander. He wrote to Sir John Wolfenden, Chairman of the UGC, expressing his concern and arguing that particular cases such as Coventry should not be dealt with prematurely. Alexander maintained that general policies and principles needed to be decided first, and he urged Wolfenden to proceed slowly with the Coventry case.[10] Wolfenden was most reassuring on this issue, and told Alexander that the UGC was 'trying, despite many pressures, not to prejudice long-term plans by short-term decisions'.[11]

Important changes, meanwhile, had taken place within the Ministry of Education/DES. In July 1963 Anthony Part, the Deputy Secretary in charge of further education, moved to the Ministry of Public Building and Works, and his responsibility in education was transferred to Toby Weaver. Part had been primarily responsible for drafting the Ministry's evidence (about further and higher education in the maintained sector) to the Robbins Committee. He expected the number of advanced courses in the technical colleges to continue to increase and he predicted that a small number of regional colleges would eventually attain university status. Essentially Part assumed that existing historical trends would continue, and he did not advocate and did not plan for basic structural changes. As will be seen later in this chapter, Weaver initiated very different ideas about how advanced courses in the further education sector should be developed and administered. Although it will not be possible to analyze the impact of this change in civil service personnel fully until the internal Ministry/DES papers are made available, there is already considerable evidence that a binary policy for higher education was being evolved before the Conservative defeat in the 1964 election. Edward Boyle acknowledged he put up a paper on the binary organization of higher education to a cabinet committee as early as March 1964.[12] Later when he knew that he was to speak in the higher education debate in the Commons during March 1965, he looked up this paper and used it considerably in his speech.[13] Herbert Andrew is reported to have been so surprised by the extent of the common ground between Crosland and Boyle in this debate that he asked Weaver how he had managed to brief *both* front benches so well.[14] Boyle knew that it was more than likely that they had both used the same departmental paper.[15] Crosland confirmed Boyle's account when he spoke to representatives of the UGC and the CVCP in April 1965. He attributed the extraordinary unanimity of view between himself and Sir Edward Boyle to the fact that they had both been working on the same DES brief.[16] From a different standpoint, Richard Crossman also claimed that the DES had evolved notions of a binary scheme before the election. He wrote, 'I became more and more convinced that one of the biggest jobs for the next Labour Secretary of State for Education was to break down the rigid division between higher education and further education and institute a unitary approach against a binary approach'.[17] The consensus between Boyle, Crosland and Crossman is remarkable, and it is clear that the origins of the binary policy are to be found in the first six months of 1964 rather than in 1965. The catalyst was almost certainly Toby Weaver.

With the creation of the DES the Conservatives settled the question of central government control of education, but the election campaign of 1964 prevented them from resolving two other outstanding issues raised by Robbins — the future of the teacher training colleges and the development of higher education courses in the technical colleges. When Labour came to power, Michael Stewart, the new Secretary of State, immediately took up the urgent question of the training colleges and dealt with this in the last few months of 1964. Understandably the DES did not wish to open up the technical college issue publicly until teacher training was settled. As soon as the latter was resolved, however, there was a cabinet reshuffle and Michael Stewart went to the Foreign Office and was succeeded by Anthony Crosland as Secretary of State. According to Richard Crossman, when Crosland first became Secretary of State he (Crosland) was not convinced that a binary policy should be pursued[18], but soon changed his mind and became a firm advocate of the scheme. Crossman said later that he much regretted that he had not made an effort to persuade Crosland against binary notions as soon as he took over at the DES. There is no doubt that Crosland, who had served as a member of the Labour Party's Study Group on Higher Education in 1963, was moving very far and very fast from the recommendations put forward in this Group's Report.[19]

Before the Government could launch its new binary policy, it had to deal with several outstanding issues. In essence, it closed several doors quite firmly before it went on to open others. On 24 February 1965 Crosland explained in the Commons that the UGC had advised him that the Robbins target of 218,000 university places by 1973–74 could be reached by the natural growth of the existing universities and the former CATs.[20] He continued that no additional universities (with the possibly exception of one in Teesside — later dropped) would be needed for ten years, and that during the same period there would be no accessions to university status from amongst existing institutions. The universities did not challenge this policy, and the CVCP agreed with Crosland that the technical colleges should stick to their last and not aspire to become universities.[21] This decision was, of course, a considerable disappointment to several of the regional colleges.[22] For the Conservatives, Boyle said that his party felt that Crosland had made the right decision.[23] He also mentioned the question of possible mergers between universities and neighbouring colleges of technology such as those proposed in Coventry and Brighton. Boyle hoped that the Government would resist 'a stampede in this direction',[24] and Crosland reassured him in general terms on this matter.[25] Later Crosland told the CVCP at a private meeting that it was important that the universities avoided 'casting covetous eyes on the leading technical colleges'.[26] Sir John Wolfenden, Chairman of the UGC, argued later that the decision to designate no new universities for ten years might easily have encouraged ambitious technical colleges to try to associate themselves with existing universities, and it was important that the Government made it clear as quickly as possible that it did not favour such mergers.[27] In 1966 Crosland himself confirmed privately that it had been necessary to be tough at the beginning over Coventry and Brighton to show that the Government meant business.[28] Plans for mergers thus came to nothing.

By the spring of 1965 the Government knew that it could depend on the support of important interest groups in pursuing its binary policy. The local authorities had been advocating such a notion since 1962, and from December 1964 Alexander conducted a vigorous campaign in the AEC journal *Education* in favour of the policy.[29] Alexander maintained that the local authority sector of higher education should not be restricted and that there should be the fullest opportunities to develop provision for research and postgraduate work.[30] In this respect Alexander had modified his views considerably, for in 1962 he had intimated that higher education institutions in the local authority sector should concentrate largely on work at ordinary degree level.

The ATTI was also increasingly coming out in favour of a binary policy for higher education. The staff in the regional colleges were certainly dissatisfied with the Robbins' recommendations for their colleges and took up their grievances with their union.[31] The proposal to develop ten colleges to university status with an indefinite date of implementation was described as having 'deplorable effects',[32] and eventually an ATTI Higher Education Advisory Panel, chaired by Eric Robinson, was established to consider and advise on the Association's higher education policy generally. Meanwhile, in its pamphlet, *Is Robbins Enough?*, published in May 1964, the Association was still thinking in terms of the Robbins' proposals. It welcomed the possibility that some of the regional colleges would be given 'autonomous status in the university field in due course'[33] and stressed that there were several colleges which were already doing sufficient work at university level to justify the speedy granting of autonomous status. It hoped that the regional colleges would be encouraged to run courses at postgraduate level and offer research facilities where these were appropriate, and it was suggested that there should be more freedom from local authority control with independent government bodies for those colleges which remained in the maintained sector.

These suggestions were not radically different from those put forward by Robbins. At the Association's annual conference in September, it was resolved to support 'a single comprehensive plan for further and higher education'[34] which seemed to imply a commitment to a unitary system, and was certainly interpreted by Alexander in this way.[35] In November 1964 Edward Britton, the General Secretary of ATTI, submitted a paper to the second meeting of the Higher Education Advisory Panel in a very different vein. Entitled *The Future of the Regional Colleges*, this paper claimed that the Robbins Committee, 'had no clear idea of what the future might be. Like the parson's nose, (the regional colleges) were neither wing, breast, nor leg, but were too tasty a morsel to be abandoned and might therefore be put on the plate of anyone which asked for them'.[36] This had led to uncertainty and insecurity. Britton mentioned that these colleges could expand university-type education but warned that 'any college undertaking only this kind of work will inevitably be looked upon as the place where students go if they fail to obtain a place at a university ... at best they can only achieve fourth division status in the university league'.[37] He felt that the alternative was to develop a form of higher education which was distinct from that normally provided in universities. He wanted to build on the 'technical college tradition' with large vocational elements in syllabuses, flexible lengths of courses and methods of study and recognition of entry qualifications other than those obtainable through the full-time educational system.[38] Existing social and industrial trends would lead to an even greater demand for this type of education. In his view CNAA would play a vital role in the development of this 'alternative and distinctive, but still equal, type of course which is the only real guarantee of a vigorous future for the colleges'.[39] The Panel asked Britton to develop the ideas in his paper and to widen the scope to 'higher education in the realm of further education'.[40] During the next few month several redrafts were made, and eventually Britton's paper was published in March 1965 as *The Future of Higher Education within the Further Education System*. In it the Higher Education Advisory Panel proposed that the technical colleges should build up vocationally orientated degree courses under the auspices of CNAA. Robinson wrote, 'Under Robbins a small number of colleges might eventually become universities. There were the ducklings of higher education and some of them might grow into swans. We are suggesting that they grow into ducks.'[41] These ideas appealed to both the Government and the Opposition, and *The Future of Higher Education within the Further Education System* was complimented by both Crosland and Boyle during the higher education debate in the Commons at the end of March. Crosland has acknowledged the influence of the ATTI on the development of the binary policy[42], but it is clear that this body was not the originator of the scheme. Alexander had developed ideas on these lines as early as 1962, and it was soon after the publication of the Robbins Report that Weaver at the DES began to formulate the binary policy. On the other hand, throughout most of 1964 the ATTI was still thinking in terms of some regional colleges gaining university status, and it was between November 1964 and March 1965 that the Higher Education Advisory Panel evolved its binary view.

According to Crosland, senior civil servants at the DES wanted to get the binary policy 'on the record' as soon as possible.[43] He admitted that, despite his own reservations, officials urged him to make the Government's intentions clear in his speech at Woolwich Polytechnic on 27 April 1965. In retrospect, he felt that he made the Woolwich speech before he had fully mastered the topic, and regretted the way in which he had presented the policy because in terms of public relations considerable harm was done.

In his Woolwich speech Crosland identified two broad traditions in British higher education. There was the autonomous university sector and the maintained sector represented by the leading technical colleges and colleges of education. Crosland stressed that the government accepted these twin traditions and rejected 'the alternative concept of a unitary system, hierarchically arranged on the "ladder" principle, with the universities at the top and the other institutions down below'.[44] He argued that the local authorities should retain a reasonable stake in higher education, and proposed that the leading technical colleges should build on their own traditions and offer a wide range of vocationally orientated degree and advanced (but sub-degree) courses. It was stressed that the maintained sector should continue to provide courses for part-time advanced (degree and sub-degree) students as well as for full-timers. Crosland also mentioned that he hoped that some of the leading technical colleges would become involved in the training of teachers. This brought the swift reaction from the colleges and institutes of education which has been discussed in the previous chapter.

Soon after he had made his Woolwich speech the Secretary of State set up an informal advisory group 'to help the Department in formulating detailed material for the discussions which are to take place with the national representative bodies about the future pattern of advanced work in the further education system'.[45] This Group was chaired by the Minister of State responsible for higher education, Reg Prentice, and consisted of 'a few friends of FE from the colleges, the LEAs and industry'.[46] The members, who served in an individual rather than a representative capacity, included William Alexander, Alec Clegg, Harry Pilkington, Lionel Russell, F R Hornby of the CNAA and E Britton and E Robinson of the ATTI.[47] The proceedings of the group were not made public, and the way in which the DES operated through this group certainly infuriated one of the national representative bodies — the CCA.[48] The Prentice group considered draft papers submitted by DES civil servants, and few major changes were made to the ideas proposed by these officials.[49] Eventually a memorandum on this subject was sent by the DES to the national representative bodies for their official reactions and comments[50], and some months later in May 1966 the Government's White Paper, *A Plan for Polytechnics and other Colleges* was published. The main contents of this White Paper had much in common with the DES papers considered earlier by the Prentice Group. The most important issue which the DES put before the Group and which had received no attention in the Woolwich speech was how the advanced courses in the further education sector were to be divided between different institutions. It was here that the origins of the Polytechnic concept were to be found and the importance of concentration into selected institutions stressed. It is now necessary to consider in some detail the key ideas which came out of the Woolwich speech and its aftermath.

Crosland's starting point in the Woolwich speech was the distinction he drew between the twin traditions in English higher education. He tended to contrast the 'pure academic education' provided in universities with, 'the applied vocationally orientated courses' put on in technical colleges. Even the ATTI in an unpublished draft policy statement prepared by Britton and J A P Hall acknowledged that this contrast was oversimplified.[51] For many years some university departments had not only provided professional (often practical) courses but also had established firm links with industry and commerce. It was equally true that some of the degree courses provided in technical colleges were 'no more vocationally committed or no more directly concerned with industry than similar degree courses in universities. Indeed, in some cases they follow exactly the same syllabus and students take the same examination.'[52] Thus, in this respect reality was much more complex than Crosland implied. Several universities (and not only ex–CATs) could trace their origins to technical college roots. In its unpublished policy statement the ATTI claimed that the essential differences between the two systems were control of syllabuses and student numbers.[53] It suggested that in the universities syllabus content and methods of approach depended upon the freedom of the teachers to expand knowledge along the lines of their own interests and the willingness of students to follow them along these lines. Britton and Hall felt that if this was the pattern in one sector of higher education, it was essential that another sector should exist where the community had a major measure of control over syllabus content. Only in this way would a technologically advanced nation be able to meet its needs for highly qualified manpower 'in numbers and in type of specialization'.[54] To suggest that the universities developed without any reference to manpower requirements was, of course, exaggerated, and, in practice, the aspect of the twin tradition notion which stood up to the closest scrutiny was the obvious administrative contrast — there were in existence relatively autonomous universities financed through the UGC and technical colleges funded and controlled by the local education authorities. Whether reference to the historical development of these two sets of institutions proved much about their intrinsic natures was doubtful.

By April 1965 Weaver and Crosland were making it quite clear that they completely rejected a unitary concept of higher education based on the 'ladder principle'. Crosland told representatives of the CVCP that technical colleges should not aspire to become universities and that he hoped by degrees to inculcate the idea that technical colleges were something worthwhile in their own right.[55] Weaver added that 'in education it was not right to build up a competitive system on the basis of a rat race'.[56] He maintained that the drift upwards had been allowed to go on for the last fifty years and a break with the policy was overdue.[57] Crosland took up the same theme a fortnight later at Woolwich where he alleged that a unitary system would be characterized by 'a continuous rat race to reach the First or University Division'.[58] He felt that there was 'a constant pressure on those below to ape the universities above, and a certain inevitable failure to achieve the diversity in higher education which contemporary society needs'.[59] In many ways this was the major plank of the binary policy. Weaver had witnessed how the Robbins proposal that ten colleges, in due course, should be granted university status had, within weeks of the publication of the Report, resulted in 'leading technical colleges that could be counted in tens rather than units urging their claims to be promoted'.[60] He was determined to stop this process once and for all as he was convinced that it was detrimental to the well-being of the maintained sector of further and higher education. There can be little doubt that Weaver developed the binary policy first and foremost as a means to bring this 'rat race' to an end.

Although Crosland gave some indications at Woolwich of the nature of the higher education to be provided in the local authority sector, he certainly did not remove all doubts in this respect. Emphasis was placed on the 'ever-increasing demand for vocational, professional and industrially-based courses'[61] and the continued need for the technical colleges to make and expand provisions in this area. It was also clear that Crosland wanted the colleges to continue to offer full and part-time courses at both degree and sub-degree levels. Crosland, moreover, proposed that the technical colleges should put on more courses in the arts and social sciences[62], despite the fact that Weaver had said only a few days earlier that he would be sorry to see many of the colleges running arts courses.[63] There was also a rather similar difference of emphasis concerning postgraduate work. Crosland indicated at Woolwich that the non-university sector should include 'an appropriate amount'[64] of this work, but Weaver was soon stressing that the technical colleges, being in the main teaching institutions with a strong vocational bias, could expect to play a much more modest role in postgraduate studies and research than the universities.[65]

The universities reacted sceptically to the Woolwich speech. Sir Charles Wilson, Chairman of the CVCP, expressed his concern in a formal letter to Sir John Wolfenden, Chairman of the UGC.[66] The CVCP felt that the speech made 'excessively rigid the division between the university and non-university sectors of higher education'.[67] It also indicated that it had misgivings over the proposed development for the CNAA. Wilson stressed that when the universities gave their support to the creation of CNAA they did so on the understanding that its purpose was to provide a means for students in non-university institutions to receive degrees. They had not conceived of it as being strongly pushed as an instrument to encourage the substantial growth of degree work in non-university institutions.[68] Wolfenden responded to this by sending the CVCP a long draft memorandum setting out the general views of the UGC on the development of the binary system.[69] This document was very much in favour of the scheme outlined at Woolwich, and Wolfenden hoped that, after the necessary discussions and clearances, it could be issued as an official UGC policy statement.

This memorandum made much of the fact that in the non-university institutions degree-level work was normally carried out in conjunction with a considerable amount of lower level work. It was stressed that these institutions should keep their degree work 'within bounds'[70] and that they should expect 'to concentrate their main efforts on meeting the equally important national need for more trained people at sub-degree level'.[71] The UGC expected the technical colleges to develop primarily as teaching institutions and not to become major centres of postgraduate work and research. The document indicated that it wanted the technical colleges to adapt in response to local industrial requirements and to transient national manpower needs, whereas the universities were to be allowed to concentrate on more strictly academic training without frequent changes in student output or course content.

The UGC draft memorandum was not well received by the CVCP. Sir James Cook, Vice-Chancellor of Exeter University, argued that the document seemed inconsistent with CNAA policy.[72] He pointed out that CNAA recognition of degree courses was often contingent on the shedding of lower level work, and he could not accept the implication in the document that the main purpose of the binary policy was to build up sub-degree work in the colleges for technicians. Several members of the CVCP felt that the real aim was to create a rival system of state sponsored institutions with degree giving powers at university level.[73] In general the CVCP felt that the UGC document was contradictory and made several questionable assertions. Eventually it was decided to ask Wolfenden for a meeting to discuss the memorandum further. This meeting took place in September 1965 and a sharp exchange of views took place.[74] The CVCP's uneasiness about how the binary policy was evolving made some impact on members of the UGC, for the plans to issue the UGC document as a policy statement were quietly dropped much to the relief of the vice-chancellors.[75]

Although the universities were able, somewhat belatedly, to bring their reservations about the binary system to the notice of the UGC and the DES, they were not in a position to influence developments. Crosland showed some sensitivity to their criticisms, however, and eventually asked for a meeting with the CVCP to discuss the implications of the Woolwich speech. This was held in November 1966[76], and Crosland set forth his ideas at some length. He stressed that he had not invented the binary system as there were already large numbers of students in higher education outside the universities. He claimed that there was never any political possibility of establishing a unitary system composed of autonomous institutions, and held that, by comparison with a unitary system under public control, the binary policy was relatively advantageous to the universities.[77] He said that the aspect of the former 'rat race' for university status which gave him most concern was the tendency of technical colleges to drop their sub-degree and part-time work. He thought that retaining institutions in the local authority sector would prevent this, and he maintained that the universities could not cater for these types of provision.

Crosland stressed that he had not intended to imply that the universities were unresponsive to social needs at Woolwich, but mentioned that the technical colleges were under more immediate public control in such matters as their courses, their class sizes and rationalization of provisions. He added that as yet there was insufficient information about the comparative costs of the two sectors, but he expected the marginal costs of the technical colleges to be lower as they had a smaller proportion of students in residence and had few commitments in postgraduate work and research.

The Secretary of State also referred to the argument put forward by Lord Robbins[78] and others that it was paradoxical that at a time when the Government was introducing comprehensive secondary education it was also embarking on a divisive selective policy in higher education. Crosland rejected this analogy completely, and claimed that 'if all full-time degree studies were confined to the universities and other institutions restricted essentially to work of a lower standard, the resulting system would be much more educationally and socially divisive'.[79]

Members of the CVCP questioned several of Crosland's arguments. It was pointed out that the technical colleges seemed to have a view of their own destiny which differed considerably from that outlined by the Secretary of State.[80] Reference was made to the proliferation of CNAA degree work, and it was claimed that many of the new courses were in the social sciences and could have been provided more appropriately and more economically in the universities.[81] Crosland answered these points by recognizing 'the difficulty of containing the ambitions of some of the institutions in the public sector'[82], but he indicated that he was prepared to use his powers to ensure that they performed the role which he had outlined. He was emphatic that 'polytechnics should not be pale reflections of universities' and affirmed that 'the Government intended to restrict large increases of readerships in polytechnics or the sort of research frequently advocated by CNAA'.[83] At the end of the meeting Crosland made it clear that his remarks were not to be interpreted as representing any change in basic policy from his Woolwich speech. A few weeks later he reiterated many of these points in a public address at Lancaster University. In retrospect he felt that his carefully prepared Lancaster speech was very much better than his original effort at Woolwich.[84] Nonetheless, it must be stressed that the commitment and content of the two speeches were essentially similar, and it was merely the public relations aspect of the policy which was presented in an alternative fashion. Crosland was quite willing to explain the binary sytem to the universities in a different way, but he was in no way prepared to abandon or alter the policy.

Although there was no reference in the Woolwich speech to the concentration of advanced courses in selected institutions, this policy was strongly favoured by several of those advocating the binary system. Even before the Woolwich speech was made, Weaver told representatives of the universities that it was wasteful to have small packets of advanced students spread over a large number of colleges and that efforts would have to be made to set up a more stratified system of colleges and concentrate degree work.[85] Alexander, who was normally in close touch with DES thinking, told the ATTI as early as March 1965 that advanced work should not be diversified to too great an extent.[86] He thought that it was inappropriate for a college to run a single advanced course, and argued that colleges should only provide advanced instruction if reasonably broad bands of higher education courses could be supplied. Crosland and Weaver continued to make similar points throughout the summer of 1965[87], and several of the DES papers submitted to the Prentice group were primarily concerned with means of concentrating advanced courses in selected institutions.[88] In the first paper prepared for the Prentice Group it was asserted that:

> The present state of affairs is unsatisfactory both educationally and from the point of view of using resources effectively. The full-time courses are scattered in too many units, most of them too small to provide a satisfactory corporate life and to sustain adequate academic standards, especially for degree work. A considerable measure of concentration will be required if the colleges are to be able to offer an alternative to the universities which is attractive to teachers and students and is capable of enjoying the public esteem that is essential to the success of the dual system.[89]

It is interesting that in this private paper the DES referred to the building up of 'an alternative to the universities' as it painted a very different picture from that presented to the universities themselves. The DES claimed that it could only achieve its aims if 'strong and broadly based centres'[90] were created, but it stressed that these centres would cater for all types of students mentioned by Crosland at Woolwich. As far as possible it intended to build upon regional and other colleges which had established reputations for advanced work and which already possessed highly qualified staff and the necessary capital resources.[91]

The DES did not believe that its objectives could be achieved within the existing three tier pattern of regional, area and local colleges which it blamed for 'much of the tension and frustration of recent years'.[92] Instead it proposed to designate about thirty polytechnic institutes (embracing a considerably larger number of existing institutions) to be strong centres of advanced work. It was suggested that 'they could be given priority in the allocation of resources in order to build up their standards and reputation, and most of the CNAA degree work would be carried out at them. Between them they should be able to deal with most of the demand likely to arise in the foreseeable future for full-time and sandwich higher education courses within the system.'[93] The DES also proposed that once the list of polytechnics had been settled there should be no additions for about ten years.

It was not envisaged that all full-time higher education courses would be incorporated in the polytechnics, and specialist centres such as art and agricultural colleges would be allowed to continue to provide full-time advanced courses in their particular fields of study.[94] The DES predicted that colleges which were not designated as either polytechnics or specialist centres would not be able to sustain advanced courses for long because of the increased competition. It did not, however, propose to curtail these courses as long as student numbers were sufficient to meet the DES requirements then in force, but it was made clear that new full-time advanced courses were not be started in these institutions.

With regard to part-time advanced courses the requirements were less stringent because of the need to provide facilities within easy travelling distance of students' homes. Institutions currently putting on part-time advanced (largely HNC) courses were to be allowed to continue, but no new centres were to be authorized 'except in quite exceptional circumstances'.[95] It was stated that these institutions were not to become involved in the provision of part-time degree courses which were only to be approved at colleges which offered equivalent full-time courses.

These DES proposals which were considered by the Prentice Group in the summer of 1965 were not well received by the ATTI. The main bone of contention was the concentration of advanced courses in a limited number of institutions. At a meeting with CNAA in June, Tom Driver of ATTI predicted a growing demand for CNAA degree courses and argued that it would be 'undesirable to start to set limits of any kind'[96] on the number of colleges which could offer them. Dr D Godfrey of CNAA felt that the ATTI should be more realistic and replied that there ought to be a limited number of centres.[97] It was also reported that Alexander had indicated that he was in favour of only some thirty colleges being selected to lead in higher education[98], and Alexander was certainly anxious to keep down the number of institutions which were recognized as 'specialist centres'.[99] Robinson soon reported to ATTI's Higher Education Advisory Panel that much of the discussion in the Prentice Group was centred around the definition of the boundary between further and higher education.[100] In November 1965 he indicated that there was 'a hardening of the attitude in official circles against the free expansion of full-time advanced work in a large number of centres',[101] and suggested that the Association could not 'avoid the necessity of rationalization, of forward planning and of compelling some colleges to recognize the necessities of economic working'.[102] He predicted that this rationalization would take the form of a 'break' across the further education field, but he particularly wanted to avoid a break which designated all full-time post-'A' level courses as advanced and segregated them into separate buildings. He proposed that higher education should be redefined to include all full-time and part-time courses normally taken by students over 18. He did not wish to see all the higher education courses in an area concentrated into one building, but thought that they could be organized through institutes of higher education which would be responsible for the higher education courses in several buildings. The control of further education (courses for the under 18s) was to remain with local education authorities, but institutes of higher education were to be put under new and larger regional authorities. Robinson's paper aroused a great deal of controversy in the Higher Education Advisory Panel.[103] One member from a regional college argued that all post-18 education could be regarded as tertiary education but only part of this could be termed higher education. He felt that 'the most important thing that would ensure the success of a binary system was the degree of esteem given to CNAA degrees, and this could only be achieved if they were available in a restricted number of colleges'. Another member suggested that the demarcation line should be between academic and craft courses which was totally unacceptable to Robinson. At the end of the discussion Britton concluded that the Panel 'was not prepared to go 100 per cent to support Robinson's scheme'.[104] On the other hand, it was agreed that the Association needed to clarify its position on this issue with a view to providing a 'follow-up statement of policy to *The Future of Higher Education within the Further Education system*'.[105]

Before agreement on this policy statement had been reached, however, the DES circulated its memorandum based on the conclusions of the Prentice Group, and the Association had to concentrate on providing a response to this initiative. The ATTI found the memorandum too 'restrictionist' and felt that in the long run it would 'seriously limit the amount of higher education that takes place in the further education system'.[106] Britton described its main proposal as the designation of 'some thirty colleges as pseudo universities', and he feared that it would give the AUT a strong fillip to revive its recruitment of members in the regional colleges.[107] This must have been a considerable worry to the ATTI as one of the results of giving university status to the CATs was that most of the teachers there joined the AUT and left the ATTI. In February 1966 an ATTI deputation led by Tom Driver met Crosland, Prentice and senior civil servants to discuss the memorandum, and on the basis of this encounter Driver predicted that the Government's White Paper on the subject 'might be couched in more favourable terms'.[108] Driver must have been disappointed in this respect for the White Paper, *A Plan for Polytechnics and Other Colleges* published in May was very similar to the memorandum. Almost immediately it was roundly condemned in an ATTI pamphlet entitled *Plan for Polytechnics*. This pamphlet claimed that the general approach adopted was too static and restrictive. It complained that the policy of concentrating advanced courses was nowhere justified in the document but its necessity merely asserted. It was felt that removing full-time advanced courses from colleges would have detrimental effects on the part-time courses provided there, and the refusal to permit part-time higher education courses to start in colleges where no other such courses already existed was regarded as extremely short-sighted. The main conclusion was that the initiative and flexibility which had character-ized further education in the 1950s and early 1960s would be stifled by the restrictions in the White Paper. Writing some years later Pratt and Burgess took much the same viewpoint. They argued that the needs of part-time students were particularly neglected[109], and claimed that 'the policy of select designation only confirmed the principle of academic drift'.[110] As Michael Locke has mentioned[111] the word 'drift' does not seem particularly appropriate in this context as the concentration of advanced courses in selected institutions was consciously and deliberately sought by government policy. Pratt and Burgess claim that between the Woolwich speech and the publication of the White Paper the essential nature of the binary policy was perverted. This interpretation fails to recognize that from the beginning the ATTI (and subsequently Pratt and Burgess) had a different conception of the whole notion from Weaver and the DES. The ATTI wanted to see the development of a flexible and open-ended system of local authority further and higher education which could be treated as one entity in the form of a continuous spectrum. Weaver, on the other hand, was much less radical and sought primarily to bring an end to the 'rat race' for university status. He hoped to create local authority institutions of higher education which could stand comparison with the universities. No doubt Weaver was well aware of the problems caused by the rigid hierarchical structure in further and higher education which had been described in great detail to the Robbins Committee by his predecessor, Anthony Part.[112] At least the DES proposals in the White Paper were more flexible than the old system, but the evidence suggests that from the outset Weaver was strongly committed to what he regarded as the rationalization of higher educational provisions in the technical colleges. He never really questioned that this meant building up advanced courses in selected institutions and discouraging them in others. To Weaver and to the DES this was an integral and essential part of the creation of a viable local authority sector of higher education.

Pratt and Burgess attached considerable importance to the fact that over the years the technical colleges have been particularly successful in providing opportunities in higher education for both mature working-class people and their children. Raafe has shown just how complex, in both educational and sociological terms, this question is.[113] Although Crosland made some reference to this issue in his speech at Lancaster University in January 1967, it received surprisingly little attention prior to this, and it is difficult to avoid the conclusion that this particular factor played little part in the decisions made earlier to develop the local authority sector of higher education. In an important sense the binary policy was primarily about preserving and developing the stake in higher education of the local authorities and of the DES. The AEC, and the local authorities generally, gave this approach an enthusiastic welcome, and, along with Weaver and the DES, they regarded the concentration of advanced courses and the designation of selected institutions as a necessary and inevitable part of the process.[114]

Notes

1   AEC, File A1132, Pimlott to Alexander, 4 November 1963.
2   *Education*, 3 January 1964.
3   LUCFO, CVCP papers, Statement by members at a meeting with ministers at the Treasury, 22 November 1963.
4   *Ibid.*, Meeting at UGC, 31 December 1963.
5   *Ibid.*
6   *Ibid.*, CVCP Minutes, 24 January 1964.
7   R CROSSMAN, *The Diaries of a Cabinet Minister*, Volume 1, (1975), p. 326.
8   *Education*, 11 September 1964.

9 *Ibid.*

10 AEC, File A1133, Alexander to Wolfenden, 14 October 1964.

11 *Ibid.*, Wolfenden to Alexander, 16 October 1964.

12 E BOYLE, *Government, Parliament and the Robbins Report*, Joseph Payne Memorial Lecture, (1979), p. 16.

13 M KOGAN, *The Politics of Education*, (1971), p. 105.

14 *Ibid.*

15 *Ibid.*

16 LUIE, File 2425, Vice-chancellor's note of meeting, 13 April 1965.

17 R CROSSMAN, (1975), *op. cit.*, p. 326.

18 *Ibid.*

19 Labour Party, Study Group on Higher Education, *The Years of Crisis*, (1963). This report advocated a unitary system of higher education and largely ignored the higher education courses in the regional and area colleges.

20 HANSARD, House of Commons, 24 February 1965, Volume 707, (1964–65), cols. 390–1.

21 LUIE, File 2425, Vice-chancellor's notes of meeting between representatives of the CVCP, UGC and Ministers, 13 April 1965.

22 E ROBINSON, *The New Polytechnics*, (1968), p. 31.

23 HANSARD, House of Commons, 25 March 1965, Volume 709, (1964–65), cols. 759–762.

24 *Ibid.*, col. 762.

25 *Ibid.*, col. 774.

26 LUIE, File 2425, Vice-chancellor's notes, 13 April 1965.

27 LUCFO, CVCP papers, Report of meeting with representatives of UGC, 14 September 1965.

28 LUIE, Vice-chancellor's notes of meeting with Secretary of State and representatives of CVCP, 11 November 1966.

29 *Education*, 18 December 1964, 2 and 16 April, 14 May 1965.

30 *Education*, 14 May 1965.

31 WUMRC, ATTI, Regional Colleges, (Ad-Hoc) Committee, Minutes, 11 March 1964.

32 *Ibid.*

33 ATTI, *Is Robbins Enough?*, (May 1964), p. 8.

34 WUMRC, ATTI, Resolution, 55th Annual Conference, September 1964.

35 AEC, File A12(b), 8 March 1965.

36 WUMRC, ATTI, Higher Education Advisory Panel, 19 November 1964, Document 520.

37 *Ibid.*

38 *Ibid.*

39 *Ibid.*

40 *Ibid.*, Notes of Meeting.

41 *Education*, 7 May 1965.

42 M KOGAN, (1971), *op. cit.*, p. 175.

43 *Ibid.*, p. 193.

44 DES, Admin. Memo. 7/65, Secretary of State's speech at Woolwich Polytechnic, 27 April 1965.

45 AEC, File A317, Mr Prentice's Advisory Group, Paper No. 1, 23 June 1965.

46   T R WEAVER addressing a joint meeting of Association of CEOs and Association of EOs, *Education*, 20 August 1965.

47   J PRATT and T BURGESS, *Polytechnics: A Report*, (1974), p. 101.

48   AEC, File A495, Parsons to Alexander, 24 January 1966.

49   AEC, File A317.

50   AEC, File A495, Pimlott to Alexander, 16 December 1965.

51   WUMRC, ATTI, Higher Education Advisory Panel, 13 December 1965, Document 274.

52   *Ibid.*

53   *Ibid.*

54   *Ibid.*

55   LUIE, File 2425, Vice-chancellor's notes, 13 April 1965.

56   *Ibid.*

57   *Ibid.*

58   DES, Admin. memo. 7/65, Secretary of State's speech at Woolwich Polytechnic, 27 April 1965.

59   *Ibid.*

60   *Education*, 20 August 1965.

61   DES, Admin. memo, 7/65, Secretary of State's speech at Woolwich Polytechnic, 27 April 1965.

62   *Ibid.*

63   LUIE, File 2425, Vice-chancellor's notes, 13 April 1965.

64   DES, Admin. memo. 7/65, Secretary of State's speech at Woolwich Polytechnic, 27 April 1965.

65   *Education*, 20 August 1965.

66   LUCFO, CVCP papers, Wilson to Wolfenden, 1 June 1965.

67   *Ibid.*

68   *Ibid.*

69   *Ibid.*, Wolfenden to Wilson, 30 June 1965.

70   *Ibid.*, UGC memorandum, *The Binary System of Higher Education*, June 1965.

71   *Ibid.*

72   *Ibid.*, CVCP, Minutes, 16 July 1965.

73   LUIE, File 2425, Vice-chancellor's notes, 16 July 1965.

74   *Ibid.*, 24 September 1965.

75   LUCFO, CVCP papers, Minutes, 24 September 1965.

76   *Ibid.*, Note of a meeting with the Secretary of State, 11 November 1966.

77   *Ibid.*

78   LORD ROBBINS and B FORD, 'Report on Robbins', *Universities Quarterly*, December 1965.

79   LUCFO, CVCP papers, Note of a meeting with the Secretary of State, 11 November 1966.

80   *Ibid.*, Vice-chancellor's notes, 11 November 1966.

81   *Ibid.*, Note of a meeting with the Secretary of State, 11 November 1966.

82   *Ibid.*

83   *Ibid.*, Vice-chancellor's notes, 11 November 1966.

84   M KOGAN, (1971), *op. cit.*, p. 193.

85   LUIE, File 2425, Vice-chancellor's notes 13 April 1965.

86   AEC, File A12(b), meeting with representatives of the ATTI, 8 March 1965.

87   *Education*, 9 July and 20 August 1965.
88   AEC, File A317.
89   *Ibid.*, Mr. Prentice's Advisory Group on Higher Education within the Further Education System, Paper No. 1, 23 June 1965.
90   *Ibid.*
91   *Ibid.*
92   *Ibid.*
93   *Ibid.*
94   *Ibid.*
95   *Ibid.*
96   WUMRC, ATTI, Higher Education Advisory Panel, Meeting with CNAA, 2 June 1965.
97   *Ibid.*
98   *Ibid.*
99   AEC, File A495.
100   WUMRC, ATTI, Higher Education Advisory Panel, Notes of Meeting, 22 September 1965.
101   *Ibid.*, Document 140.
102   *Ibid.*
103   *Ibid.*, Notes of Meeting, 4 November 1965.
104   *Ibid.*
105   *Ibid.*
106   *Ibid.*, Notes of Meeting, 4 March 1966.
107   *Ibid.*, Universities Committee, Notes of Meeting, 14 March 1966.
108   *Ibid.*, Higher Education Advisory Panel, Notes of Meeting, 4 March 1966.
109   J PRATT and T BURGESS, (1974), *op. cit.*, p. 41 and 44.
110   *Ibid.*, p. 43.
111   M LOCKE, *Traditions and Controls in the Making of a Polytechnic: Woolwich Polytechnic 1890–1970*, (1978), p. 160.
112   ROBBINS COMMITTEE, Evidence, pp. 1943–5.
113   D RAAFE, 'The "Alternative Route" Reconsidered: Part-time Further Education and Social Mobility in England and Wales', *Sociology*, January 1979.
114   AEC, Files A317 and A495.

Chapter 4

New Arrangements for Governing the Institutions

Once it had been decided to set up polytechnics, the question of how these new institutions were to be related, through their governing bodies, to their local education authorities had to be considered. In June 1965 the DES prepared a paper for the Prentice Group about the internal government of further education colleges engaged in higher education.[1] This set out the existing provisions at some length summarizing both Circular 7/59 which advised local education authorities about such matters and the Robbins Report's recommendations for reforms. The paper posed many questions but offered few answers, and it gave little indication of the Department's thinking in this area. In its conclusion it admitted that detailed consideration of the issues involved would be too time-consuming for the Prentice Group and suggested two possible ways of proceeding. Either the national representative bodies could be asked to nominate members to a small working party which would draft detailed recommendations or the Department itself could prepare a detailed draft which would be considered in turn by the Prentice Group and the representative bodies.[2] Members of the Prentice Group, however, were well aware of the work of the Weaver Study Group on the government of colleges of education, and, no doubt, realized the importance of comparability between provisions for governing bodies in the two areas. It was soon agreed that the question of internal government of further education colleges involved in higher education should be considered later in the light of the Weaver Group.[3] Toby Weaver himself realized the importance of this decision, and he knew well before his Group reported that its recommendations would have implications for the whole of local authority higher education and not just for teacher training.[4]

By the mid-1960s there was considerable feeling in the further education colleges that their governing bodies should be given more freedom from local authority control. Normally college governing bodies were sub-committees of local education authorities and the extent to which powers were delegated to them varied considerably from authority to authority. Circular 7/59 encouraged delegation, but this clearly remained at the discretion of the individual authority. In a few instances the college principal was a member of the governing body, but more often he was only allowed to attend in an advisory non-voting capacity. Comparatively few colleges included teaching staff on their governing bodies. There were sometimes complaints that local authority procedures obstructed the smooth running of the colleges and caused resentment amongst the staff.[5] By 1965 the ATTI had already asked the Secretary of State to set up a working party to study this question, and it argued that:

> the college governing body should be free to spend money within estimates approved by the local education authority; that the college administration should be free from day-to-day control by the education authority; that the college principal and several members of the teaching staff should be full members of the governing body; and that the academic and staffing policies of the college, including the appointment of all except the most senior members of staff, should be largely in the hands of a college academic board.[6]

The ATTI acknowledged that important changes in the internal government of colleges were encouraged in Circular 7/59, but its central grievance, that many local education authorities had failed to implement them, remained. Later in 1965 CNAA stressed that the teaching staff in colleges offering a range of degree courses would be expected to play a responsible part in deciding the academic policy of the college. It proposed that academic boards should be created for this purpose, and it was also suggested that representatives of the teaching staff should serve on governing bodies.[7]

The Weaver Study Group reported in February 1966 when the DES was still preparing its White Paper, *A Plan for Polytechnics and other Colleges*, which has published in May. The question of polytechnic government was not considered in the White Paper as consultations with the national representative bodies still had to take place. At this stage, however, it was made clear that the arrangements for the government of a polytechnic would have to be approved by the DES before it was designated.[8] In June the DES put a paper about the government of further education colleges engaged in higher education before the Prentice Group (now renamed the Roberts Group as Goronwy Roberts had succeeded Prentice as Minister of State). In the paper it was proposed 'to use the (Weaver) Study Group's report as the basis for considering the arrangements proposed for polytechnics, and proposals would be expected to conform to them in spirit, though not necessarily in detail'.[9] The Roberts Group agreed to tackle the government of the polytechnics first and to leave the question of the other colleges until later[10], and in August the DES produced a much more detailed paper. Members of the Group were invited to submit comments in writing on this draft, which eventually formed the basis of *Government and Academic Organisation of Polytechnics. Notes for Guidance*, Appendix A of Administrative Memorandum 8/67 issued in April 1967.

In this memorandum it was made clear that the governing bodies of polytechnics would not be sub-committees of education committees, and that their instruments and articles of government would have to be submitted for DES approval. J A R Pimlott of the DES described this document as 'a radical departure from past practice in further education'.[12] The government of polytechnics was seen as of 'great importance in their full development as major institutions of higher education complementary to the universities'.[13] It was acknowledged that the polytechnics required highly qualified academic staff who should participate fully in the government and management of their academic communities. The memorandum attempted to indicate the various responsibilities of central government, local education authorities, governing bodies and academic boards in this area, but, as Michael Locke has pointed out, there was vagueness and lack of clarity in some respects.[14] It would be tedious to summarize this lengthy memorandum, and it is intended to consider only those points which proved particularly controversial. Even as early as when the AEC discussed the pre-publication draft of this memorandum, it was clear that some LEAs were doubtful about certain aspects. Eventually the AEC accepted its general approach, but Alexander warned the DES that LEAs had assumed that it was not intended to be 'rigidly prescriptive'[15] and that individual education committees might wish to make their own representations.

The main bones of contention were the clerkship to the governing body and the control of finance (including staffing establishments and grading). As in the case of the colleges of education, some authorities wanted the clerkship to be the responsibility of the CEO, but the DES, in line with the policy of the ATTI, remained adamant that this duty should be performed by the polytechnic's own senior administrative officer. The question of financial control aroused even more controversy. The DES proposed that governing bodies should be responsible for drawing up annual estimates which were to be submitted to LEAs for approval. Within approved estimates there was to be freedom for the governors to incur expenditure without further reference to the authority and there were to be provisions for virement between different headings of expenditure. These suggestions were different from existing local authority practices and there was considerable opposition to them. J C Swaffield of the AMC took up these matters with Weaver in the spring of 1968 prompting Patrick Gordon-Walker, the Secretary of State, to reiterate his belief in autonomy for the polytechnics.[16] Soon afterwards the DES gave more detailed guidelines about financial controls to the local authority associations[17], making it clear that the DES would not approve articles of government which gave governing bodies less generous terms than the guidelines specified. Several LEAs remained unhappy[18], but they had little option but to acquiesce. A further issue which became entangled with polytechnic and college government in this period was student representation. This important subject was broader than the local authority sector involving the whole of post-school education. It would not be appropriate to pursue this in detail here, but, suffice it to say that, Shirley Williams, the Minister of State dealing with this matter, had sympathy for the students' case. She insisted that all articles and instruments of government fitted in with her own convictions about educational democracy and student representation. In some instances this resulted in LEAs having to revise and resubmit their drafts, and there were consequent delays in designation.

In October 1968 a meeting of CEOs whose authorities were involved in the development of polytechnics was arranged in London.[19] From this it is clear that some authorities had found their negotiations with the DES over articles and instruments a protracted and difficult business. The Chairman, Sir William Houghton of ILEA, suggested that the local authorities were 'in a delicate and even dangerous position'.[20] It was widely felt that 'the principle of freedom and independence for the polytechnic may conflict with the role and responsibility of the local education authority'.[21] The CEOs were clearly uneasy and on the defensive. J H Taylor of Leeds maintained that 'the DES often gave the impression of wishing to counter the restrictive instincts of authorities',[22] but, compared with the problems encountered over the government of colleges of education, the LEAs had a relatively smooth passage with the polytechnics.

Some local authorities continued to have serious doubts about certain recommendations in the Weaver Report. Although, under Alexander's influence, the AEC accepted and commended the whole Report, the AMC and CCA expressed reservations about the composition of the governing body, the clerkship to the governors, the methods of appointing staff and the financial arrangements. When the Report was considered by the Leeds LEA, for example, the Education Committee did not favour the suggestion that college principals and academic staff representatives should be full members of governing bodies, and proposed that they should be allowed to attend meetings as non-voting members.[23] It also maintained that the CEO should continue to act as clerk to the governors. Leeds was certainly not alone in adopting such attitudes, and the ATCDE soon set up an Action Committee to keep up the pressure on the Government and the local authorities to implement Weaver.[24] This Committee was very active during 1966 and 1967.

In February 1967 the DES issued Circular 2/67 which committed the Government to implement the Weaver Report and to introduce the necessary legislation. This encouraged the ATCDE which tried to ensure that the government of every individual college came into line with the letter of the Weaver recommendations. Problems soon arose in Kent where the principals of the maintained colleges wished the CEO to continue to clerk their governing bodies.[25] The ATCDE opposed this, and John Haynes, the CEO, took up this matter with the AEC. Alexander felt, however, that his intervention could easily make matters worse, and he was not disposed to start 'a further argument with the ATCDE at Association level'.[26] Haynes remained dissatisfied, and believed that the ATCDE was attaching 'undue importance to what they regarded as status symbols because they were still licking the wounds they received when the Robbins' proposals for the colleges were rejected'.[27]

During 1967 the ATCDE was concerned about the slow progress being made. It was convinced that some authorities were determined to thwart the full implementation of the Weaver Report. The publication of Administrative Memorandum 8/67 did not help matters. This gave the polytechnics a form of government which the ATCDE had been seeking for the colleges throughout, and it appeared at a time when it looked possible that this might still be denied to at least some of the colleges.[28] Some of the ATCDE's fears were allayed in November when the Education Bill was introduced in the House of Lords, but it was still dissatisfied with two omissions from the Bill.[29] Firstly, it was perturbed that only the articles and not the instruments of government required the approval of the Secretary of State. The articles of government regulated the powers of the governing body and the instruments its composition and membership. Even the ATCDE had to admit that approval of instruments was not mentioned in the Weaver Report, but this was now regarded as an important matter. Secondly, there was no requirement that the clerkship to the governing body should be held by the college's own senior administrative officer. This worried the ATCDE as it had collected evidence that in only twenty-three out of fifty-eight cases of local Weaver implementation had this provision been included.[30] Lord Aberdare, the Conservative spokesman who was in close touch with the ATCDE[31], pressed these issues strongly in the debates stressing that in the case of the polytechnics both points had been conceded.[32] At this stage the

Government made no changes and the Bill passed to the Commons. The local authority associations, meanwhile, informed the DES that they supported the Government in its rejection of the controversial amendments put in the Lords.[33] The CCA stressed that, regarding the instruments, the Bill was in line with the Weaver Report, and that it would regard a decision by Parliament which varied this 'as impugning the competence of LEAs and as reopening the question of our acceptance of the report as a whole'.[34] In an interesting personal note Hetherington of the CCA told Alexander that in practice he did not think that it made very much difference whether the instruments were approved by the Secretary of State or not.[35] He felt that the ATCDE's move was 'one of those irritatingly ill-advised proposals which could do a lot of harm'[36], and added that he gathered that Weaver himself fully shared this view.[37] As the local authorities lined up against the ATCDE again, the CVCP[38] and UCET[39] predictably indicated to the DES that they supported the college teachers.

In the Commons Shirley Williams, the Minister of State, came under similar pressure from *both* sides of the House concerning the instruments of government. She clearly had some sympathy with the Bill's critics in this respect[40], but she stressed that any change would lead to difficulties with the local authorities. Sir Edward Boyle was particularly unhappy about the discrepancy between the polytechnics and the colleges of education and found it 'difficult to accept a solution which gave the impression that the colleges of education were the cinderellas of the education system'.[41] Towards the end of the debate Williams admitted that, with regard to the instruments, she seemed 'to be clinging to nothing but a rather insubstantial piece of paper'.[42] She promised to take members' views seriously, but she asked them to take the local authorities' opposition seriously.[43]

By this stage the ATCDE considered that it had pushed its case concerning the instruments as far as it dared, although it was still concerned that without the requirement of DES approval some local authorities would deny voting rights to teacher representatives on governing bodies. The ATCDE was worried that the whole Bill might be withdrawn if pressure was maintained[44], and it issued a circular to members suggesting that the Bill should now be allowed to go through its remaining stages without further amendment.[45]

ATCDE officers met Shirley Williams a few days later, and discovered that local authority association opposition was weakening. At a meeting between the Minister of State and the local authority associations it was agreed to amend the Bill so that instruments of government of colleges of education (but *not* of further education colleges) had to be submitted for DES approval.[46] It was argued that it would cause too much extra work and be too expensive to include the further education colleges. The DES was also anxious to keep the further education colleges in line with schools in this respect[47] as were the local authorities. The exclusion of the further education colleges from this amendment brought strong protests from the ATTI.[48] A A Evans, General Secretary of the ATCDE, was jubilant pointing out that the change would make it much more difficult for authorities which had held out for large majorities on college of education governing bodies and which had proposed to withhold voting powers from staff representatives.[49]

Still the vexed question of the clerkships to governing bodies remained. On 18 April 1968 Williams announced that the Government would require, as a clause in the articles, that the senior administrative officer of a college should be the clerk, but that the small size of some colleges and certain administrative problems in others might prevent immediate implementation in all cases.[50] Some CEOs remained hostile to this, but the local authority associations began to take a more conciliatory attitude. The debates in Parliament had shown that there was little sympathy for the local authorities' position on this issue.[51] Leonard Brown, Education Secretary of the CCA, told Alexander that he wished that 'some of our more militant education officers could be made to realize how thin is the ice on which the binary system is skating'.[52] Alexander agreed and admitted that he was 'increasingly concerned by the attitude of some of our colleagues as to whether we were right to fight for the binary system. They merely give colour to the arguments which were used against authorities at earlier stages in these discussions.'[53] Eventually Hetherington proposed a compromise solution to the DES. Where there was agreement about the future of the clerkship between all the parties concerned (the authority, the governors, the principal and the staff representatives), that agreement should be respected. Although where the clerkship was to remain with the CEO, the situation should be reviewed after a specified period of time. In cases of disagreement, provided that the Secretary of State approved, the clerkship would remain with the CEO for a limited period only, after which the situation would be reviewed.[54]

Hetherington's proposal was severely criticized by one county CEO who felt that it continued local authority weakness in the face of the ATCDE.[55] Hetherington predicted that in two or three years time people would wonder what all this fuss was about[56], and his suggestion proved acceptable to Herbert Andrew, Permanent Secretary at the DES.[57] The CCA's proposals were formally agreed at a meeting between Shirley Williams and the local authority associations early in 1969[58], and Williams intimated that, 'if at the end of the review period the authority, the governors and the staff all still wanted the CEO to continue to act as clerk it was unlikely that the Department would demur.'[59]

When the DES applied this formula to the colleges of education in Buckinghamshire, there was concern about the considerable diminution in local authority powers on the part of some leading members of the Education Committee (including two who had attended the January meeting at the DES with Shirley Williams).[60] One or two senior members were very critical of the weakness of the CCA over this, and the CEO only just managed to prevent the complete rejection of the compromise proposals.[61] The CEO told Alexander that in Buckinghamshire members rarely took such a strong line as this, and he stressed that all those concerned wished the CEO to continue to clerk the governing bodies of the colleges and that no difficulties had ever arisen over this matter before. He concluded that he agreed with members who claimed that local authorities' discretion was being removed to the Secretary of State.[62] Alexander confirmed that the DES was acting according to the agreement with the local authority associations, but added 'I do not suggest that this was a very satisfactory arrangement but it was the best we could get'.[63] He went on to criticize the attitude of certain local authorities and of the Minister of State. He claimed that there were authorities (but stressed that he did not include Buckinghamshire in this category) 'where basically the whole concept of the Weaver Report is unacceptable. My personal view is wholly in favour of a high degree of delegation of authority to governing bodies of colleges, and indeed of schools.'[64] On the other hand, he was 'increasingly concerned at the attitude of Mrs Williams to local authorities. Recent announcements seem to indicate that she takes the view that she is directly responsible for higher education and that the local authority associations are of no importance in this field.'[65] It is interesting that Alexander attributed the local authorities' frustrations in this area to Shirley Williams in particular and not to the DES in general, and the available evidence suggests that he was not very wide of the mark.

By the summer of 1969 about 40 per cent of the maintained colleges had made arrangements under which the CEO continued as clerk to the governing body[66], but there were still problems in some localities. In Kent, for example, Sittingbourne College of Education found itself in the centre of a dispute between its LEA and the London University Institute of Education. Lionel Elvin indicated that the Institute did not approve of the CEO continuing to act as clerk to the governing body, and implied that, if this was more than a temporary arrangement, the Institute would have to consider its continued recognition of the College.[67] This incensed John Haynes who was completely familiar with the terms of the agreement with Shirley Williams which Kent had followed to the letter. Alexander strongly supported Haynes over this, and Shirley Williams was approached. At first she responded by stressing that 'we share the wish of the London Institute that in the long run the senior administrative officer should be clerk to the governors and expect that in due course this will be the wish of the staff and the governing body'.[68] Alexander and Haynes regarded this response as unsatisfactory as it implied that the Department might be prepared to try to influence the staff and governors to reach this conclusion. Haynes replied that he thought that when this matter was reviewed there should be freedom of choice and opinion for all the parties.[69] Shirley Williams conceded this, and, to Haynes satisfaction she reiterated her previous statement to the local authority associations.[70] Thus this particular dispute was eventually resolved amicably, but clearly feelings were still running high.

With hindsight it is perhaps surprising that these details of college government aroused so much controversy in the late 1960s. It is easy, however, to underestimate the magnitude of the changes. Contemporaries certainly felt that they were involved with issues which were vital to the future of their institutions and their working lives. With respect to the polytechnics Michael Locke has argued that disproportionate time and attention was devoted by the DES to constitutional questions.[71] He has pointed out that this led in certain instances to long delays in designation and that little guidance came from central government on other issues which were vital to the future development of the polytechnics. These are fair comments as long as they are not interpreted to mean that the question of government was unimportant.

The discussions about college government were significant not only because they reflected increased concern in society as a whole about matters such as participation and democracy, but also because they were concerned with the prestige and status of the institutions involved. In many ways the latter were the more important. The teachers' associations felt that greater institutional autonomy was essential to meet the justified aspirations of their members, and in the case of the ATCDE there was particularly strong respect for university forms of government which it hoped would be emulated in the local authority sector. The local authorities, having been promised their own sector of higher education, found themselves, almost immediately, in a difficult position. They felt increasingly squeezed between DES requirements and initiatives on the one hand and increased institutional autonomy on the other. In general they were more willing to grant increased autonomy to the newly-created polytechnics than to colleges of education and further education colleges which were more numerous and which had formed part of the local authority domain for decades. They were prepared to pay the price for the increased status being accorded to the polytechnics, but could see little reason to disturb established relationships in other spheres despite the recommendations of the Weaver Report. It is interesting that the local authority associations, especially the AEC led by Alexander, were usually more amenable to the changes than individual LEAs and particularly certain CEOs. At a time of increasing economic difficulty with consequent financial pressures on the education service the local authorities feared that the changes would lead to less detailed and effective control of expenditure. There is evidence to suggest that senior civil servants at the DES shared at least some of the misgivings of the local authorities, and in the end the reforms owed much to the interest and persistence of certain politicians. Sir Edward Boyle, the Conservative education spokesman, was fully committed to these changes and refused to allow them to fall from the political agenda. Shirley Williams, who was the Minister of State during the crucial period, never made a secret of her enthusiasm for these reforms, and, according to Alexander[72], her considerable contribution in this area was the main achievement of her period of office.

Notes

1   AEC, File A317, DES memorandum, 23 June 1965.
2   *Ibid.*
3   *Ibid.*, 14 July 1965.
4   *Ibid.*, File A713, Weaver to Alexander, September 1965.
5   J PRATT and T BURGESS, *The Polytechnics: A Report*, (1974), p. 151.
6   ATTI, *The Future of Higher Education within the Further Education System*, (1965), p. 21.
7   CNAA, Statement No. 3, (November 1965) pp. 9–10.
8   DES, *A Plan for Polytechnics and Other Colleges*, (May 1966), Paragraph 25.
9   AEC, File A713, DES memorandum for meeting of Roberts Advisory Group, 13 June 1966.
10   *Ibid.*, File A731, Peters to Alexander, 22 August 1966.
11   *Ibid.*
12   *Ibid.*, File A190, Minutes of the National Advisory Council on Education for Industry and Commerce, 22 November 1967.
13   DES, Administrative Memorandum 8/67.
14   J PRATT and T BURGESS, (1974), *op. cit.*, pp. 165–6.
15   AEC, File A731, Alexander to Peters, 1 December 1966.
16   *TES*, 8 March 1968.
17   AEC, File A731, Pimlott to Swaffield, 14 March 1968.
18   *Ibid.*, Houghton to Pimlott, 8 April 1968, Hetherington to Pimlott, 19 April 1968.
19   *Ibid.*, Meeting of CEOs at AEC Building, 1 October 1968.
20   *Ibid.*
21   *Ibid.*
22   J H TAYLOR, *The Polytechnics and the LEAs*, (July 1970), in *Coombe Lodge Reports*, Volume 3, No. 16, p. 9.

23 LUIE, File 3091, Leeds Education Committee, October 1966.
24 ATCDE, *The Government of Colleges of Education*, p. 9.
25 AEC, File A713, Haynes to Alexander, 20 March 1967.
26 *Ibid.*, Alexander to Haynes, 4 April 1967.
27 *Ibid.*, Haynes to Alexander, 3 April 1967.
28 ATCDE, *op. cit.*, p. 11.
29 *Ibid.*, p. 12.
30 ATCDE, Analysis of Replies received from Principals re progress on Weaver implemention, January 1968.
31 ATCDE, *op. cit.*, p. 12.
32 HANSARD, House of Lords, 23 November 1967, cols. 1177–8, 5 December 1967, col. 550.
33 AEC, File A731, Hetherington to Weaver 20 December 1967, Alexander to Weaver, 5 January 1968.
34 *Ibid.*, Hetherington to Weaver.
35 *Ibid.*, Hetherington to Alexander, 10 January 1968.
36 *Ibid.*
37 *Ibid.*
38 ATCDE, *op. cit.*, p. 13.
39 LUIE, File 3093, UCET Committee Minutes, 7 December 1967.
40 HANSARD, House of Commons, 7 February 1968, col. 575.
41 *Ibid.*, col. 581.
42 *Ibid.*, col. 610.
43 *Ibid.*, cols. 615–6.
44 ATCDE, *op. cit.*, p. 14.
45 *Ibid.*
46 AEC, File A731, Alexander to Drew, 8 April 1968.
47 *Ibid.*, Pimlott to Alexander, 12 June 1967.
48 *TES*, 12 July 1968.
49 *Education*, 17 May 1968.
50 ATCDE, *op. cit.*, p. 14.
51 AEC, File A731, Hetherington to Wigfall, 23 August 1968.
52 *Ibid.*, Brown to Alexander, 11 September 1968.
53 *Ibid.*, Alexander to Brown, 13 September 1968.
54 *Ibid.*, Hetherington to Wigfall, 23 August 1968.
55 *Ibid.*, Hetherington to Harding, 11 September 1968.
56 *Ibid.*
57 *Ibid.*, Alexander to Brown, 13 September 1968.
58 AEC, File A1119, Note of a meeting at DES, 13 January 1969.
59 *Ibid.*
60 AEC, File A713, Harding to Alexander, 21 March 1969.
61 *Ibid.*
62 *Ibid.*
63 *Ibid.*, Alexander to Harding, 25 March 1969.
64 *Ibid.*
65 *Ibid.*
66 AEC, File E38, Haynes to Alexander, 8 July 1969.
67 *Ibid.*, Elvin to Haynes, 2 July 1969.

68 *Ibid.*, Williams to Haynes, 22 July 1969.
69 *Ibid.*, Haynes to Williams, 4 August 1969.
70 *Ibid.*, Williams to Haynes, 24 September 1969.
71 J PRATT and T BURGESS, (1974), *op. cit.*, pp. 149–71; M LOCKE, *op. cit.*, in *Coombe Lodge Reports*, Volume 5, No. 15.
72 *Education*, 31 October 1969.

Chapter 5

Unresolved Issues in the Advanced Further Education Sector

Defining the Polytechnics' Functions

It has often been pointed out that central government gave the nascent local authority sector of higher education little guidance about its nature, philosophy and principles. It was certainly true that, with the exception of forms of government, detailed requirements were not laid down. When asked by the ATTI about the philosophy behind the structure of the polytechnics, J A R Pimlott, Assistant Under-Secretary at the DES, replied that, 'the broad philosophy had been laid down in the White Paper, but it was his impression that it would be wrong at this stage, and against our interests, if authorities were to lay down the philosophy of the polytechnics when, in fact, the people deciding this were non-academics'.[1] He thought it would be more advisable if the machinery of polytechnics was established first, then the academic boards allowed to establish what the philosophy was in the development of that polytechnic. Robinson and Britton were dissatisfied with this response, and Britton commented, 'they were producing a machine to do a job when, in fact, a job analysis had not been carried out to find out what the machine was required to do'.[2] The DES kept firmly to this line, and the Minister of State, Shirley Williams, is on record as saying in early 1969, 'only the polytechnics themselves will decide what they become . . . it is a role that the DES itself cannot determine'.[3] This was, of course, very much in tune with the approach traditionally adopted by central government in relation to educational institutions in this country.

A theme which ran through Crosland's Woolwich and Lancaster speeches and which was present in the 1966 White Paper was that the local authority sector would cater for both full and part-time students who were attending courses at both degree and sub-degree levels. This was sometimes described as 'comprehensive' higher education and was contrasted with the provision made in the universities where, it was claimed, full-time under-graduate and postgraduate studies dominated.

In February 1968 Pimlott told CEOs that these points remained basic to government policy.[4] He criticized those who thought that the polytechnics would be primarily concerned with degree courses and 'as alternatives to universities with another name'.[5] Those who claimed that polytechnics were a means to provide university education 'on the cheap'[6] were denounced. He went on to give the current DES definition of comprehensive higher education. It applied 'broadly to all courses aimed at students of 18 or over with a normal minimum standard of entry of five 'O' levels or the equivalent and rising to a standard above 'A' level'.[7] This is interesting in the light of earlier discussions of this question. In 1965 it was stated that, although polytechnics should shed all courses aimed at the 16–18 age range, 'the presumption would be that unless there was good reason to the contrary in a particular case all courses catering for over 18 students at entry were appropriate'.[18] The definition which Pimlott mentioned in 1968, and which was the same as the one used by the Robbins Committee, was narrower than the one employed in earlier discussions. Now a minimum entry requirement of five 'O' levels was specified whereas the phrase mentioned earlier was 'irrespective of entry requirements'.[9] Pimlott repeated that the polytechnics would concentrate on the 18+ age group, but stressed that 'tendencies to shed non-degree and part-time courses such as have occurred in the past will be vigorously resisted'.[10]

In the next few years ministers often reiterated these basic points. Although emphases varied slightly, Patrick Gordon-Walker, Edward Short and Shirley Williams for Labour and Margaret Thatcher, William van Straubenzee and Norman St. John-Stevas for the Conservatives developed these themes in speeches made in the period 1968 to 1972. The DES, however, did not provide guidelines about the proportions of full and part-time students it expected to find in the polytechnics. Nor did it indicate how they should divide their resources between degree and sub-degree courses. This led some commentators[11] to question whether there was real commit-ment to part-time students and to sub-degree work on the part of the DES.

Several studies of the emerging polytechnics were carried out in the 1970s, and they were unanimous in their findings that part-time and sub-degree work declined in comparison with full-time degree course provi-sion.[12] Cantor and Roberts estimated that there were 67,000 full-time and 96,000 part-time students in polytechnic colleges in 1969, but by 1975 there were 108,000 full-time and only 54,000 part-time.[13] Similarly Burgess calculated that at the time of designation sub-degree courses accounted for 70 per cent of the total work of the polytechnics, but by 1974 this had fallen to 50 per cent and was still falling.[14] Commentators have been less unanimous in their views about the causes of these trends. Pratt, Burgess and Robinson have argued that the DES gave little impetus to these areas of work, and they also felt that polytechnic directors and many of their staff had insufficient commitment to this level of work preferring to concentrate on higher status full-time degree work.

Robinson claimed that the DES gave a poor lead in this respect as early as 1967.[15] During salary negotiations in that year the authorities panel (representing both the DES and the LEAs) countered the claim from the ATTI that there should be parity between the pay of university and polytechnic lecturers by stressing that some of the work in the polytechnics was at sub-degree level. According to Robinson this encouraged the polytechnics to shed their sub-degree work as soon as possible, and, with hindsight, Anthony Crosland agreed that a mistake had been made.[16] On the other hand, Cantor and Roberts were sceptical of these arguments and have suggested that the greater emphasis on full-time degree courses was in large measure a result of students 'voting with their feet'.[17] The Committee of Directors of Polytechnics, with obvious but not necessarily distorting vested interests, took much the same line. Sir Alex Smith, Director of Manchester Polytechnic, told a House of Commons Committee in 1976

> Most polytechnics that I know would just love to lay on more part-time courses for HNC-type students, but they are not forthcoming; the students are not there. They are preferring to go on to full-time degree courses and I personally think this is a trend in education the effect of which we shall feel for a long time in our industry. There is going to be a dearth of senior technicians.[18]

His colleague, Dr A Suddaby of City of London Polytechnic, added

> The 1966 White Paper concentrated higher education at degree level in a few institutions and so of course the degree work expanded in polytechnics. The part-time work could not expand in proportion because at a time when you are expanding the places for full-time higher education the part-time demand cannot increase very easily: in fact it tends to decrease.[19]

In 1977 Shirley Williams, now Secretary of State, chastised the polytechnics for the disappointing level of expansion achieved in part-time higher education[20], but governments continued to deal in exhortations rather than requirements or incentives in this matter. Central government also gave little guidance to the polytechnics about their curricula. In his Woolwich speech

Anthony Crosland put great emphasis on vocational, professional and industrially-based courses. Ministers from both political parties continued to stress the importance of this approach and it has been widely accepted in principle by those who work in the polytechnics. It is not proposed to try to consider curriculum development in the polytechnics here. This complex subject is worthy of a book in its own right.

The question of research in the local authority sector of higher education, particularly the polytechnics, proved interesting. By the mid 1960s the ATTI was already stressing that research was important for the vitality of institutions of higher education[21], and in 1965 it had been agreed to introduce posts of reader into the technical colleges. Although the ATTI was generally pleased by this development, it made it clear that it had reservations about research becoming a major criterion in the upgrading of departments. Edward Britton told the Burnham Committee, 'we are a little disturbed that this may encourage the kind of attitude that exists in some departments in universities where the standard of teaching is almost irrelevant but where the department is judged by the number of research papers that the staff of the department can publish'.[22] Despite these fears, the ATTI continued to argue publicly for the development of research. CNAA also encouraged research in institutions which taught its degree courses.[23] Its chief officer, F R Hornby, admitted that it was unrealistic to expect all the colleges teaching CNAA degree courses to have a volume of research work comparable to that existing in universities, but stressed

> A degree course conducted in a bleak atmosphere where there was no prospect of research work or advanced study would indeed be a poor thing: the Council has no intention of approving a course as leading to its degrees where such an atmosphere exists.[24]

The DES, meanwhile, remained almost silent on this subject. No indication of policy was given in either the Woolwich speech or the White Paper of 1966. In private Crosland told the CVCP that the Government did not intend to push research in the polytechnics.[25] In his public speech at Lancaster University soon afterwards, Crosland seemed more positive. Although he reiterated that the balance between teaching and research in the polytechnics would be different from the universities, he claimed, 'when we say that the polytechnics will be primarily teaching institutions, of course we do not wish to deny the staff opportunities for research to serve the needs of local industry, or to enlarge their knowledge and understanding of their own disciplines'.[26] These assurances were regarded with scepticism by an anonymous writer in the *Times Educational Supplement* who described them as 'half-truths'.[27] In the light of what had been said to the CVCP this scepticism seemed justified and the Lancaster speech did little to clarify the position. In some ways the DES was already committed to research in technical colleges, for as early as 1946 the Ministry of Education had issued a circular[28] encouraging research there. In April 1967 the DES updated its thoughts in Appendix B of Administrative Memorandum 8/67 entitled *Research in Polytechnics*. Its first sentence indicated that 'the main responsibilities of the polytechnics will be as teaching institutions',[29] but allowed that provision for research 'which is essential to the proper fulfilment of their teaching functions and the maintenance and development of close links with industry'[30] should be made. It stressed that teachers should have the chance to study for higher degrees and 'adequate opportunities of keeping abreast with new knowledge in their fields and should be given the necessary facilities to do so.'[31] It hoped that polytechnics would be 'ready to undertake *ad hoc* research projects on behalf of industry or under contract from research councils and other bodies'.[32] On the other hand, it argued that research activities should be carried out 'without prejudice to other necessary work and without adding to the permanent establishment'.[33] The DES did not envisage that there would be members of academic staff who devoted the whole or most of their time to research, and it did not expect full-time research assistants to be employed on any considerable scale.[34] Polytechnics, therefore, were not to be deprived of research, but, despite these new guidelines, the whole subject remained shrouded in doubts and ambiguities. It is difficult to avoid the conclusion that these doubts and ambiguities were in the Department's interests, for to have denied the polytechnics research opportunities would have reduced their status and would have prompted strong protests, but to have given them their head in this respect would have been expensive and would have brought criticisms that they were becoming inseparable from universities.

During the period in which Administrative Memorandum 8/67 was being prepared the DES remained silent about the appointment of readers in technical colleges. This led the ATTI to believe that the DES was 'dragging its feet' over this matter[35] and the AEC was approached. Alexander denied that the LEAs were responsible for the delay, and eventually raised the question with Crosland.[36] The latter explained that when applications began to arrive from colleges in 1966 they did not follow a common pattern or reflect consistent policies. Most colleges had put up one or two cases where the CNAA had specifically suggested that there should be readers, but one authority proposed that there should be a first instalment of eighteen readers (towards a projected total implement of forty-seven) in one of its colleges.[37] In view of the difficulty of arriving at common criteria and because of other complications arising out of the reorganization of further education, Crosland proposed to suspend the consideration of applications until after the polytechnics were designated.[38] This brought a strong protest from Sir William Houghton of the ILEA.[39] He claimed that this would be 'a considerable blow to morale' and that 'it will certainly recreate the suspicions which are not yet dead, that in the Department's thinking research will have no place in the new institutions'.[40] In practice in the 1970s very few readers were appointed in polytechnics, for in 1977 there were only forty-seven readers out of a full-time teaching staff of over 15,000.[41] In the light of these figures, Houghton's obvious doubts concerning the Department's commitment seemed vindicated.

During 1967 the Department also became concerned about the practice of certain LEAs which charged expenditure on research studentships to the advanced further education (AFE) pool. Sunderland had done this for some years, but was informed early in 1968 that the DES had taken legal advice and had been told that such expenditure was not poolable. This opinion was questioned by Sunderland, and eventually the Department asked the newly-created Pooling Committee[42] whether it thought research studentships ought to be poolable.[43] It was pointed out that in the period 1961–66 there had been fifty-seven research students at Sunderland Technical College but very few of them had been supported by industry or research councils.[44] The DES also stressed that Sunderland was not an isolated case and that the AFE pool was carrying 'an appreciable but unidentifiable amount of expenditure on research studentship'.[45] The Pooling Committee decided that the pooling of expenditure on research studentships should cease, although the local authority associations were concerned that the Pooling Committee was close to overstepping its proper functions in dealing with this 'policy' matter.[46] Sunderland felt that this decision 'would inevitably have an adverse effect on the development of research',[47] but Alexander pointed out to LEAs that there was 'widespread concern that the rate of increase in pooled expenditure had far outstripped increase in expenditure in other sectors of education'.[48] In this context there was little chance that the DES view would be seriously challenged.

References in ministerial speeches to research in polytechnics kept strictly within the guidelines laid down in Administrative Memorandum 8/67, but were usually restrictionist in tone. In March 1968 Patrick Gordon-Walker emphasized that polytechnics would be 'primarily teaching institutions and less of their effort would therefore be devoted to research than at universities',[49] and he hoped that polytechnics would attract staff whose main interest was in teaching. They would, however, be encouraged to develop applied research which arose naturally from their teaching activities, sponsored by industrial and other agencies. In June 1969 Shirley Williams took very much the same line.[50] The change in government in 1970 made little difference in this respect. William van Straubenzee, Under-Secretary of State, said that he did not see polytechnics as major centres of fundamental research.[51] He expected 'their research philosophy to be in close parallel with their teaching aims — the application and development of existing knowledge to meet contemporary needs'.[52] Margaret Thatcher put these points more strongly and made it clear that polytechnics would receive no encouragement 'to undertake scientific research without practical application'.[53] She stressed that they were primarily teaching institutions and their research was to be different from that of the universities 'in both nature and degree'.[54]

During this period the ATTI, the CDP[55] and the CNAA consistently advocated the development of research in polytechnics. In 1974 a CNAA working party chaired by Professor George Rochester reported on resources for research.[56] It emphasized that the CNAA expected staff teaching on degree courses to participate in research, and it expected polytechnics to provide the necessary time and equipment. CNAA also made it clear that it regarded all styles of research including 'fundamental' and 'pure' research, as suitable for polytechnics. It proposed that the DES should be more liberal in its appointment of readers to polytechnics, but it stressed that there should be no division between staff 'who do research' and others 'who carry the teaching load'. In many ways this Report strengthened CNAA's initial comments made on research in 1965. Nonetheless, the polytechnics did less well in obtaining grants from the research councils than the universities. In 1979–80, for example, the polytechnics received 2.8 per cent of the Social Science Research Council's budget and 3.5 per cent of the Science and Engineering Council's[57], but this disparity was hardly surprising when the terms of Administrative Memorandum 8/67 and the economic constraints of the 1970s are taken into account. NATFHE (ATTI's successor), CDP and CNAA all remained committed to the development of research in the local authority sector of higher education, but in the context of the 1980s Sir Norman Lindop, former Director of Hatfield Polytechnic, was almost certainly correct when he said, 'We have always had to fight for research on the margins of things. Now under pressure it is going to be even more difficult'.[58] In many ways Administrative Memorandum 8/67 obfuscated, rather than clarified, the position regarding research in the local authority sector of higher education, and successive governments have done little to change this situation. It is difficult to avoid the conclusion that the DES's interests continued to be well served by the existing ambiguities.

Devising National Organizational Structures

During 1969 and 1970 tensions between the local authorities and central government over aspects of the implementation of the binary policy were much in evidence. In January 1969 Shirley Williams, the Minister of State, exacerbated an already delicate situation when she suggested at a conference that polytechnics needed to develop a sense of autonomy and confidence, and that to help achieve this she hoped the directors of polytechnics would set up a committee which could play a similar role to the CVCP.[59] The local authorities which did not want to see the polytechnics engaging in direct negotiations with central government regarded this suggestion, which was repeated on several occasions, as provocative. A few weeks later the Government announced plans to increase student numbers in higher education, and, Alexander, along with other local authority spokesmen, objected strongly that this matter had not been discussed with their associations.[60] It was also reported that the Government accepted the view of Kenneth Berrill, the new Chairman of the UGC, that a unitary plan for higher education was necessary if costs were to be kept down.[61] Later in May and June Edward Short, now Secretary of State, and Shirley Williams, denied a spate of rumours that 'the Government had abandoned the binary policy at birth'.[62] Williams argued that the binary policy should not prevent cooperation between universities and polytechnics, but she confirmed that basic policies had not changed. Soon afterwards the binary policy was questioned from another quarter. The House of Commons Select Committee on Student Relations reported that it had received little evidence in support of the dual system of higher education and much against it.[63] The Committee recommended the establishment of a Higher Education Commission across the binary line, and suggested that the Government should consider how all institutions of higher education could be financed in the same way.[64] During the next two years there was much speculation in the educational press about the creation of polyversities or comprehensive universities, and groups including the AUT, the NUT and the NUS came out in favour of a unitary system of higher education. The available evidence suggests that neither the DES nor the local authorities took these ideas particularly seriously.

During the spring of 1970 Shirley Williams's suggestion that a Committee of Directors of Polytechnics should be formed was taken up. The first Secretary, George Tolley, Director of Sheffield Polytechnic, assured the local authorities that this new body wanted the polytechnics to remain within their sphere of influence.[65] He was on record as rejecting the Select

Committee's notion of a Higher Education Commission, but he favoured the creation of a 'representative Polytechnics Commission to assist the LEAs'.[66] A Polytechnics Grants Committee soon became CDP policy, and the directors also indicated that they were interested in the question of charters for polytechnics to award degrees but they emphasized that university status was not sought.[67] The CDP continued to stress, however, that it favoured local authority involvement in the polytechnics and in higher education.[68] The fears of chief education officers were not allayed by these reassurances, and a meeting of CEOs with polytechnic responsibilities was held at Oxford to exchange views. It was generally agreed that there were dangers to the position of CEOs in the present situation and that the DES had not been helpful in this respect.[69] The CEOs decided to continue to observe developments carefully. Alexander, who was in touch with the CEOs, took the view that the AEC could do little. He was not as anxious as the CEOs, and he felt, with the newly-elected Conservative Government in power from June 1970, that there was not 'such close contact or sympathy' between the DES and the CDP as when Shirley Williams had been in office.[70]

Even before the new polytechnics came into operation there was considerable concern amongst local authorities about the rate of growth of pooled expenditure. In part this was a reflection of the general unease concerning the growth of education expenditure particularly in the light of Britain's poor economic prospects. During the late 1960s Alexander regularly pointed out that since the war the cost of the education service had increased more rapidly than the wealth of the nation. In 1945 education required less that 2 per cent of the gross national product, but by 1969 it needed over 6 per cent.[71] He stressed that education was a labour-intensive service in which costs were likely to rise more steeply than in the economy as a whole, and he concluded that it was most unlikely that education's current growth rate would be sustained in the future. It is against this background of increasing economic difficulty in the late 1960s that concern over pooled expenditure must be seen.

The practice of 'pooling' expenditure was introduced for teacher training in 1945 and for advanced further education in 1958. Its aim was to spread costs fairly amongst all LEAs, and it was based on the principle that 'it would be a hardship for the maintaining LEA to bear the full cost of colleges and courses which attract a considerable proportion of students from the areas of other authorities'.[72] Expenditure on approved courses was charged to the pool by the providing authority, and, according to a formula, all LEAs made sufficient payments to cover the total cost of the pool.

By 1966 some authorities were so concerned about increases in rates that a resolution was submitted to the AEC Conference that the financial responsibility for pooled expenditure should be transferred to national taxation.[73] Although this motion was severely criticized and eventually lost, it was indicative of the depth of feeling in some areas. During the following year the AMC approached the DES and expressed the view that

> having regard to the extent of the sums now involved in pooling arrangements and the prospect of further widening of the area of expenditure to be pooled, there is a need for greater local authority participation in the oversight of pooled expenditure, with the object of keeping the grand total within limits which may be regarded as tolerable by local authorities in relation to the share which they have to bear.[74]

Although the DES did not entirely share the AMC's views, it recognized that there was anxiety and arranged a meeting of officers from the AMC, the CCA, the ILEA and the DES to discuss the matter. Eventually the DES agreed to set up a standing committee to provide a forum for discussion of pooling problems. This was welcomed by the local authority associations. The Committee's terms of reference were 'to consider and keep under review the arrangements for pooling educational expenditure with particular reference to teacher training and advanced further education and to make recommendations to the Secretary of State or to the local authority associations, as may be appropriate'.[75] The first Chairman of the Pooling Committee was J A Hudson, Accountant-General at the DES, and it was composed of four representatives from the AMC, four from the CCA, two from the ILEA, two from the AEC and one from the Welsh Joint Education Committee. Both local authority treasurers and chief education officers were strongly represented, but it did not include elected councillors in its membership. Very early in the Committee's proceedings the local authority associations, led by Hetherington of the CCA, made it clear that they felt that it should not be concerned with policy matters and this was accepted by the DES.[76] Consequently, the Pooling Committee concentrated mainly on technical exercises such as analyses of cost factors in teacher training and advanced further education. These were undertaken with a view to establishing norms for staffing and other items of expenditure.

The creation of the Pooling Committee did not alleviate the local authorities' concern over the growth of pooled expenditure. On the contrary, in many ways feelings intensified as education's growth rate was curtailed. During 1969–70 the Government expected LEAs to limit their growth rate to $3\frac{1}{2}$ per cent but authorities were faced with contributions to the pool which were 11 per cent higher than the previous year.[77] Kathleen

Ollerenshaw, the Conservative Chairperson of the AMC Education Committee, estimated that pooled expenditure would continue to grow at twice the pace of all LEA expenditure.[78] From time to time individual LEAs took up this issue with their associations, for example, in 1970 Warwickshire complained to the AEC and the CCA about 'the excessive growth of pool expenditure in 1969–70 and 1970–71'.[79]

The main criticism of the pooling system was that individual authorities made decisions involving large sums of money which were ultimately charged to other authorities. Some members of authorities which were 'payers' rather than 'providers' wondered whether this could be squared with local independence and democratic control[80], and there was resentment about it.[81] It was often alleged that as providing authorities had to find only a small proportion of the total cost of their colleges their sense of financial responsibility was eroded. In some quarters it was felt that 'neither the burdens of extravagance nor the benefits of sound planning and economical administration were effectively brought home to the local authorities concerned'.[82] The AMC claimed that pooling 'tended to be inflationary',[83] and this was echoed by Kathleen Ollerenshaw when she wrote, 'We ardently hope that all providing local authorities take an equally responsible view about economies of cost. The evidence suggests that they do not'.[84] She also pointed out that pooling encouraged an individual authority to expand its provisions in the relevant areas as much as it could as it gained in capital development, population, local employment, commercial income and grant from the expansion but shared the cost with other authorities.[85] Alexander accepted Ollerenshaw's basic points that pooling could be both inflationary and expansionary (it is important to recognize that these are separate issues although they can have similar effects on total costs), but, with regard to the latter, he stressed that in the 1960s it was deliberate government policy to expand the main items of pooled expenditure more rapidly than the education service as a whole.[86]

The CDP was particularly annoyed by the AMC's allegation that pooling by its nature was inflationary.[87] This claim was often repeated by other people and it soon became widely accepted as correct. It was included in the Second Report of the House of Commons Expenditure Committee[88], and the former Minister of State, Gerald Fowler, made the same point writing in August 1970.[89] The CDP completely refuted this claim and contended that pooling could only be called 'inflationary' if it was shown that 'there has been wasteful and unnecessary duplication, if costs have been increasing out of proportion to real provision or if there has been misallocation of resources'.[90] The Society of Education Officers was probably accurate when it maintained that authorities were not claiming that pooling led to waste and inefficiency but were suspicious that the rate of growth was uncurtailed.[91] Kathleen Ollerenshaw remained concerned about 'the open-endedness of this financial commitment'.[92] She mentioned that there were plans to increase student numbers in polytechnics, and with national salary scales and conditions of service there was little scope for economies on staffing. She also stressed that polytechnics and colleges had recently been given relatively independent governing bodies with a considerable degree of financial freedom. By the late 1960s some local authority members and officers argued that having their own distinctive sector of higher education had brought them diminished influence and control over their colleges and, at the same time, had committed them to meet high and ever increasing costs.

Under Kathleen Ollerenshaw the AMC's Education Committee pressed for further action. It argued that the present arrangements in the Pooling Committee, with financial advisers compiling useful statistical information, were good within their limitations but it wanted a new body 'with more teeth'. It suggested that

> as a matter of urgency there should be introduced into the machinery a more positive means of controlling the total of pooled expenditure. We therefore propose to ask the Department and the other Associations to discuss the desirability of establishing a committee with elected member representation to exercise central oversight of pooled expenditure, with, (if necessary), executive responsibilities.[93]

Swaffield of the AMC told Sir Herbert Andrew, Permanent Secretary at the DES, 'what I think we are inclined to hanker after is something not dissimilar from the UGC in exercise of a controlling function and a much more definite central oversight of the expenditure charged to the pool'.[94] He accepted that development on these lines 'must lead towards a diminution of local independence since a central body to be effective would have to have some measure of executive responsibility'.[95] He concluded, 'I cannot believe that any of the Associations or, indeed, the Department could be happy about this area of educational expenditure whilst the whole of the public sector of expenditure is under such strain'.[96] The Pooling Committee, meanwhile, was grappling with the problem of the future of the AFE pool. The CCA representatives argued that the whole case for the pooling of expenditure should be reviewed as it 'militated against the rationalization of the provision of courses and detracted from the independence of authorities'.[97] It suggested that recoupment offered a suitable, practical alternative. This was rejected by the AMC representatives because they considered 'it overlooked the fundamental question of controlling the level of expenditure'.[98] The ILEA was also sceptical of recoupment pointing out that as the new polytechnics were regarded as national institutions it was likely that costs there would be higher than at other establishments. It felt that if recoupment rates reflected this there would be a danger that certain courses in certain polytechnics would be starved of students. As there was no general agreement about changes, it was decided to carry out further investigations into the existing position and possible alternatives.[99] The AMC, however, continued to work on its policies and remained convinced that there was a need for a committee 'to plan the development and regulate the extension of advanced further education'.[100] Eventually in January 1970 it forwarded its own scheme for the allocation of resources in the local authority sector of higher education to the other associations and to the DES.

Radical changes were advocated by the AMC.[101] It was suggested that a Polytechnics Grants Committee (PGC) should be established as soon as possible, and that a College of Education Grants Committee (CEGC) should follow in due course although it was acknowledged that the voluntary colleges were a complicating factor in this case. The PGC would be made up of nominees from the local authority associations, the teachers' associations and industry and commerce. The DES and CNAA would appoint assessors, and the PGC would establish links with the UGC. Polytechnics would formulate their estimates for poolable work for submission direct to the new body. The PGC would then relate these estimates to its long-term development plans, and there would be consultations with the local authority associations and central government to settle the total approved recurrent expenditure for all polytechnics for a given period. Responsibility for allocating funds to individual institutions would also rest with the PGC. The DES and the PGC would share 'a broad oversight of approval of courses'.[102] It was suggested that the relationship between the PGC and the polytechnic directors 'would be similar to that existing between the UGC and vice-chancellors'.[103] The AMC envisaged a reduced role for the Regional Advisory Councils for Further Education, but stressed that they would continue to be concerned with part-time and non-advanced courses.

The AMC's proposals were received with some hostility by the other local authority associations, and J C Swaffield, the Secretary of the AMC, was easily persuaded to amend the title Polytechnics Grants Committee to Advanced Further Education Committee.[104] The majority of the local authority leaders took the view that to make provisions for polytechnics separately from non-polytechnic colleges would lead to deep and undesirable cleavages in the local authority sector. Swaffield, however, was under some pressure to move swiftly as he knew that the DES was anxious to commence discussions on these matters.[105] Toby Weaver was particularly interested in the AMC's scheme, and, according to Alexander, Weaver took the view that something on these lines was 'essential in order to bring higher education in the public sector into a planned structure — the plan necessarily from national level'.[106] Eventually the local authority associations and the ILEA agreed to take part in informal discussions on the AMC's paper with the DES as long as it was clear that they were in no way committed to its contents. Before these discussions took place, Sir William Houghton, CEO of ILEA, expressed his doubts about the proposals to Alexander.[107] Houghton maintained that the AMC's approach involved LEAs working within fixed financial limits for higher education, which meant, in practice, a predetermined limit on student numbers. In Houghton's view this marked a fundamental change in the philosophy of the further education system, and as such should be treated as a major policy issue in its own right and not as a mere side-effect of a piece of administrative machinery designed to control expenditure.[108] He felt that the Advanced Further Education Committee (AFEC) would be put in a position of great power and would directly determine a major part of each polytechnic's expenditure and hence its work. This would lead to strong and understandable pressures for direct negotiations between individual polytechnics and the AFEC. Houghton concluded that there was 'a strong possibility that polytechnics would cease to be, in any meaningful sense, LEA institutions at all', and he predicted that the AMC's proposals would have much more significant and far-reaching effects than the new schemes of internal government recently instituted. Alexander shared Houghton's reservations. At the meeting with the DES in June it was clear that Weaver was sympathetic to the AMC's paper but Leonard Brown and Sidney Broad for the CCA expressed serious doubts. Houghton, Alexander and Andrew Davies, for the Welsh Joint Education Committee, were also unenthusiastic.[109] Alexander felt that it was 'an indefinite meeting',[110] and Swaffield was left 'to pick up the pieces' by organizing another meeting between the associations.

Before this took place, Swaffield drafted another paper. This proposed the creation of a new Local Authority Higher Education Committee (LAHEC) whose functions 'would be necessarily limited, and to a considerable extent advisory in character'.[111] Its objectives would be 'to advise both the Government and the LEAs on a long-term development plan for higher education'. Swaffield argued that 'it would not be unreasonable for LAHEC to set a limit on any expenditure subject to pooling arrangements'.[112] Expenditure in excess of such a limit could be borne solely by the authority responsible for the college. This paper stressed that LAHEC 'was not intended in any way to alter or limit the present functions of individual LEAs in relation either to their own institutions of further education or to the DES',[113] and it was clear that LAHEC was a much less radical departure than the AMC's previous proposals. Swaffield's new approach proved acceptable to the associations although Andrew Davies commented that the regional advisory councils were also interested in these matters and he suggested that the Standing Conference of Regional Advisory Councils might be consulted.[114] The associations took up this suggestion, and they also agreed to set up an interim joint committee, representative of the associations and the ILEA, to consider matters preparatory to the establishment of a more formal body.[115] The Joint Committee worked on Swaffield's draft, and soon increased the role of the regional advisory councils[116] as it was agreed that practical considerations entailed that a development plan should be built up on a regional basis. Swaffield approached Weaver with a view to discussing the Joint Committee's proposals with the DES, but the DES was not prepared to enter into discussions on this basis. It was critical of the proposals 'on the grounds that they will not produce a sufficiently effective machinery and are too dependent on the regional advisory councils'.[117] Eventually it was agreed that the DES would put its own paper before another meeting.

William Pile, the newly-appointed Permanent Secretary at the DES, claimed that the Government's proposals were 'new and radical', and changed 'both the nature and the level of local authority participation in the development and planning of the polytechnics'.[118] This was not disputed by the local authority associations which agreed that 'the alternative proposals put forward by the Department involved a more radical approach than the Joint Committee had previously envisaged as being possible on the part of Government'.[119] The DES wanted to set up a new body 'to supervise the advanced further education sector of higher education defined initially to cover the polytechnics only'.[120] It was argued that 'to be effective the proposed body must be more than advisory in function, that it must in fact be put in a position to make its decisions effective'.[121] The two main functions of the new body were to be 'the planning of courses and the allocation of resources'. To the local authorities' surprise, 'in a wider context of positive planning' the DES was prepared to contemplate 'giving up its own present course approval procedure (through the regional staff inspectors)'.[122] With regard to full-time advanced courses, the DES's scheme implied demotion for the RACs, and the DES fully recognized that in the new circumstances the proposed national body would require a strong supporting administrative and secretarial unit. In many important ways these

DES proposals were strikingly similar to those which had been put foward several months previously by the AMC and which had proved so completely unacceptable to the other local authority associations.This did not augur well.

During the next few months these DES proposals were discussed at length. The main points at issue in the debate were: (i) the powers of the proposed body; (ii) the range of institutions which would come under its jurisdiction; (iii) the question of regional structure; (iv) the composition of the new body; and (v) the fundamental issue of how the non-university sector of higher education was to be regulated and controlled. It is proposed to discuss each of these issues separately, although, in many ways, they were, of course, interdependent.

The Powers of the Proposed Body

The local authorities, at first, held to their ground that the proposed body should be advisory in character. They argued that 'ultimate control must continue to rest with the government in any case'[123] and pointed out that local authorities 'might not feel able to take on responsibility for a full-scale administrative machine'. The DES, on the other hand, doubted the need for the insertion of an advisory committee into the existing system and claimed that this would complicate arrangements and give 'a power of intervention without responsibility'.[124] It pointed out that the existence of certain ultimate government controls did not prevent the UGC from being 'an effective decision making body in a rather similar situation'.[125] To try to find a compromise the associations began to consider whether Government confirmation of the new body's decisions would meet their requirements. It was felt that in these circumstances disagreement with an individual authority would in the last resort be between that authority and the Department, 'thus preserving the normal relationship between central and local government'.[126] Swaffield, who invested considerable personal effort into these matters, drafted new papers which attempted to show that 'the differences between the associations and the Department were not as numerous or as fundamental as might appear at first sight'.[127] The local authority associations tried to make their notions of the proposed body 'slightly more executive',[128] but the majority view was that a procedure for appeal to the Secretary of State by individual authorities which were not satisfied with the recommendations of the proposed body was essential. In rejecting the associations' ideas on an appeals procedure, the Under-

Secretary of State, William van Straubenzee, expressed fears that they would lead to duplication of work and would weaken the new body's 'authority and effectiveness'.[129]

The Range of Institutions under the Jurisdiction of the Proposed Body

This question had been discussed earlier by the local authority associations, and it had been agreed that all local authority institutions providing higher education courses should eventually come under the purview of common national machinery. The DES wanted the proposed body to deal initially with the polytechnics only because it wished to start on a scale which was 'administratively feasible'.[130] For a time local authority representatives, especially Swaffield, were reluctantly prepared to accept this, but in May 1971 they informed the DES that from the outset the new machinery 'must cover the whole field of advanced further education'.[131] The authorities argued that the scope of the proposed body should 'coincide with the limits of the pooling system'.[132] They claimed that, as one-third of the expenditure fell outside of the polytechnics, 'it would be pointless to set up a mechanism to plan and control polytechnic expansion and leave the rest free'.[133] It was stated, quite explicitly, that 'any difference in treatment between polytechnics and other colleges would produce rigidity and resentment (based partly on fears that the polytechnics would be taken out of local authority control)'.[134] This 'formidable change in the scale of the operations envisaged'[135] proved totally unacceptable to the DES which questioned 'whether the associations would be able to sustain an organization of the necessary strength and size'.[136] Weaver later argued that 'instead of trying to tackle the whole thing simultaneously', it would have been better 'to attack at the point where improvement seemed most likely to be capable of being made, and that was in the management of the polytechnic programme. But this gradually broadened out to such an extent that we began to find difficulty in seeing how to control it'.[137] The local authorities' holistic approach, involving hundreds of institutions, was consistently rejected by Weaver and his colleagues who felt that it lacked administrative viability.

Regional Structure

In building up a national plan for advanced further education the local authority associations believed that the proposed new body should rely on the expertise of the RACs. It was suggested that the RACs, which were composed largely of local authority representatives, could formulate and submit regional plans to the new body. The latter could then put these into a national context and make amendments accordingly. No doubt the local authorities felt that, as all advanced further education (excluding teacher training) came under the jurisdiction of the RACs, the risk of isolating the polytechnics would be avoided. Alexander had already developed ideas for reconstituted and strengthened regional councils for higher education[138], and the associations' position was much in line with his thinking. Furthermore, Alexander argued that a large central secretariat for the new body would be unnecessary as most of the detailed work could be done by the regional councils and the DES.[139] Predictably the Standing Conference of RACs supported the local authority associations, but the CDP could not see the value of the RACs advising on the planning and financing of courses which recruited nationally rather than regionally.[140] The DES remained sceptical about the involvement of the RACs[141], and was unwilling to comment on their future role at a time when local government reorganization was being considered.[142] Weaver gave away his real feelings about the potential of these councils when he described them as 'advisory bodies with no powers whatever at the moment'.[143] The DES, in complete contrast to the local authorities, continued to regard regional structures, in William Pile's words, 'as second order issues'.[144]

The Composition of the Proposed Body

This matter did not prove as contentious as others at this stage. The DES recognized that membership could not be on the UGC pattern, but it maintained that there should be some representation for polytechnic and teacher interests as well as participation by the local authorities and the Department itself.[145] From the outset the local authority associations indicated that in their view local authority interests should not be in a minority[146] and Alexander urged the AEC to press for majority representation.[147] For the AMC, Swaffield took the same point of view, and eventually the associations informed the DES that they regarded majority representation as essential.[148] The DES never indicated whether it found this acceptable or not because other issues led to the abandonment of the proposals before the issue was settled.

Regulation and Control of the Non-University Sector of Higher Education

This was the fundamental question at the crux of these debates, and in many respects the issues discussed in the previous sub-sections grew out of this. The Government tried to assure the associations that it had 'no intention of assuming central responsibility for local authority higher education'.[149] It argued that it wanted to set up machinery so that the local authorities would be able 'to speak collectively and with authority on higher education matters'.[150] Some of the local authority representatives remained uneasy, however, feeling that the creation of the new body would reduce the existing powers of individual local authorities.[151] There were clearly some differences of emphasis amongst local authority spokesmen. One line of thought, often put forward by AMC representatives, was that 'the development of the local authority sector of higher education necessitated the taking of decisions to which individual authorities cannot effectively be party'.[152] Although she acknowledged that many difficulties still had to be overcome, Kathleen Ollerenshaw stated unequivocally that, 'some more effective mechanism for collective local authority representation at member level and for policy discussion *vis-à-vis* ministers is required'.[153] On the other hand, an alternative viewpoint maintained that, even if the local authority associations were in a substantial majority on the proposed body, 'it would still be difficult to convince a local authority that it was associated with decisions made by indirectly appointed representatives from other authorities'.[154] Alexander feared that an 'individual local authority providing higher education would very quickly wish to be relieved of the financial responsibility of a service in which they apparently had no power of decision'.[155] At times the local authority associations expressed this position in forthright terms:

> the Department's proposals were dependent on a concept of collective local government responsibility which was not wholly compatible with reality. It is not a weakness in local government which makes local authorities reluctant to accept as binding decisions which are taken collectively on their behalf. On the contrary, it is the diversity of local opinion, circumstances and needs which constitutes both the strength and raison d'être of local government.[156]

The local authorities particularly feared that it might become their collective responsibility to implement policies which had been imposed upon them entirely by central government restrictions on expenditure. In essence, they continued to feel that individual authorities would see the new body as 'an extended arm of central government'[157] which gave responsibility without power. With these feelings in the background compromise and agreement were impossible.

After negotiations lasting several months, the DES proposed in July 1971 that the discussions should be suspended.[158] Van Straubenzee stressed that the difficulties had not been resolved and that the creation of a new central body was not feasible in the immediate future. He argued that both sides would be in a better position to reappraise the situation after the James Committee on teacher training had reported and after local government reorganization had advanced further. The local authority associations were not able to insist on DES involvement, but they were unwilling to allow these matters to rest. They soon proposed that 'the associations and the ILEA should set up a body of their own'.[159] It was hoped that this might 'prepare the way for a central body when the time was opportune'.[160] This accorded with the views of the Standing Conference of Regional Advisory Councils which was featuring increasingly in the local authorities' plans. SCRAC stressed that it had already appointed a working party under Sir Eric Richardson to consider cooperation and coordination in the planning and development of higher education. It also claimed that the RACs already possessed a structure on which the organization of the local authority sector of higher education could be built.[161]

From October 1971 Swaffield, with the help of others, especially Jamieson, the Secretary of SCRAC, worked on the details of a scheme. A constitution, terms of reference and a possible programme of work were drafted and proved acceptable to the associations and the ILEA. Eventually it was agreed in July 1972 to set up a Local Authority Higher Education Committee consisting of representatives of the AMC, CCA, AEC, ILEA and the Welsh Joint Education Committee. Almost immediately Sir Eric Richardson, former Director of Regent Street Polytechnic, who had recently completed his report for SCRAC, was invited to undertake an enquiry into methods by which LAHEC could best perform its functions.[162] Given the lengthy discussions which had already taken place, it was surprising that further enquiries were still required. The choice of Sir Eric Richardson was more predictable as the views expressed in his report to SCRAC[163] were similar to those of the local authority associations.[164] Swaffield acknowledged that LAHEC was much narrower in its membership than the national committee envisaged by Richardson in his report to SCRAC, but he stressed that the associations had come to the conclusion that 'constitutional problems of representation would be so difficult that the establishment of the Committee would be yet further delayed'.[165] He hoped that the basis of the Committee would be broadened 'as work proceeds',[166] and the Chairman of LAHEC, Alderman F Hatton from Manchester, wanted the new Committee to form 'a close relationship with the ATTI and the CDP' and expected that 'eventually representatives of these and other bodies would be included on the committee'.[167] Richardson accepted these assurances and agreed to undertake the enquiry.

From the outset the CDP gave LAHEC a very cool reception and doubted whether it would be 'either credible or effective'.[168] The DES immediately offered its 'cooperation' to LAHEC,[169] but for the time being largely kept its own counsel. LAHEC had emerged in a very different form from either that originally envisaged by the AMC or that proposed by the DES. Its parentage was obvious, and this, coupled with the struggles surrounding its birth, hardly gave it an auspicious start to life. It was difficult to see how it could develop into anything other than 'just another pressure group representing a sectional interest in higher education'.[170] The creation of LAHEC was in itself of considerably less importance than the circumstances which surrounded it. The negotiations of the early 1970s clearly exposed radically different conceptions of how the local authority sector of higher education was to be managed and controlled. DES civil servants and the local authority associations were pulling in different directions and little common ground could be found. These underlying tensions were to persist well beyond the early 1970s.

Notes

1   WUMRC, ATTI, Higher Education Advisory Panel, Minutes 31 October 1967. Report of meeting at DES, 3 October 1967.

2   *Ibid.*

3   S WILLIAMS, 'Progress with the plan for polytechnics', in *Coombe Lodge Reports*, Volume 2, No. 8, (January 1969), p. 3.

4   AEC, File A1038, Minutes of Thirteenth Annual Meeting of Association of Chief Education Officers, 1 and 2 February 1968.

5   *Ibid.*

6   *Ibid.*

7   *Ibid.*

8   AEC, File A317, R Prentice's Advisory Group, Paper No. 5 (nd).

9   AEC, File A495, DES memorandum, Future Pattern of Higher Education within the Further Education System, 1965, p. 10.

10 AEC, File A1038, Minutes of Thirteenth Annual Meeting of Association of Chief Education Officers, 1 and 2 February 1968.

11 J PRATT and T BURGESS, *The Polytechnics, A Report*, (1974); E ROBINSON in *TES*, 26 May 1972.

12 J PRATT and T BURGESS, (1974), *op. cit.*; L DONALDSON, *Policy and the Polytechnics*, (1975); J WHITBURN, M MEALING and C COX, *People in Polytechnics*, (1976); P VENABLES, *Higher Education Developments: Technological Universities*, (1978); L M CANTOR and I F ROBERTS, *Further Education Today*, (1979).

13   L M Cantor and I F Roberts, (1979), *op. cit.*, p. 93.

14   T Burgess, *Education after School*, (1977), p. 239.

15   E Robinson, *The New Polytechnics*, (1968), p. 212.

16   *THES*, 16 June 1972.

17   L M Cantor and I F Roberts, (1979), *op. cit.*, p. 93.

18   House of Commons, Tenth Report of the Expenditure Committee, *Policy Making in the DES*, (1976), Minutes of Evidence, Q 1018.

19   *Ibid.*, Q 1020.

20   *THES*, 3 March 1977.

21   ATTI, *The Future of Higher Education within the Further Education System*, (1965), p. 15.

22   AEC, File A115(d), Minutes of the Burnham Further Education Committee, 7 November 1966.

23   CNAA, Statement 3, (November 1965), pp. 10–11.

24   *TES*, 25 February 1966.

25   LUCFO, CVCP papers, Vice-Chancellor's notes of CVCP meeting with Secretary of State, 11 November 1966.

26   J Pratt and T Burgess, (1974), *op. cit.*, p. 212; A Crosland's speech at Lancaster University, 20 January 1967.

27   *TES*, 27 January 1967.

28   Ministry of Education, Circular 94, *Research in Technical Colleges*, 8 April 1946.

29   DES, Administrative Memorandum 8/67.

30   *Ibid.*

31   *Ibid.*

32   *Ibid.*

33   *Ibid.*

34   *Ibid.*

35   WUMRC, ATTI, Higher Education Panel, Minutes, 24 May 1966.

36   AEC, File A731, Hardyman to Alexander, 6 April 1967.

37   *Ibid.*

38   *Ibid.*

39   *Ibid.*, Houghton to Mrs. Sloman, no date, (1967).

40   *Ibid.*

41   L M Cantor and I F Roberts, (1979), *op. cit.*, p. 159.

42   *Infra*, this chapter.

43   AEC, File A215, Pooling Committee, DES memorandum on AFE pool, May 1968.

44   *Ibid.*

45   *Ibid.*

46   *Ibid.*, Hetherington to Hudson, 18 July 1968.

47   AEC, File A731, Meeting of CEOs on Polytechnic Developments, 1 October 1968.

48   *Ibid.*

49   *TES*, 8 March 1968.

50   *TES*, 6 June 1969.

51   *TES*, 4 December 1970.

52   *Ibid.*

53   *THES*, 3 August 1973.

54   *Ibid.*

55   *Infra*, this chapter.

56   CNAA, *Report of the Working Party on Resources for Research in Polytechnics and other Colleges*, (1974).

57   *THES*, 25 September 1981.

58   *Ibid.*

59   S WILLIAMS, (1969), *op. cit.*, p. 3.

60   *Education*, 28 March 1969.

61   *TES*, 28 March 1969.

62   *TES*, 6 June 1969.

63   Select Committee of House of Commons, Education and Science (1968–9), Report on Student Relations, Volume 1, p. 156.

64   *Ibid.*

65   *Education*, 29 May 1970.

66   *Ibid.*, 16 January 1970.

67   AEC, Files A1039–40, Meeting of AMC and CDP, 29 September 1970.

68   *Ibid.*

69   *Ibid.*, File A728, Informal meeting of CEOs, St. Catherine College, Oxford, 9 July 1970.

70   *Ibid.*, Alexander to Aitken, 2 October 1970.

71   W P ALEXANDER, *Towards a New Education Act*, (1969). p. 66.

72   SCRAC, *Cooperation in the Planning and Development of Higher Education*, Appendix 11, (1972), p. 47.

73   *Education*, 1 July 1966.

74   AMC, Report of Education Committee, 17 May 1967.

75   AEC, File A215, Pooling Committee, Terms of reference and composition, May 1968.

76   *Ibid.*, Hudson to Alexander, 9 August 1968.

77   J H TAYLOR, 'The polytechnics and the LEAs', in *Coombe Lodge Reports*, Volume 3, No. 16, (July 1970), p. 7.

78   K OLLERENSHAW, *Higher Education and Planning*, Old Queen Street Paper, Conservative Research Department, (1971), p. 12.

79   AEC, Executive Committee Minutes, 19 March 1970.

80   K OLLERENSHAW, (1971), *op. cit.*, p. 13.

81   J H TAYLOR, (1970), *op. cit.*, p. 7.

82   AEC, File A350, Memorandum for Pooling Committee prepared by Durham County Treasurer, 23 April 1969.

83   Expenditure Committee of House of Commons, (Education and Arts sub-committee), *Further and Higher Education*, (1972–3), Evidence of AMC, p. 423.

84   K OLLERENSHAW, (1971), *op. cit.*, p. 13.

85   *Ibid.*

86   W P ALEXANDER, (1969), *op. cit.*, p. 27.

87   EXPENDITURE COMMITTEE, *op. cit.*, Evidence of CDP.

88   *Ibid.*

89   *TES*, 7 August 1970.

90   EXPENDITURE COMMITTEE, *op. cit.*, Evidence of CDP.

91   *Ibid.*, Evidence of Society of Education Officers, Q 881.

92   K OLLERENSHAW, (1971), *op. cit.*, p. 12.

93 AMC, Report of Education Committee, 25 September 1968.

94 AEC, File A215, Swaffield to Andrew, 10 October 1968.

95 *Ibid.*

96 *Ibid.*

97 *Ibid.*, File A350, Minutes of Pooling Committee, 30 April 1969.

98 *Ibid.*

99 *Ibid.*

100 AMC, Report of Education Committee, 23 July 1969.

101 AEC, Files A1039–40, AMC Paper 44–70, The Financing and Control of Local Authority Higher Education.

102 *Ibid.*

103 *Ibid.*

104 *Ibid.*, AMC Paper 354–70, (March 1970).

105 *Ibid.*, Swaffield to Alexander, 13 April 1970.

106 *Ibid.*, Alexander to Houghton, 21 May 1970.

107 *Ibid.*, Houghton to Alexander, 15 May 1970.

108 *Ibid.*

109 *Ibid.*, Alexander to Hutty, 18 June 1970.

110 *Ibid.*

111 *Ibid.*, AMC Paper 803–70, (June 1970).

112 *Ibid.*

113 *Ibid.*

114 *Ibid.*, Davies to Swaffield, 1 July 1970.

115 *Ibid.*, Swaffield to Alexander, 21 July 1970.

116 *Ibid.*, LAHEC, Joint Committee, 23 September 1970.

117 *Ibid.*, Swaffield to Alexander, 5 and 9 November 1970.

118 *Ibid.*, Meeting between representatives of the DES and the local authority associations, 24 November 1970.

119 *Ibid.*, LAHEC, Joint Committee, 10 December 1970.

120 *Ibid.*, DES paper, Local Authority Higher Education.

121 *Ibid.*

122 *Ibid.*

123 *Ibid.*, Meeting between representatives of DES and local authority associations, 24 November 1970.

124 *Ibid.*

125 *Ibid.*

126 *Ibid.*, LAHEC, Joint Committee, 10 December 1970.

127 *Ibid.*, Meeting between representatives of DES and local authority associations, 20 May 1971.

128 *Ibid.*

129 *Ibid.*, Van Straubenzee to Alexander, 21 July 1971.

130 *Ibid.*, Meeting of representatives, 24 November 1970.

131 *Ibid.*, Meeting 20 May 1971.

132 *Ibid.*

133 *Ibid.*

134 *Ibid.*

135 *Ibid.*, Van Straubenzee to Alexander, 21 July 1971.

136 *Ibid.*

137 House of Commons, Expenditure Committee, *Further and Higher Education*, (1972–3), Evidence of T WEAVER, Q 1230.

138 W ALEXANDER, (1969), *op. cit.*, p. 16 and 42.

139 AEC, Files A1039–40, Meeting 20 May 1971.

140 EXPENDITURE COMMITTEE, *op. cit.*, Evidence of CDP.

141 AEC, Files A1039–40, Meeting 20 May 1971.

142 *Ibid.*, Van Straubenzee to Alexander, 21 July 1971.

143 EXPENDITURE COMMITTEE, *op. cit.*, Evidence of T WEAVER, Q 1222.

144 AEC, Files A1039–40, Meeting 24 November 1970.

145 *Ibid.*

146 *Ibid.*

147 *Ibid.*, Haynes to Alexander, 2 December 1970.

148 *Ibid.*, Meeting 20 May 1971.

149 *Ibid.*, Meeting 24 November 1970.

150 *Ibid.*

151 *Ibid.*

152 *Ibid.*, AEC, File A838, AMC General Meeting 15 September 1970.

153 K OLLERENSHAW, (1971), *op. cit.*, pp. 13–14.

154 AEC, Files A1039–40, LAHEC, Joint Committee, 10 December 1970.

155 *Ibid.*, Alexander to Swaffield, 17 December 1970.

156 *Ibid.*, LAHEC, Joint Committee, 10 December 1970.

157 *Ibid.*

158 *Ibid.*, Van Straubenzee to Alexander, 21 July 1971.

159 *Ibid.*, LAHEC, Joint Committee, 29 September 1971.

160 *Ibid.*

161 *Ibid.*, Jamieson to Swaffield, 28 September 1971.

162 *Ibid.*, LAHEC, Minutes, 24 July 1972.

163 SCRAC, *Cooperation in the Planning and Development of Higher Education*, (March 1972).

164 AEC, Files A1039–40, Swaffield to Richardson, 1 August 1972.

165 *Ibid.*

166 *Ibid.*

167 *THES*, 18 August 1972.

168 AEC, Files A1039–40, Tolley to Swaffield, 21 December 1971.

169 *Ibid.*, Weaver to Swaffield, 2 August 1972.

170 *THES*, 18 August 1972.

Chapter 6

Wresting the Colleges of Education from the University Institutes

During 1965 ATCDE and CID feared that the colleges of education were to be removed from the university institutes of education and placed entirely on the local authority side of the binary divide. They had no doubts that the instigators of these policies were Weaver of the DES and Alexander of the AEC. In the event a stubborn rearguard action was fought, and the university connection survived — albeit in a context in which it was continually vulnerable. During 1967 plans to incorporate neighbouring colleges of education into the proposed polytechnics at Leeds and Huddersfield caused concern. In Leeds the LEA wanted to include the Yorkshire College of Education and Home Economics in its new polytechnic, but this was opposed by the College's governing body, its staff and the ATCDE. The College staff felt particularly strongly that their interests would be overlooked in a predominantly technical institution. They were also disappointed that they would be denied the independence promised by the new arrangements for college government. Their objections were put to the DES, but the Department stressed that it had not taken the initiative with these proposals.[1] They had arisen locally, and the DES refused to stand in the way of such mergers if they were desirable on educational grounds.[2] It also pointed out that there could be clear advantages in such arrangements. When UCET considered these developments, it decided not to take up the specific cases, but it condemned 'incorporation in principle as weakening the college ties with universities'.[3] It agreed to contact the Minister of State, Shirley Williams, with a view to arranging a meeting to discuss these issues. This meeting eventually took place at the end of May 1968, and Williams stressed that 'the Department had no plans to introduce teacher training in other polytechnics, either by the creation of new education departments or through the absorption of existing colleges of education'.[4] She added that 'she could not give an assurance that this policy would continue for all time',[5] but promised that UCET would be consulted if any change was contemplated. With regard to the colleges in Leeds and Huddersfield, she argued that 'incorporation in a larger institution of higher education seemed a sensible way of securing the future of these two particular colleges, whose viability as separate institutions must, because of their relatively small size, be in doubt'.[6] At about the same time Edward Britton, the newly-appointed General Secretary of the NUT and formerly of the ATTI, was advocating that teacher training should take place in technical colleges rather than specialist institutions. He maintained

> there would be much to be gained from a closer working of the two sections of local authority higher education. There is little to be said for running them as two completely separate systems. The colleges of education would stand to gain from much of the specialist subject teaching that could be given by the staffs of the technical colleges, while the technical colleges would gain greatly in breadth of outlook from the presence of the colleges of education. The students in each would gain considerably.[7]

Britton was regularly supported in these contentions by Eric Robinson who regarded the incorporation of two colleges of education in polytechnics as 'very significant'.[8] Robinson maintained that 'the development of teacher training is being badly hindered by the university connection ... Mr. Crosland did not press the logical implications of the binary policy — that colleges of education should be included in polytechnics'.[9] In this increasingly hostile climate UCET and ATCDE could only cling to Shirley Williams' reassurances and await further developments.

In the late 1960s increasing publicity was given to concern about teacher training in this country. In many ways the issues raised are beyond the scope of this study, but in certain respects the debates which took place had important bearings on the future development of the local authority sector of higher education. In 1967 the Plowden Committee on Primary Education argued that, because of the rapid turnover of teachers, colleges of education were at that moment in a more influential position than in more settled times, and it recommended that there should be 'a full study of the whole subject of teacher training'.[10] During April 1968 William Taylor, Director of Bristol University Institute of Education and at that time a part-time member of the DES Planning Branch, arranged a major symposium entitled *Towards a Policy for the Education of Teachers*.[11] This was attended by many of the leading public figures involved in the field. In connection with the symposium Taylor commented accurately, there are very few people in the universities or the DES, in local authorities or teachers' organizations, in ATCDE or UCET, or in the colleges or departments themselves, who have a clearly developed idea of the way in which the structure and content of teacher education should develop during the next twenty years. Even if such a vision existed in a form capable of giving rise to a coherent policy, the business of convincing the various partners in the enterprise of its merits and feasibility would be both difficult and long-drawn out.[12]

According to Margaret Maden, a participant in the symposium,

it became clear that there was a recognizable division of opinion on the fundamental needs of a policy for the education of teachers. Established figures like Sir Derman Christopherson (Vice-Chancellor of Durham University), Dr K G Collier, Mr E G Peirson and Miss J D Browne (all principals of colleges of education and prominent figures in the ATCDE) argued essentially for consolidation. They implied rather than positively asserted that the main policy lines had been drawn, that significant structural changes had been made, and that the major issues were now problems of academic and institutional development within existing colleges and universities. On the other hand, educators more removed from the colleges of education, such as Stuart Maclure, Edward Britton and Eric Robinson together with some of the less orthodox teacher trainers, notably Professor Rée, made a strong plea for the need to re-examine fundamentals.[13]

The latter, who was the Professor of Education at York University, was a particularly vociferous critic of the existing structure of teacher training, and he pressed strongly for a major enquiry.[14] One of the results of this Bristol conference was the creation of a new pressure group, SPERTT (Society for the Promotion of Educational Reform through Teacher Training). This 'ginger' group was set up by the more radical element at Bristol and aimed at a fundamental restructuring of the teacher training system.

The DES did not respond favourably to this demand for a major enquiry into teacher training. UCET was told that a royal commission on the subject might be set up in the mid-1970s, and institutes were asked to encourage their colleges to experiment with different forms of teacher training in the interim period.[15] The DES made it clear that it was unhappy with area training organizations which looked after very small numbers of colleges, and also recognized that the creation of new universities put the boundaries of existing ATOs into a new perspective.[16] It was felt that these issues would have to be considered after local government reorganization. When questioned about an enquiry, Herbert Andrew, the Permanent Secretary, replied that the Department had no plans for one.[17] He pointed out that the teacher training system had expanded greatly in the last few years and had had heavy demands placed upon it. In his view 'a period of consolidation' was required 'with perhaps a little more administrative and financial assistance'.[18] He argued that it had done 'a very good job under very difficult conditions', and 'the institutions and the people in them would do best to have a year or two of relative quiet'.[19] M J G Hearley for the Inspectorate took the same view and praised the efforts of the ATCDE and its members.[20] The DES was widely condemned at the time for complacency and indifference to this question. In many ways this was too simplistic and underestimated the tensions and complications involved. From the evidence available for the second half of the 1960s it is clear that the Permanent Secretary, Herbert Andrew, was broadly satisfied with the existing structure of the teacher training system , but his colleague, Deputy Secretary, Toby Weaver, wanted to see basic changes. From the mid-1960s Weaver hoped to see the colleges of education placed much more firmly on the local authority side of the binary line, but this involved the demise of the university institutes of education which Andrew was not prepared to contemplate. A full scale enquiry could easily have made these differences of opinion within the Department much more obvious, and Andrew wanted to avoid this. He was also aware that the views of the various bodies involved in this field were still as entrenched as ever, and realized that an enquiry would only underline their differences. There were, moreover, further important factors emerging in the late 1960s. It was becoming apparent that the demand for teachers in the 1970s was likely to be much smaller than during the 1960s. Conversely, the estimates of the demand for higher education in the 1970s were growing bigger and bigger. The crucial questions of whether and in what ways the colleges of education could contribute to the satisfaction of this demand had yet to be considered both inside and outside the Department. A long enquiry into teacher training would, almost certainly, have delayed the resolution of these issues. In all these circumstances Andrew's response to a call for an enquiry is more easily understood. His answer was probably not the result of indifference and complacency but of careful consideration. It was certainly not in the interests of this senior planner to embark on a long enquiry at this juncture. Late in 1968 the question of an enquiry moved out of the hands of the DES and was taken up by the House of Commons Select Committee on Education and Science. On the initiative of its Chairman, Fred Willey, the Committee announced that it intended to consider teacher training after it had completed its work on student relations. It started its investigations in July 1969 and these continued well into 1970.

Much of the evidence presented to the Select Committee was concerned with the quality of the students leaving the colleges of education and their readiness for the practical activity of teaching in schools. Some of the issues raised, however, proved important to the future development of teacher training and to the local authority sector of higher education. These issues are discussed in the following four sections.

The Bachelor of Education Degree

Perhaps the largest task faced by the colleges of education in the late 1960s was the introduction of the BEd degree. In this the colleges, of course, required the cooperation of the universities (senates as well as institutes of education). There were considerable variations between the BEd schemes devised by different universities. These variations were not confined to contents and course structures, but extended to admissions criteria, selection procedures and standards of award. One university commentator pointed out: 'The courses offered for first degrees by different universities do vary in virtually all the traditional fields, but it would be difficult to find any field in which there was greater diversity than the proposed first degrees in education'.[21] Differences in admissions criteria led to a number of startling anomalies in individual cases which were highlighted in the educational press from time to time.[22] Another result of the diversity was that very different proportions of students in different colleges stayed on to take BEd degrees, but the aspect of the situation which aroused greatest controversy was that some universities offered BEd honours degrees and others only ordinary degrees. Apart from the question of status, 'these arbitrary arrangements'[23] introduced serious anomalies as the NUT and others quickly pointed out. Firstly, graduate teachers with ordinary degrees were denied the 'good honours' increment through their teaching careers; secondly their promotion prospects were probably affected detrimentally; and thirdly their chances of being accepted to read for higher degree courses were reduced. Even the ATCDE, which normally gave strong support to the universities, echoed the NUT's criticisms and argued that some students suffered injustice.[24] E G Peirson, Principal of Worcester College and a leading member of ATCDE, was so disillusioned by his experience with the Birmingham University BEd that he reluctantly came to the conclusion that colleges should seek CNAA validation if they were not satisfied with the BEd schemes offered by their neighbouring universities.[25] The universities, particularly the institutes of education, were well aware of the problems which had been created. As early as January 1968 UCET urged individual universities to take measures to ensure that high standards of performance in the BEd were fully recognized.[26] This move was supported by ministers at the DES and by the CVCP, but, as Stanley Hewett of ATCDE pointed out, 'UCET had no power to act'.[27] In many ways the diversity of different BEd schemes was an extension of the existing wide variation between teacher's certificate courses.[28] In turn this was a reflection of the British university tradition, for throughout their existence the universities had zealously protected their individual autonomy and resisted the standardization of courses. Herbert Andrew accepted and respected this position.[29] Fred Willey, Chairman of the Select Committee, also recognized it but was much more critical.[30] By the early 1970s the universities had moved to 'a much more homogeneous BEd pattern'.[31] In 1971 BEd honours degrees were available from fifteen of the twenty-two universities involved, and four others were in the process of introducing them[32], but in many ways the changes which the universities made came too late to stem the criticisms.

Initially some universities were reluctant to accept certain practical subjects (for example, art, domestic science and physical education) commonly found in the school curriculum as suitable for graduate studies.[33] According to the ATCDE these problems were soon overcome[34], but not before those who saw the universities as narrowly academic and restrictive institutions could claim that their viewpoint had been vindicated. Many universities were also criticized for being slow to approve arrangements which enabled serving teachers (largely two-year trained at this time) to obtain BEd degrees. Several witnesses to the Select Committee (particularly supporters of SPERTT and some school teachers) maintained that the intoduction of the BEd had accentuated the divorce between theory and practice in teacher training. They argued that, under university influence, too much emphasis in the BEd had been placed on narrow academic 'book-learning'. Consequently, they claimed, the practicalities and rigors of classroom teaching were relatively neglected. They sometimes implied that the theoretical knowledge gained by students on BEd courses made them more remote from the crucial issue of classroom survival during their first teaching posts. College and institute of education spokesmen denied these allegations, and the issues, not surprisingly, remained unresolved. Although the ATCDE claimed that 'a significant and promising start had been made'[35] and college staffs generally believed that academic quality had been improved by the BEd[36], the local authority associations[37], the chief education officers[38] and the teachers' unions all remained sceptical. Despite the problems experienced with some BEd schemes, the NUT still argued for the development of comprehensive universities incorporating the colleges of education.[39] On the other hand, local authority spokesmen cited problems with the BEd as further evidence of the universities' failure to grasp and deal with the real needs of teacher training. There can be little doubt that those universities which initially set up restricting BEd schemes played into the hands of those who sought to reduce the universities' role in teacher training.

The Area Training Organizations

The evidence submitted to the Select Committee about the ATOs was unsurprising. Alexander felt that they were unduly dominated by the directors of the university institutes[40], and the Association of CEOs argued that they were insufficiently imaginative.[41] It is clear that the Chairman of Committee, Fred Willey, strongly agreed with these views.[42] Predictably ATCDE and UCET were much more sympathetic. Sir Herbert Andrew was also supportive, and he said of the ATO system, 'It has worked pretty well ... We do not have great feeling that it is unsatisfactory ... There are criticisms of it, of course, as there are of all human institutions, but we do not have any feeling that there is anything there which is decaying or liable to cause a break-down, or that it is manifestly worse than some alternative system'.[43] As long as Andrew remained Permanent Secretary at the DES the demise of the ATOs was unlikely.

Throughout 1969, partly because of the activities of the Select Committee, the pressure to hold a further enquiry into teacher training grew. In November the Secretary of State, Edward Short, told the Commons that he regarded many of the recent criticisms of college courses as 'mischievous and based on inadequate evidence'.[44] He announced, however, that he was considering how colleges could be helped to adapt their courses to 'the changing methods and patterns of organization in schools'.[45] He acknowledged that a general enquiry was among the possibilities, but he doubted whether it would be the best course of action.[46] It seems probable that Andrew's influence was important here, but this cannot be substantiated until internal DES papers are available. Short came to the conclusion that the best way to meet the demand for an enquiry was to ask ATOs, in association with the Inspectorate and schoolteacher representatives, to review their structures and activities. These proposals were put to a small number of educational leaders, including Alexander, before they were announced. Although Alexander expressed reservations about the BEd, which were shared by Short, he was prepared to go along with the Secretary of State's suggestion.[47] This form of investigation was well received by the ATCDE and the universities (except Professor Rée), but did not satisfy the system's radical critics. It was felt in some quarters that Short had merely asked the ATOs 'to do what they were set up to do in the first place',[48] and there was a call for a 'full-scale inquiry into the structure and control of all tertiary education'.[49] Before the ATOs completed their task, however, this review was superseded by another enquiry into teacher training which had much broader ramifications.

Estimates of the Demand and Supply for Teachers in the 1970s

During 1968 the DES gave the first indications that the national teacher shortage was being solved. In a letter to an LEA it was stated that 'the Government's target of 110,000 teacher training places in England and Wales by 1973–4 is likely to be achieved ahead of time without any further capital expenditure'.[50] Later in the year, however, the Department felt that 'in areas of growing population' there was still a need for expansion and announced its intention to approach the LEAs concerned.[51] Fears of teacher unemployment were voiced particularly amongst the students in the colleges, but the DES found no evidence for this and predicted that there would be no difficulties in 1969 'as long as authorities continue to give priority to the employment of teachers and in particular give first choice to those who are immobile, and as long as those who are mobile move where the jobs are'.[52] In the longer term the DES held 'the total supply of teachers will continue to increase faster than the school population ... the target will be reached about 1976–77 on the more favourable assumption on wastage rates or in 1978–79 on the less favourable assumption'.[53] Andrew told the Select Committee, 'The gap between supply and demand has narrowed very rapidly recently, therefore there is great anxiety that it might cross over. But if things go as we expect they will, this should not happen'.[54] According to Joan Browne of the ATCDE, the DES was 'the reverse of alarmist'[55] in the late 1960s, and as late as June 1970 estimated that initial teacher training places in the colleges would increase by 15,000 throughout the decade.[56] Hugh Harding, a senior civil servant in the DES at this time, has since acknowledged how wide of the mark these DES estimates were and has suggested reasons why the Department failed to detect the trends accurately.[57] Although the DES did not foresee the major problems which emerged in the 1970s, certain educationalists learned enough to realize that existing policies would have to be reviewed. William Alexander, for example, quickly stressed the financial pressures which would face the educational system in the 1970s, and he pointed out again and again that the rate of expansion experienced in the 1960s could not continue in the 1970s. More narrowly concerned with the future of the colleges of education, the

ATCDE had to devise policies for a changing situation. In March 1969 Stanley Hewett tried to persuade the ATCDE Executive that 'thought should be given to the position in the late 1970s when the teacher supply problem would be solved and there would be spare capacity in the colleges'.[58] In practice, of course, the timescale proved much shorter than Hewett (or virtually anyone) realized. In response to Hewett's proposal the ATCDE decided to 'investigate further the relationship between the colleges of education and other institutions of higher education'.[59] It is in this context that further developments must be considered.

The Diversification of the Colleges of Education

The idea that the colleges of education should broaden their scope beyond teacher training courses was not new. It was implicit in some of the evidence submitted to the Robbins Committee (notably that of the local authority associations), and the Robbins Report itself supported this suggestion. Dividing such ideas into two categories the Robbins Report made the following comments:

> Some colleges will wish to broaden their scope by providing courses, with a measure of common studies, for entrants to various professions in the social services. We think that they should be allowed to do so as soon as practicable, although we believe it would be wrong to suppose that the needs of these professions are likely to be such as to require large-scale provision in the generality of colleges. Other colleges may wish to provide general courses in arts and science subjects ... the scope for such developments as these will be restricted during the next ten years or so, because the whole capacity of the colleges will be needed to match the demand for teachers; but ... there will be opportunities for a good number of experiments with such courses later in the 1970s.[60]

The Robbins' predictions for the mid-1960s were correct, but, during 1968 and 1969, as the estimates for the demand and supply of teachers came closer together, these suggestions came into prominence again.By the end of 1969 the local authority associations, the NUT, the NUS and many other commentators were all stressing the virtues of diversification and urging the demise of 'monotechnic' teacher training institutions. It was suggested that it was wrong on educational grounds to isolate intending teachers from students who were preparing to enter other professions or planning different careers. It was argued that this isolation gave college of education students an unnecessarily narrow experience of life, and it was also stressed that the age of 18 was too young for students to commit themselves to a career in teaching. The NUS complained that a teacher's certificate was an unsaleable commodity outside of teaching and it limited the employment prospects of students from colleges of education.[61] Finally, it was widely pointed out that some students entered colleges of education, not because they wished to teach, but because they sought some form of full-time higher education after the age of 18. It was alleged that in the 1960s the colleges of education, to some extent, had become overspill institutions for the universities. Given the increasing demand for higher education and the pressure for university places, it was almost inevitable that this happened; and the growth of this trend was one of the strongest arguments employed by those who wanted colleges of education to offer a broader range of courses.

During 1969 the issue of whether colleges of education should be diversified was subsumed to a considerable extent into the larger question of how higher education could be expanded in the 1970s. Early in the year Government spokesmen made it clear that estimates of the number of higher education places required were being revised upwards, but no detailed figures were made public. Shirley Williams, the Minister of State, stressed that increases in places had to be related to manpower needs, and she suggested that industry required 'more general first degrees'[62] than were normally provided. Speculation in the press about numbers continued throughout the year, and Shirley Williams and Edward Short showed particular interest in how unit costs in higher education could be reduced.[63] On 25 September Shirley Williams and a team of senior civil servants met representatives of the UGC and the CVCP at University College, London, to discuss the latest DES projections and their implications. At this meeting Williams raised for discussion a series of thirteen ways in which university costs could be reduced. These were not put forward as Government policies or opinions, but as suggestions for further consideration. The CVCP undertook to ask individual universities for their views on each of these thirteen possibilities. At the same time the point was made that non-university institutions would also be required to provide more places in the 1970s. It was commented, 'there seems scope for further thought about possible future development of the colleges of education in directions other than simply the training of teachers',[64] and the universities were asked for observations. In October Shirley Williams was replaced by Gerald Fowler who soon outlined the essence of the debate thus:

> If in a decade we shall be faced with a demand for student places in
> higher education which is composed of over 20 per cent of the age

group and still rising, we are undoubtedly moving towards a mass higher education system different from that which we have traditionally known in this country. Certainly in a period of rapid expansion we shall need to consider nationally, against the best advice we can receive, the problem of where to concentrate resources or how to divide up the resources which are available for higher education as a whole.[65]

The attitude of the ATCDE to these issues was both interesting and important. When the Association submitted its evidence to the Select Committee in July 1969 there was little discussion of possible diversification in the colleges of education. It was mentioned that the colleges were appropriately fitted to provide training courses for the social professions and experiments in this field were encouraged.[66] No prominence, however, was given to this question, and David Hencke's comment that 'the colleges' role as exclusive centres to train teachers was predominantly defended' was justified.[67] The ATCDE's position in this respect moved sharply during the early months of 1970. A working party, considerably influenced by Stanley Hewett, produced a Report *Higher Education and Preparation for Teaching* which set out radically new departures in ATCDE thinking. The Association maintained that the colleges of education should share at least proportionately in the expansion of higher education planned for the 1970s. In the ATCDE's scheme the colleges were in future to provide three year degree courses in the arts, sciences and social sciences as well as teacher training courses. These new courses were not intended to be 'a replica of traditional honours degrees', but could be broadly based and interdisciplinary. It was argued that this would allow many of the college students to keep their career options open longer and also meet criticisms that teachers in training were isolated from other groups of students. The Association claimed that 'the goal of an all graduate entry (to the teaching profession) . . . would be brought within striking distance',[68] and it was proposed to raise minimum entry qualifications progressively to bring them into line with those required by the universities.[69] ATCDE maintained that unit costs in the colleges were much lower than in the universities, and that expanding the colleges provided a most economical way of increasing the total number of places in higher education. It was recognized that these proposals offered very different futures for different colleges, and it was expected that some would provide a wide range of courses whereas others, especially smaller colleges, would be restricted to a much narrower range of activities. The unifying element in the scheme was that all the colleges were to strengthen their links with a 'parent' university 'which would be responsible for overseeing, developing and validating courses and awards'.[70] ATCDE argued that 'trying to live in both halves of the binary system at one and the same time is placing increasing strains on the colleges',[71] and the Association proposed that the local authorities should lose their administrative and financial controls over the colleges and that a central grants committee should be created. In this respect the ATCDE still urged an only slightly modified Robbins' solution, but their suggestion for academic diversification was a radical departure and, according to Joan Browne, 'was becoming the chief preoccupation of the Executive'.[72]

During the early months of 1970 some influential university spokesmen also made it clear that they favoured the diversification of the colleges of education as a means to expand higher education. Sir Derman Christopherson and Fred Dainton, Vice-Chancellors of Durham and Nottingham universities respectively and both members of the CVCP deputation which met Shirley Williams at University College, London, publicly advocated this approach.[73] Alan Bullock, Vice-Chancellor of Oxford, and Alec Ross, Professor of Educational Studies at Lancaster, took a similar line.[74] UCET considered the question, but was slow in making its views known despite the efforts of William Taylor to expedite matters.[75] When the CVCP's response to Shirley Williams' 'thirteen points' was published[76], it became clear that the CVCP in particular, and the universities in general, favoured the diversification of the colleges.[77] It was reported, however, that the UGC preferred the creation of new universities to 'the college of education alternative'.[78]

In general the CVCP and the universities reacted negatively to Shirley Williams' 'thirteen points' concerning possible economies. The one suggestion which the CVCP thought worthy of further serious consideration was the possibility of introducing 'a two-year course of study leading to a specific qualification'.[79] In the press and in popular discussion this was often referred to as 'a two-year degree', but the CVCP was careful to avoid the word 'degree' in this context in its document. It stressed that this question of course structure needed to be raised in a much broader context than that of costs.[80] The CVCP emphasized that the universities were virtually unanimous that it was 'fallacious to suppose that it is possible in two years to achieve the same result as is achieved by the conventional three-year honours degree course'.[81] The Committee acknowledged that 'a two year course of study, to a sub-honours level, might well have a part to play in the future'.[82] It envisaged that some students would leave for employment after two years, and others would proceed to honours degree studies or to professional training. Honours degree studies were to be restricted to the universities, but the two-year basic courses and the professional training could be offered by the whole range of existing higher education institutions. Although some vice-chancellors, for example, Christopherson (Durham) and Carter (Lancaster) made it clear that they were opposed to two year degrees, others[83], such as Thistlethwaite (East Anglia)[84] and James (York) seemed prepared to consider such developments. Lord James, in particular, linked the proposal for the diversification of the colleges of education with those for two-year higher education courses.[85] This link, which was included as at least a possibility in the CVCP document, was strongly opposed by the ATCDE. It did not want the colleges of education relegated to the position of junior colleges on the American pattern, and it argued that the professional training of teachers would deteriorate within such a structure.[86] With relatively recent memories of two-year teacher training courses, the ATCDE was firmly against the colleges being used primarily as providers of two-year degree or sub-degree courses. The American junior college pattern, however, clearly appealed to some vice-chancellors, but the views of the DES, which had yet to declare its hand, were crucially important to the resolution of these issues.

DES views on the diversification of the colleges were not made public for some considerable time. In March 1970 Hugh Harding, now in charge of the teacher training branch at the DES, told UCET that 'financing the expansion of higher education was going to be very difficult and it looked as if it would not be possible to cater for the higher education of the future numbers of school leavers on the same lines as at present. We had to think of various ways of either cutting down the number or providing some forms of higher education that were less expensive'.[87] He argued that the colleges 'were not monolithic, but fell into groups which were considerably different from each other',[88] but he did not see much future in the social work link as student numbers on that side were small. Harding acknowledged that there was strong support for concurrent teacher training in the colleges, but suggested that 'social and logistic factors' pointed to 'consecutive courses'.[89] He concluded that some of the problems could only be solved by restructuring the teaching profession. A few weeks later, when Herbert Andrew was asked about the same subject, he replied somewhat cryptically, 'There is a widespread view — I do not know that the Department as such has any particular view on the matter — that if teachers were educated along with other people, this would be good for them. One also has to consider the effect on the other people'.[90] During June 1970 Harding returned to this subject at a conference of principals of colleges of education at York. The timing, as well as the contents, of this speech was interesting. Firstly, it came in the middle of an election campaign which was a strange time for a civil servant to deal with controversial issues. Secondly, Herbert Andrew, the Permanent Secretary of the DES who was sympathemtic to the university/college connection in teacher training, was due to retire at the end of July, and it had already been announced that his successor was to be William Pile who had worked in the Teacher Supply Branch of the DES in the early 1960s. In Pile's time this Branch had been strongly opposed to the Robbins' solution for teacher training and had favoured local authority retention of the colleges.[91] It was during this uncertain period that Harding made his controversial and important York speech.

In his introduction Harding said that his speech was prompted by the ATCDE statement of policy on college diversification.[92] He gave an account of the latest DES projections for the demand and supply of teachers in the 1970s which, although the fall in the birth rate was mentioned, were far from gloomy. Negative comments were made on how the universities had coped with BEd degrees particularly in subject areas unfamiliar to them, and it was also alleged that few ATOs were equipped to organize the in-service programmes which would be required in the 1970s. The main part of the speech was a response to the ATCDE's scheme for 'liberal arts colleges associated in groups with parent universities'.[93] Harding indicated that the ATCDE justified this scheme on three main grounds: (i) economy; (ii) administrative unity; and (iii) educational desirability. He reviewed the economic arguments and doubted their validity, and he concluded that there did not seem to be 'any long run cost advantage in expanding one sector of higher education rather than another'.[94] On the question of administrative control, Harding argued that even if the colleges were diversified they would still be responsible for initial and in-service professional training and thus 'the teaching profession and its employers must remain associated with academic supervision'.[95] He also pointed out that if universities received earmarked grants for colleges, academic and financial control would be divorced, and if grants were not earmarked the colleges 'would be dependent on university senates in competition with other university expenditure'.[96] Considering the educational issues, the dilemma between the colleges' preference for concurrent courses and students' desires to postpone career choices was highlighted. Harding suggested that one way around this problem was for some students to spend an initial period of two years on a course which 'led to a qualification comparable with the Higher National Diploma'.[97] Then, potential teachers could proceed to a two-year professional training course in which the second year would be largely school-based and would replace the existing probationary year. Harding concluded by asking several rhetorical questions which were very much in the spirit of the whole speech. The most important of these questions were:

1   Might the CNAA be a more appropriate degree awarding body

than a parent university? What conclusions should we draw from experience with the BEd and the London external degree?

2   What are the implications for the two cultures, if, outside the universities, science and technology are based on polytechnics and arts on colleges of education? If monotechnics are bad are polytechnics good?

3   Would development of liberal arts colleges weaken professional education and the standing of education departments (cf. standing of UDEs in university world)?

4   Is a frontal attack on the 'Binary Line' a constructive policy for those actively concerned to improve relations with the teaching profession, their employers and the schools? Is there scope for combining the principle of local authority maintenance with a greater measure of central supervision by a committee on which colleges as well as local authorities are represented?[98]

Although Harding warned his audience that his paper should not be interpreted as the advice which would be given to ministers, he, no doubt, realized that it would be seen as a reflection of thinking from a high level in the DES. Certainly, the college principals, institute of education directors and the ATCDE, all took the speech to mean that in the DES's view the future of the colleges was not to be with the universities. When Harding was asked about this by members of UCET, he stressed that the speech was a personal statement activated by the ATCDE policy document.[99] At this private meeting he said that he did not envisage any change in government policy about ATOs in the near future and he predicted that their structure was secure in the short term which he defined as five to ten years.[100] He explained that he had posed the question about CNAA/university validation because of the implications of introducing two-year courses of higher education. The polytechnics, in his view, were poised for great expansion on the arts side, and he felt that the colleges could be squeezed out between the universities and the polytechnics. Harding was not opposed to a pattern in which some of the colleges went to the CNAA for validation and others stayed with the universities. He emphasized that if colleges were validated by the CNAA this did not necessarily imply the demise of the ATOs, and he argued that the future of validation and of the ATOs should be regarded as separate issues.[101] Despite the reassurances, Harding's speech was seen as an important semi-public announcement of DES thinking. It is difficult to ignore its timing. It is unlikely that ministers wanted these potentially contentious issues raised in the middle of a general election campaign, and they were almost certainly preoccupied with pressing party political matters. At the same time senior civil servants at the DES were aware of basic changes which were about to affect them. It has already been mentioned that Herbert Andrew, who supported the university/college connection, was about to be replaced by William Pile who had opposed the Robbins' solution to teacher training. Toby Weaver remained the Deputy Secretary in charge of higher education, and it has already been shown that he was sceptical of the university role in teacher training and wished to see CNAA more active in this area. With the impending departure of Andrew and the imminent arrival of the potentially more sympathetic Pile, it is likely that Weaver and his Under-Secretary Harding took the opportunity to get their views, albeit relatively tentatively, on to the record.

During the 1970 election campaign Margaret Thatcher hinted that the Conservatives 'might expand the colleges of education to take students other than intending teachers', and she made a firm commitment to hold a major enquiry into teacher training.[102] After consulting her senior civil servants and various interest groups, the new Secretary of State set up such an enquiry under the chairmanship of Lord James of Rusholme, Vice-Chancellor of York University and former Highmaster of Manchester Grammar School. James's views on the nature of universities — he believed that vocational and professional education were outside the scope of their primary functions — were well known. With these presuppositions it was not surprising that he was a long-standing critic of the existing university institutes of education. Lord James was fearful of the consequences of the projected expansion of the universities in the 1970s, arguing that teaching rather than research would suffer. As recently as July 1970 he had told the House of Lords that 'a significant number of those 400,000 (the projected total of university students) might be happier and more successful in places other than universities'.[103] He hinted that diversified colleges of education, which he supported, could accommodate some of these students, and he maintained that some colleges 'could most profitably experiment with two-year courses of a general character which could provide suitable education for those uncertain as to whether a full degree course is what they really want'.[104] There were six other members of the Committee of Enquiry: Elizabeth Agett, Headmistress of a London primary school, Cyril English, Director of the City and Guilds, Harry Judge, headmaster of Banbury School, Patrick Milroy, CEO for Gloucestershire, James Porter, Principal of Berkshire College of Education and Roger Webster, Professor of Education, University of Wales. Both Judge and Porter were on record as supporting radical changes in teacher training, and Judge had been the chairman of a joint working party of the Headmasters' Association and the Headmasters' Conference which was critical of the BEd degree and which advocated more school-based teacher training.

From the outset the DES favoured a small committee[105], and it resisted representations to increase its size.[106] There was also some considerable feeling that the membership was unrepresentative.[107] The DES, moreover, asked the Committee to undertake an intensive enquiry and report within one year. This emphasis on speed was yet another source of criticism, and it was felt that a combination of the above factors made it inevitable that the Committee would be much more dependent on DES inputs than other national education enquiries in the post-war period.[108] The Committee's terms of reference prompted considerable comment. From the outset the Department was prepared to spell out in detail the kind of enquiry which was intended. Thatcher stated that, in addition to the content and organization of teacher training courses, she wanted the Committee to consider 'a way to break down the isolation of the colleges of education so that a growing proportion of intending teachers are trained side by side with students who are either vocationally uncommitted or committed to other careers'.[109] She acknowledged that this would inevitably lead the Committee into other areas of higher education, but she stressed that these areas would only be considered 'in relation to the training of teachers'.[110] The Committee was asked to assume that the local authorities were to continue to play a major part in the provision of higher education but it was not to regard 'the distinction between colleges of education and further education colleges as immutable'.[111] Given Weaver's views and Harding's hints at the York Conference, it was significant that the DES chose to make these particular considerations quite explicit. It is interesting that at this juncture no mention was made of the in-service training of teachers, and, although this had a prominent place in the Committee's Report, its inclusion owed more to pressure from bodies as diverse as the local authority associations and UCET than to DES initiative. A wide range of interest groups, including the local authorities, the universities and the polytechnics, were doubtful about the terms of reference. The local authority associations were not convinced that the Committee could be kept narrowly to teacher training and felt that consideration of others forms of higher education were implied. They suggested that the proposed committee should undertake a short survey of the content and nature of teacher training courses, but advocated that a more widely based body with more time should consider 'the longer-term problems of a structural nature'.[112] Although the CDP and UCET did not propose two enquiries, they took up a similar position on the main issue. These representations were ignored by the DES and the enquiry went ahead, with the exception of the inclusion of in-service training, much as originally envisaged. By this time, the main interest groups agreed with the DES that the question of the diversification of the colleges of education was both important and urgent, and they also grasped that this question was inseparable from the issues of student numbers in, and future patterns of, higher education in the 1970s. Many felt that the size, composition, terms of reference and planned duration of the James Enquiry were unsuitable for the tasks to be performed, and some were suspicious that the James Committee would be used mainly to present the Department's own preferred solution to the problem.

By July 1971 the James Committee was informing interest groups of its likely recommendations, and this practice, along with other factors, led to leaks being reported in the press. A short, but comprehensive account, in *The Guardian* presaged many of James's recommendations very accurately.[113] In future intending teachers could take two possible routes. During the first stage they would follow either three-year degree or two-year diploma in higher education courses. The latter were to be made available mainly in colleges of education. The second stage was to consist of one year of college-based professional training and one year of school-based teaching. Successful completion of the second stage was to carry the award of BA (Ed). In-service education and training, which was to be expanded, was to form a third stage. It was also proposed by a majority of the Committee to abolish the university institutes of education, and to transfer the control and validation of college of education courses to a new, specially constituted, national body. The idea of severing the college links with the universities, hardly surprising given the composition of the Committee, caused consternation in UCET, which was also sceptical of the concept of a 'third force' in higher education from the outset.[114] In essence James was proposing three separate strands in higher education: (i) the universities which controlled their own courses; (ii) the polytechnics and advanced further education under CNAA jurisdiction; and (iii) the colleges of education whose courses were to be validated by a new national body. UCET and ATCDE wanted to counter such proposals, but they did not know how far the universities would be willing to validate qualifications other than BEds and certificates in education. The CVCP evidence to James was non-commital and not particularly encouraging in this respect. Stanley Hewett of ATCDE feared that the universities might be 'very grudging',[115] and the validation of non-teacher awards in the colleges of education was, of course, essential to their proposed diversification. The James Committee saw this as a weakness in the universities' position and placed emphasis upon it. UCET contacted CVCP and found that this body had already expressed its concern to the James Committee.[116] ATCDE hoped that the CVCP would make a positive, public statement in the near future, but the Chairman of UCET felt that this was unlikely before the report was published although individual vice-chancellors might make their personal views known.[117] The idea of a 'third sector' of higher education posed considerable tactical problems for ATCDE. The General Secretary realized that if the Association publicly discredited the notion, its members could easily be forced by the Government to operate it. Thus, having undermined the concept, the Association would then have to try 'to make it credible' to its own members and to potential students.[118] UCET decided that its best course of immediate action was to sound out the views of other bodies particularly the teachers' associations. In general these associations and the NUS shared the views of UCET and ATCDE, although the Headmasters' Association and the Headmasters' Conference supported James.[119] The NUT was so concerned about the James leaks that it organized a meeting of those opposed to the proposals. As a result of this and further meetings a joint committee was formed to lead a public campaign against the James' proposals.[120] This Committee was composed of representatives from the AUT, ATCDE, ATTI, UCET, NUT and NUS. The other school teacher's associations were also asked to join, and the CVCP was invited to send observers. Months before the James Report was published, *The Times Higher Educational Supplement* commented that, against such united opposition the proposals 'were doomed to failure',[121] and, while continuing their opposition, the main interest groups turned to preparing counter-proposals.

Notes

1 LUIE, File 3092, Notes of Directors' meeting with DES officials, 23 October 1967.
2 *Ibid.*
3 *Ibid.*, File 3093, UCET, Main Committee, 7 December 1967.
4 *Ibid.*, UCET meeting DES representatives, 30 May 1968.
5 *Ibid.*
6 *Ibid.*
7 W Taylor (Ed), *Towards a Policy for the Education of Teachers* (1969), p. 187.
8 *TES*, 16 May 1969.
9 *Ibid.*
10 Central Advisory Council for Education, *Children and their Primary Schools*, (1967), p. 339.
11 W Taylor, *Towards a Policy for the Education of Teachers*, Proceedings of a Symposium held in Bristol University, April 1968, (1969).
12 *Ibid.*, p. ix.
13 M Maden, 'Educational reform through teacher training', *Higher Education Review*, Autumn (1969), p. 28.
14 H Rée, 'Wanted: A royal commission', *Higher Education Review*, Autumn (1968), pp. 55–67.
15 LUIE, File 3364, Meeting of H Harding with UCET Committee A, 2 May 1969.
16 *Ibid.*

17 House of Commons Select Committee, (Session 1968–9), Education and Science, Evidence of H Andrew, Q 2.
18 *Ibid.*
19 *Ibid.*
20 *Ibid.*, Evidence of M J G Hearley, Q 10.
21 P Gosden, 'The BEd Degree', *British Universities Annual*, (1968), p. 115.
22 *TES*, 2 May 1969.
23 House of Commons, Select Committee, (Session 1969–70), Education and Science, Evidence of NUT, p. 148.
24 *Ibid.*
25 J D Browne, *Teachers of Teachers*, (1979), p. 205.
26 LUIE, File 3093, Tibble to UCET members, 4 January 1968.
27 House of Commons, Select Committee (1969–70) Evidence of S Hewett, Q 1212.
28 P Gosden, (1968), *op. cit.*, p. 119.
29 House of Commons, Select Committee (1969–70), Evidence of H Andrew, Q 1236.
30 F T Willey and R E Maddison, *An Enquiry into Teacher Training*, (1971), p. 69.
31 *THES*, 15 October 1971.
32 *Ibid.*
33 House of Commons, Select Committee (1969–70), Evidence of ATCDE, p. 336.
34 *Ibid.*
35 *Ibid.*
36 F T Willey and R E Maddison, (1971), *op. cit.*, p. 73.
37 *Ibid.*, p. 71.
38 *Education*, 30 January 1970.
39 House of Commons, Select Committee (1969–70), Evidence of NUT, p. 149.
40 *Ibid.*, Evidence of W Alexander, Q 374.
41 F T Willey and R E Maddison, (1971), *op. cit.*, p. 86.
42 *Ibid.*, p. 102.
43 House of Commons, Select Committee (1968–69), Evidence of H Andrew, Q 12.
44 J D Browne, (1979), *op. cit.*, p. 206.
45 *Ibid.*
46 *Ibid.*
47 AEC, File A870, Short to Alexander, 25 February 1970.
48 *TES*, 27 February 1970.
49 *Ibid.*
50 AEC, File A194, Marshall to Stone, 4 April 1968.
51 *Ibid.*, Harding to LEAs, ATOs and College Principals, 19 June 1968.
52 DES, Reports on Education (51), *The Supply of Teachers*, (December 1968).
53 *Ibid.*
54 House of Commons, Select Committee (1968–9), Education and Science, Evidence of H Andrew, Q 24.
55 J D Browne, (1979), *op. cit.*, p. 203.
56 DES, Planning Paper 2, *Student Numbers in Higher Education in England and*

Wales, (June 1970).
57   *Education*, 29 December 1978.
58   J D Browne, (1979), *op. cit.*, p. 203.
59   *Ibid.*, p. 204.
60   Robbins Report, (1963), p. 108.
61   J D Browne, (1979), *op. cit.*, p. 197.
62   Conference Report, Caius College, Cambridge, 6–8 January 1969, *Universities Quarterly*, Summer (1969), p. 304.
63   B MacArthur, 'Who plans higher education?', *Higher Education Review*, Spring (1970), pp. 32–3.
64   *Ibid.*, p. 38. MacArthur quotes the CVCP letter to the universities verbatim.
65   *Ibid.*, p. 34.
66   House of Commons, Select Committee (1968–9), ATCDE memorandum, pp. 16–17.
67   D Hencke, *Colleges in Crisis*, (1978), p. 41.
68   ATCDE, *Higher Education and Preparation for Teaching*, (1970), p. 9.
69   *Ibid.*, p. 3.
70   *Ibid.*, p. 4.
71   *Ibid.*, p. 1.
72   J D Browne, (1979), *op. cit.*, p. 207.
73   *Education*, 16 January 1970; *TES*, 16 January and 9 May 1970.
74   *Education*, 10 April 1970; *TES*, 15 May 1970.
75   LUIE, File 3537, Minutes of UCET Research Committee, 23 April 1970.
76   CVCP, *University Developments in the 1970s*, (1970).
77   *Ibid.*, p. 6.
78   *TES*, 29 May 1970.
79   CVCP, (1970), *op. cit.*, p. 12.
80   *Ibid.*
81   *Ibid.*
82   *Ibid.*
83   *TES*, 16 January and 15 May 1970.
84   *TES*, 15 May 1970.
85   Hansard, House of Lords, Volume 311, 15 July 1970, col. 636.
86   *TES*, 12 June 1970.
87   LUIE, File 3391, UCET, Working Party on the Future of Teacher Education, Minutes, 13 March 1970.
88   *Ibid.*
89   *Ibid.*
90   House of Commons, Select Committee (1969–70), Education and Science Evidence of H Andrew, Q 1415.
91   E Boyle, *Government, Parliament and the Robbins Report*, Joseph Payne Memorial Lecture, (1979), p. 15.
92   LUIE, File 3537, H A Harding, Some Reflections on the Problems of Teacher Education over the next 10 years, York Conference, 10 June 1970.
93   *Ibid.*
94   *Ibid.*
95   *Ibid.*
96   *Ibid.*

97 *Ibid.*
98 *Ibid.*
99 LUIE, File 3391, Note of UCET meeting, 14 July 1970.
100 *Ibid.*
101 *Ibid.*
102 *TES*, 29 May and 5 June 1970.
103 HANSARD, House of Lords, Volume 311, 15 July 1970, col. 636.
104 *Ibid.*
105 AEC, File A1098, Thatcher to Alexander, 13 August 1970.
106 B FORD, 'Report on James', *Universities Quarterly*, Spring (1972), p. 132.
107 *Ibid.*, pp. 131–2. Also D HENCKE (1978), *op. cit.*, p. 39; P GOSDEN, *Education since 1944*, (1983), pp. 115–6.
108 *Ibid.*, p. 131.
109 AEC, File A1098, Thatcher to Alexander, 13 August 1970.
110 *Ibid.*
111 *Ibid.*
112 *Ibid.*, Local authority associations to Thatcher, 8 October 1970.
113 *The Guardian*, 24 July 1971.
114 LUIE, File 3624, UCET, Executive Committee Minutes, 2 July 1971.
115 *Ibid.*
116 *Ibid.*, 30 September 1971.
117 *Ibid.*
118 WUMRC, ATCDE, Memo from General Secretary to the James Committee Working Party, 4 October 1971.
119 LUIE, File 3624, UCET, Standing Committee A, Minutes, 5 November 1971.
120 *THES*, 12 November 1971.
121 *THES*, 5 November 1971.

Chapter 7

Picking and Choosing from the James Report

When the James Report appeared it contained few surprises and the leaks were confirmed. Notes of reservation and extension[1], written jointly by the university representative and the college of education principal, had not been leaked, and they illustrated clearly how the interest groups had taken up their expected positions in the Committee. The authors of these notes completely rejected the Committee's severe criticisms of the influence of the universities on the colleges. They advocated the retention of the university/college connection, and hoped that academic awards would continue to be validated by universities or CNAA. They did not want to see the colleges' academic courses restricted to diplomas in higher education and stressed that 'first degrees of many kinds'[2] including four-year honours BEd courses should be offered there. In many respects these proposals were radically different from those in the main report, and it was strange that such important differences were only recorded in brief notes of reservation and extension. On several crucial issues the Committee itself remained almost as divided as the educational world outside.

During the early weeks of 1972 the James Report was greeted with enthusiasm by the media. Margaret Thatcher had promised that wide consultations would take place before decisions were taken, and Toby Weaver later acknowledged that throughout 1971 and 1972 a large number of DES staff was working on a Government White Paper on education.[3] It is important that the James Report and its aftermath is seen in this wider context, for the decisions ultimately taken related to a much broader field than teacher training. Most well-informed educationists were well aware of this at the time, and they grasped that the James Report was merely the prelude to the recasting of the higher education system. If emphasis is placed here on criticisms of certain of the James proposals, this is because criticisms of, and alternatives to, James soon became central to the debate concerning the future development of higher education. This emphasis does not imply that certain aspects of the James Report were not widely supported. Its proposals, for example, for the expansion of the in-service education of teachers were almost universally applauded, and many also agreed with its severe castigation of some of the university institutes of education. Influential bodies such as the National Association of Head Teachers and the local authority associations, especially the AEC, welcomed the whole Report with considerable enthusiasm.

According to UCET, 'potentially the most far-reaching'[4] recommendation in the James Report was the proposal to set up the Diploma in Higher Education. Almost all the interest groups warmly welcomed this proposed award for a two-year course of general higher education, seeing it as a possible solution to the diversification of the colleges. Similarly almost all regarded university and CNAA recognition as essential to its credibility. This did not create a problem as CNAA announced that it would validate the DipHE and the CVCP indicated that it expected universities to be willing to do the same. The CVCP also predicted that the new award would be taken 'primarily in non-university institutions'.[5] It was recognized that some holders of the DipHE would eventually seek entry to degree courses and hope to obtain some credit for their previous study. The CVCP envisaged that the amount of credit would be 'a matter for detailed discussion in individual cases . . . but the impression was that in dealing with such cases universities would be likely to consider one year (exceptionally two) as appropriate exemption from a three-year degree course'.[6] It was also stressed that 'chances of acceptability would be greatly enhanced if universities could assure themselves of the standards of the diploma by validating it themselves'.[7] To develop into a major force in higher education, the DipHE also needed credibility outside of the academic world. It required to be generally acceptable as a qualification for entry to various forms of employment and to professions other than teaching. During 1972 the James Committee, the local authority associations and the DES were sanguine about this, although UCET and ATCDE were more guarded and Laurie Sapper, General Secretary of the AUT, extremely sceptical.[8] Views on this subject remained impressionistic, and little, if any, attempt was made to test the market.

The James Report set the DipHE very firmly in the context of teacher training, and, although it mentioned briefly that the award could be offered in institutions other than colleges of educaton, it failed to develop this point in any detail. The Committee may not have been helped by its terms of reference in this respect, but its failure to discuss the proposed diploma in the broad setting of higher education as a whole brought severe criticism from almost all quarters. The CDP was particularly displeased by this and made the point, echoed by several other groups, that 'a DipHE intended to prepare for a range of professions other than teaching, if it is confined to existing teacher training institutions, would only not be credible, but would perpetuate the very difficulties of isolation which the James Committee has drawn attention to in the existing situation'.[9] It complained that 'The Report pays scant attention to those institutions, the polytechnics, which are currently providing the great majority of courses, at sub-degree level, for other professions'.[10] It was the CDP's view that 'the DipHE concept, to be viable and acceptable, must be refined and finalized in the light of the considerable experience of the polytechnics'.[11]

DES civil servants agreed with much of this criticism and were unhappy with the James Report's presentation of the DipHE. According to Gerald Fowler, a former Minister of State, 'Toby Weaver complained that James had taken one of his favourite ideas, that of a two-year degree, and damaged it by making it a DipHE in the context of teacher education'.[12] Hugh Harding has made much the same point.[13] Later in 1972 the idea of the DipHE was taken up in the Government's White Paper, but it was there proposed to introduce 'this new option . . . in each of the main sectors of higher education'.[14] In the longer term the DipHE made little impact in English education. It did not develop into a major avenue to employment, and, in comparison with three-year degree courses, it recruited very few students. To preserve standards its minimum entry requirements were made the same as for degree courses[15], and, in these circumstances, it was hardly surprising that almost all students preferred direct entry to degree courses. In Harding's words the DipHE became 'an optional extra'[16] in English higher education, and it must be added an 'extra' which was very largely ignored. It must be remembered that in this period economies were already being sought in education, and many in the DES and the local authorities hoped that economies could be found in the introduction of a DipHE-type qualification. They believed that such an award might 'break the mould' in higher education and introduce different (and for many students shorter) course patterns. Senior staff in polytechnics were enthusiastic about these new course patterns which were remote from the universities' experience and much closer to their own. They seemed to offer the local authority sector considerable opportunity for expansion. On the other hand, there was little chance that the DipHE could compete successfully with the three-year degree. If the original Weaver inspired proposal to make the two-year degree (or diploma) common throughout higher education had been accepted, circumstances would have been very different, but as soon as this was defeated the fate of the DipHE was sealed.

Representatives of the colleges and the universities opposed the James proposal to abolish the BEd as an initial teacher training award. They argued that the Committee had underestimated the considerable achievements made by the colleges in this field in a short time. The main Report, although not the note of extension, had proposed that degree teaching in the colleges should be considerably curtailed, and, indeed, removed from many colleges altogether. This was completely unacceptable to the ATCDE which received support from UCET and the CVCP. The latter bodies stressed the important progress which had been made with the BEd. The CVCP admitted that the universities had been cautious in framing their regulations for this degree initially, but claimed that it was now viewed with 'increasing confidence'[17] within the universities. It was also contended that the development of the BEd 'offered the prospect of true academic status and flexibility of approach'.[18]

The James Report put strong emphasis on consecutive, rather than concurrent, teacher education and training. This permitted students to delay their career choices, and made it easier for those controlling teacher supply to make adjustments relatively quickly. Nonetheless, a large number of bodies including ATCDE, UCET, CVCP, CNAA and certain local authorities felt that James had been too rigid in rejecting opportunities for concurrent training. Local authority concern was expressed by Sir William Houghton, Education Officer of ILEA, when he doubted whether one year of vocational training was 'sufficient to provide local authorities with an adequate supply of well-trained primary teachers ready to go into the schools even if their first year in the schools is regarded in some sense as a fourth year of training'.[19] Alexander of the AEC agreed with this[20], and, although the local authority associations did not give wide publicity to it, it was mentioned to Pile at the DES.[21] In its White Paper the DES claimed that during its consultations it found 'much greater support for concurrent courses . . . than there appeared to be when the Committee were engaged on their task'.[22]

Central to the James recommendations was the proposal to institute the BA(Ed) degree. This was to be a professional award conferring both graduate and qualified teacher status. All teachers were to enter their profession by this route whether they were already graduates or not. The BA (Ed) course incorporated one year of professional study in college and one year of practical teaching experience in school, and the award of the degree was to be made at the end of the second year. James envisaged that the BA (Ed) would be validated, at least initially, by the proposed new National Council for Teacher Education and Training. These arrangements implied that teacher training was to be made into the so-called 'third force' in higher education separate from and independent of both the universities (the 'first force') and the polytechnics (the 'second force').

From the outset spokesmen for the universities, polytechnics, colleges and schools were sceptical about the BA(Ed) degree. They argued that is was likely to be in no way comparable with degrees awarded by universities and CNAA, and they feared that it would become a debased qualification. Later, when interest groups produced their considered reactions to the Report, the condemnation was even clearer. The CVCP contended:

> The proposed BA(Ed) could be expected to have little standing; it would be open to candidates without the present university minimum entrance qualifications, it would be awarded on work done for other qualifications and after attendance at up to three institutions/centres and finally the scope of study would be unrelated and diffuse. On this account the degree would not be acceptable as a means of achieving an all-graduate profession.[23]

A few weeks later the CVCP issued a public statement which claimed that,

> It is most unlikely that the academic content of such a course will merit comparison with any other British first degree ... The impression so far received is that universities would be likely to accord it no more favourable recognition than the existing Certificate in Education in relation to admissions to advanced courses. The qualification has therefore little chance of achieving the status claimed for it in the Report.[24]

This devastating criticism was supplemented by UCET[25] and ATCDE[26] which argued that the BA(Ed) was neither credible nor acceptable as a degree as it did not indicate intellectual achievement but was a recognition of professional competence. CDP[27] took a rather similar view, and even the AMC pointed out that an all-graduate profession 'must not be achieved at the expense of graduate status'.[28] It added that there was no point in introducing the BA(Ed) if it was to be regarded as 'a second class type of degree'.[29]

There was considerable concern that the BA(Ed) proposals would perpetuate, even exacerbate, the existing divisions in the teaching profession. The authors of the note of extension were 'disturbed that divisiveness will persist in that area where it causes most concern: differences in the length of initial higher education received by teachers of different kinds which are in turn reflected in differences of salary and career expectations'.[30] NUT spokesmen, such as Edward Britton and Alan Evans, consistently attacked these recommendations pointing out that two classes of teachers would emerge. 'First class' teachers would start their careers with three-year university or polytechnic honours degrees and BA(Ed)s, and 'second class' teachers with two-year college diplomas and BA(Ed)s. Evans had no doubt that the former with two degrees would have 'more attractive employment opportunities'.[31] He argued that the BA(Ed) would be and would be seen as a sub-standard degree, and as such could not be acceptable to teachers as a means to an all-graduate profession.

The proposal to create new machinery to validate awards for teacher training institutions was opposed by almost all the main interest groups. It was stressed that such an innovation would isolate the colleges of education even further from the mainstream of English higher education, and this isolation was one of the main failings of the existing system which Margaret Thatcher had asked the James Committee to rectify.[32] Separate validation of teacher training was the cornerstone of the 'third force' policy. Britton of the NUT equated this 'third force' with the 'third division in a severely competitive higher education league'.[33] He predicted that students would apply to universities as their first choice, to polytechnics as their second and to colleges as their third.[34] Alec Ross of Lancaster University maintained that it was lamentable that, in practice, the vast majority of the teachers of young children in primary schools would be trained in the sector of higher education with the lowest status.[35] To most realists the 'pecking order' described by Britton seemed a likely development, and it was soon widely argued that the James Committee had not produced compelling reasons for the creation of a separate 'third force' in English higher education.[36] The obvious solution, which avoided the isolation of the colleges, was to abandon James and incorporate teacher training into the two existing sectors of higher education.

Many of the critics of James commented adversely on the Report's lack of statistical information concerning the projected demand for teachers. Several interest groups were frustrated by this during 1972 and pressed the DES for details. The DES responded by claiming that no figures could be supplied at this time as they depended on policy decisions still to be taken such as class sizes and the balance between provisions for primary and secondary education.[37] The James' Report gave little prominence to the question of the future demand for teachers, although it did warn that planners should not overlook 'the possibility that some colleges might close or be made over to other educational uses'.[38] It also added later in the Report: 'To put it bluntly, the supply of new teachers is now increasing so rapidly that it must soon catch up with any likely assessment of future demand, and choice will have to be made soon between various ways of using or diverting some of the resources at present invested in the education and training of teachers'.[39] It was surprising that the Report devoted so little attention to this crucial issue, for the comments quoted were not in prominent positions in the text and were left undeveloped. Some felt that the James' Report gave a misleading impression in this respect. It is now clear[40] that 'the numbers issue was considered by the Committee in greater detail than was ever made explicit in its final report'.[41] Several writers have speculated about the reasons for the Report's omissions in this area. Hencke, for example, has suggested that the DES may have prevented the publication of the figures for its own rather sinister reasons,[42] but this has been strongly denied by Hugh Harding of the DES.[43] With hindsight, it is difficult to avoid the conclusion that the DES made a tactical error in withholding their projections (albeit unsophisticated and imperfect ones). Such secrecy was bound to fuel suspicions. Apart from the psychological effects, the withholding of these figures in all probability made little difference. Although the various interest groups did not know the latest figures, it had been common knowledge since 1969–70 that the demand for teachers would be significantly reduced in the 1970s.[44] By 1971–72 all the groups were fully expecting reductions in teacher training numbers and they certainly would not have been shocked by government announcements of such. Their reactions to the James' Report were prefaced on such assumptions, and it seems unlikely that their responses would have been different with detailed knowledge of the DES's current forecasts.[45]

As has been shown the James' proposals for the BA(Ed) and the creation of a separate 'third force' in higher education received little support. Harding has made it clear that he supported the critics of James on these issues[46], and there is no evidence to suggest that his views were different from those of his departmental colleagues. When representatives of the CVCP met Toby Weaver and others from the DES in April 1972, it was clear that the DES was not pursuing the idea of the BA(Ed) and was looking for other ways of conferring professional degrees in education.[47] DES warned on 'resource grounds'[48] that it was 'unrealistic to assume that any pattern of study involving a *minimum* period of four years initial education and training would be introduced'.[49] The CVCP was asked whether there would be university support for 'the establishment of a three-year BEd course at pass level, combining academic and professional elements'.[50] The CVCP's preliminary reply was encouraging provided that 'the minimum entry requirements were as for other first degree courses'.[51] It was also envisaged that four-year BEd honours degrees would continue to be available in the colleges for some students. The idea of a three-year ordinary BEd degree had first been put forward in the ATCDE's original submission to James[52], and the DES could expect support from this quarter. The NUT was also known to favour the development of such degree schemes.[53] Before the publication of the James' Report UCET and CVCP had insisted that a minimum period of four years was necessary to produce a trained graduate teacher, but at its Brighton conference in March 1972 UCET, recognizing constraints in a pragmatic way, moved towards support for a three-year ordinary BEd degree. This was mentioned to Weaver and DES representatives at a meeting on 12 May, and UCET's new schemes were published about the same time.[54] Very soon afterwards CNAA announced that it was willing to validate three-year BEd degrees, also mentioning that it would consider three-year honours schemes.[55] When representatives of the DES, including Margaret Thatcher, met the local authority associations in August, the misgivings about the BA(Ed) and the new proposals for BEds were explained.[56] The latter were acceptable to the local authorities, but doubts were expressed about whether three-year BEds justified the award of honours. William Alexander was unenthusiastic about the new proposals because he felt that 'it could well appear that the only outcome of the James Report was to give a degree at the end of a three-year course — the course being more or less as it is at present — provided the student had two 'A' levels at the point of entry'.[57] The DES also indicated that it envisaged the continuation of certificate in education courses for students who could not meet the minimum entry requirements for degree courses. The local authorities doubted 'the wisdom of maintaining the dichotomy which would thus be continued apparently indefinitely' and they argued that 'this would defeat the purpose of creating a trained graduate profession'.[58] Alexander felt strongly that all teachers should be given a degree on the successful completion of a three-year course, and he feared that in practice most of those taking the certificate course would subsequently become infants' teachers. Despite these reservations the plans for the three-year ordinary BEd degree went forward.

No attempt was made by the DES to develop the James' notion of a 'third force' in higher education, and, when in discussions interest groups such as CVCP, UCET, ATCDE and CNAA pressed that teacher training awards should be validated by existing institutions, this was accepted by the DES. The attitude of the various groups to CNAA validation was both interesting and important. In the mid-1960s, Weaver, in attempting to bring teacher training and advanced further education together into one united sector of local authority higher education, had tried to break the university institute of education monopoly control of teacher training awards.[59] This had been resisted by the universities and ATCDE, and, with some assistance from Herbert Andrew, this resistance proved at least partially successful. The institutes retained their control of professional teacher training awards, although CNAA was authorized to validate academic BEd degrees. In practice in the early 1970s all certificate and nearly all BEd courses were still validated through the university institutes. At York in June 1970 Harding gave strong indications that the DES still favoured the development of a local authority sector of higher education with awards validated by CNAA. In its evidence to James ATCDE came out strongly against a merger between advanced further education and teacher training and against CNAA validation of college courses.[60] UCET and CVCP in their evidence did not refer to this possible merger, but maintained that 'no single arrangement would be equally appropriate to all colleges and the position of each college would need to be examined in the light of its own particular circumstances'.[61] Both bodies urged that teacher training awards should continue to be controlled by the university institutes. Later in their attempts to defeat the proposals for the BA(Ed) and the new validating body for college of education courses, ATCDE, CVCP and UCET all agreed, following the lead given by Porter and Webster in the note of extension to the James' Report[62], that CNAA was a suitable body for validating academic and professional awards for teachers. This was a most significant change of position as it conceded that the university institutes were to lose their monopoly control of initial training courses. Henceforth the colleges could be moved more easily from the university camp, and a merger between teacher training and advanced further education became a much more viable proposition. In May 1972 CNAA expressed its willingness to validate teacher training awards, and in November Margaret Thatcher announced that CNAA was to be fully recognized for such purposes.[63] Stanley Hewett of ATCDE commented on this: 'It is too early to say if it will affect a lot of colleges . . . The decision is a logical development from the fact that CNAA exists'.[64] Neither the universities nor ATCDE were now in a position to oppose this change, and they tried to console themselves that it had been inevitable.

After the publication of the James' Report ATCDE was almost alone in its total opposition to mergers between colleges of education and polytechnics and further education institutions. At Easter 1972 at its Worcester conference ATCDE moved from this unequivocal position[65] and soon acknowledged that in the future no uniform pattern could be expected for all colleges. It predicted that different colleges would need to adopt different roles, and that some would continue in close association with universities while others would move to CNAA.[66] These views were close to those which had been held by UCET for some time.[67] In a very different context — the meeting between the DES and the local authority associations in August — similar issues surfaced. The question of merging colleges with polytechnics or of retaining them as monotechnic institutions was discussed and it was agreed that 'both of these possibilities would remain open, according to particular circumstances one or the other being preferred'.[68] The local authority associations also pointed out that 'the smaller colleges would become virtually redundant for the purpose of preparing teachers and could well be embodied in the further education arrangements'.[69] DES suggested that some colleges were too small to offer degree work and proposed that they might teach certificate courses only. This stratification was unacceptable to the local authorities which maintained that 'all colleges should be enabled to offer degree courses'.[70] Later in the year, when Margaret Thatcher and her officials met representatives of ATCDE and UCET, the Department's thinking on these lines was confirmed.[71] Professor Norman Haycocks told UCET: 'Arrangements are unlikely to be uniform — they are more likely to be *ad hoc* arrangements, to cope with the varying circumstances in the different colleges and areas'.[72] He later pointed out that there was nothing 'to prevent complete absorption of a college within a university, if this was what everyone concerned wanted'.[73] He felt that 'the DES seemed to be assuming that the majority of colleges would remain linked with a university for their courses and awards',[74] but, with hindsight, it is clear that this was wishful thinking. On a more realistic note, Haycocks predicted that any absorption was more likely to be into a polytechnic than a university.[75] Stanley Hewett of ATCDE made a similar point when he addressed the UCET conference at York. He posed but did not answer the pointed question: 'What will be the effect on the universities and ATOs of the fact that the bulk of teachers will inevitably be trained in the public sector of higher education?'[76] UCET, however, put on a brave face and took comfort from the defeat of the James proposals for the BA(Ed) and the 'third force'. Although UCET had been informed that the Government intended to set up new regional councils for teacher education, for a brief period at the end of 1972 UCET was under the false impression that there was a reasonably long-term future for the university institutes of education.[77] It also at first underestimated the importance of the recognition of CNAA as a validating body for initial training awards, and it expected that colleges moving to CNAA would still be involved with their local institutes of education.[78] UCET took a little time to grasp that, in essence, the DES had accepted the James recommendation for the abolition of ATOs although it wanted them to continue to perform their functions for an interim period. In general, UCET was pleased by its post-James consultations with Margaret Thatcher and the DES[79], and it felt that UCET and ATCDE had had an influence on some of the government's decisions.[80] This was partially true and some of the government's final proposals were closer to the views of

UCET and ATCDE than had been expected earlier in the year. On the other hand, the post-James changes led directly to the demise of the university institutes of education and to the incorporation of most of teacher education into the local authority sector of higher education.

There can be little doubt that the DES took what it wanted from the James Report and 'ditched' the remainder. The available evidence suggests that the DES was pleased to find opposition to the notions of the BA(Ed) and the 'third force', and it soon gave support to this opposition. To replace the BA(Ed), DES took up ATCDE's idea of a three-year ordinary BEd and took the initiative in putting this proposal to the CVCP and CNAA. It did not attempt to disguise that financial considerations ruled out four-year courses of education and training for all teachers. From the outset it was unlikely that the 'third force' idea would appeal to the senior civil servants in the DES, as Toby Weaver had been largely responsible for developing the binary theory and policy. In the mid-1960s he had tried hard to merge local authority teacher education with local authority advanced further education, but had been thwarted by the opposition of the universities and ATCDE and the scepticism of his Permanent Secretary, Herbert Andrew. Andrew had been replaced in 1970 by the more sympathetic William Pile. In the post-James negotiations Weaver and the DES were able to drop the almost universally condemned 'third force' notion, and they replaced it with their well-established scheme to merge teacher education with advanced further education. The case for the latter was presented shrewdly. It was stressed that different colleges would need to develop different roles in the future and that no one pattern or solution could be expected. Some colleges might have their awards validated by universities, others by CNAA. Some might merge with polytechnics, some with further education colleges, some with universities. In some instances two or more colleges of education could be brought together to diversify, in others larger colleges might remain free-standing and diversify. Some colleges could offer a wide range of courses, some could continue to concentrate on initial teacher training, some could switch to in-service training, others might abandon teacher training altogether and make a contribution to further education. These possible variations suggested that the future of individual colleges was open-ended. In particular, those voluntary colleges which did not want a future with the local authorities were offered other routes. On the other hand, the DES expected that the majority of the local authority colleges would be merged into local authority advanced further education. The fall in the birthrate and consequent fall in the demand for teachers reinforced Weaver's case for merging teacher education with advanced further education. After a merger spare capacity in the training colleges could easily be transferred to more general uses in higher education in the local authority sector. Margaret Thatcher acknowledged that finding mechanisms to control the supply of teachers had been an important factor influencing the DES in its post-James decisions. Early in 1973 she wrote: 'it is my hope that the new pattern of courses together with the merger of colleges of education with advanced further education will enable teacher supply to be adjusted more flexibly to meet the demand than has been so far possible'.[81]

Notes

1   DES, *Teacher Education and Training*, (1972), p. 54 and 78–9.
2   *Ibid.*, p. 78.
3   *THES*, 2 March 1973.
4   UCET, *UCET on James*, (May 1972), p. 4.
5   LUIE, File 3621, CVCP meeting, 18 February 1972.
6   *Ibid.*
7   *Ibid.*
8   *THES*, 19 May 1972.
9   AEC, File A1099, CDP, *Statement of Views upon the Report on 'Teacher Education and Training' (James Report)*, (May 1972), p. 4.
10   *Ibid.*, p. 4.
11   *Ibid.*, p. 1.
12   G Fowler, 'Policy formulation and administration: A critique', in R J Alexander, M Craft and J Lynch, *Change in Teacher Education*, (1984), p. 269.
13   *Education*, 29 December 1978.
14   DES, *Education: A Framework for Expansion*, (December 1972), p. 32.
15   *Ibid.*
16   *Education*, 29 December 1978.
17   *THES*, 14 April 1972.
18   LUIE, File 3621, CVCP, Meeting 18 February 1972.
19   AEC, File A1098, Houghton to Alexander, 5 November 1971.
20   *Ibid.*, Alexander to Houghton, 11 November 1971.
21   *Ibid.*, Alexander to Pile, 11 November 1971.
22   DES, (December 1972), *op. cit.*, p. 21.
23   LUIE, File 3621, CVCP meeting, 18 February 1972.
24   *THES*, 14 April 1972.
25   LUIE, File 3624, UCET, *Alternatives to James*, (1972), p. 2.
26   ATCDE, *Statement by the Executive Committee on Teacher Education and Training*, (1972), p. 10.
27   AEC, File A1099, CDP, *op. cit.*, p. 3.
28   AEC, File A1099, AMC, Teacher Education and Training (May 1972), p. 2.
29   *Ibid.*
30   DES, *Teacher Education and Training*, (1972), p. 79.
31   *THES*, 15 October 1971.
32   AEC, File A1098, Thatcher to Alexander, 13 August 1970.

33   *THES*, 15 October 1971.
34   *Ibid.*
35   *Ibid.*
36   *THES*, 28 January 1972.
37   LUIE, File 3621, CVCP meeting with DES, 28 April 1972.
38   DES, (1972), *op. cit.*, p. 62.
39   *Ibid.*, p. 75.
40   Stuart Maclure made this point in articles in the *TES*, 5 May and 24 November 1972. David Hencke mentioned it in *Colleges in Crisis*, (1978), p. 40. HUGH HARDING (formerly DES) confirmed it in *Education*, 29 December 1978.
41   D Hencke, (1978), *op. cit.*, p. 40.
42   *Ibid.*, pp. 45–7.
43   *Education*, 29 December 1978.
44   Supra, Chapter 6.
45   With hindsight, it is now known that these forecasts considerably underestimated the fall in the demand for teachers, but later in the 1970s the DES was as surprised as others by the extent of this fall.
46   *Education*, 29 December 1978.
47   LUIE, File 3621, Meeting of CVCP and DES representatives, 28 April 1972.
48   *Ibid.*
49   *Ibid.*
50   *Ibid.*
51   *Ibid.*
52   ATCDE, *The Professional Education of Teachers*, (1971), p. 10 and 26–7.
53   *THES*, 10 March 1972. Also 'Report on James', *Universities Quarterly*, Spring (1972), p. 160.
54   UCET, (May 1972), *op. cit.*
55   LUIE, File 3754, CNAA Report on Lord James Committee, May 1972.
56   AEC, File A1099, Memorandum on the James Report, 9 August 1972.
57   *Ibid.*
58   *Ibid.*
59   Supra, Chapter 2.
60   ATCDE, (1971), *op. cit.*, pp. 13–4.
61   LUIE, File 3535, Memo from CVCP to James Committee, 7 April 1971.
62   DES, (1972), *op. cit.*, p. 78.
63   *THES*, 17 November 1972.
64   *Ibid.*
65   LUIE, File 3757, UCET, Standing Committee A, Minutes, 27 April 1972, Statement by N Haycocks.
66   ATCDE, *Statement of Executive Committee on Teacher Education and Training*, (1972), pp. 13–14.
67   LUIE, File 3757, UCET, 27 April 1972, N Haycocks.
68   AEC, File A1099, Memorandum on the James Report, 9 August 1972.
69   *Ibid.*
70   *Ibid.*
71   LUIE, File 3757, UCET, Executive Committee Minutes, 26 October 1972.
72   *Ibid.*

73 *Ibid.*, Standing Committee A, Minutes, 10 November 1972.
74 *Ibid.*
75 *Ibid.*
76 *Ibid.*, UCET York Conference, 3–5 November 1972, notes of a Leeds University representative.
77 *Ibid.*, Executive Committee Minutes, 26 October 1972, Council Minutes, 14 December 1972.
78 *Ibid.*, Standing Committee A, Minutes, 10 November 1972.
79 *Ibid.*, Executive Committee Minutes, 8 December 1972.
80 *Ibid.*, Council Minutes, 14 December 1972. Also WILLIAM TAYLOR in *THES*, 15 December 1972.
81 LUIE, File 3757, Thatcher to Boyle, 23 February 1973.

Chapter 8

The 1972 White Paper and the Merger of the Two Sub-sectors of Local Authority Higher Education

Many of the provisions for teacher training included in the White Paper had been negotiated with the main interest groups during 1972 in the aftermath of the James Report. In *Education: A Framework for Expansion* the Government announced the introduction of the Diploma in Higher Education and the three-year ordinary BEd degree both of which could be validated by either a university or CNAA. Commitments to in-service training and the induction of teachers were confirmed, but the demise of the university-based ATOs was outlined. The White Paper also stressed the need to adjust to the projected fall in demand for teachers in the 1970s, but encouraged colleges of education to diversify their courses so that they could 'share in the expansion of higher education'.[1] These proposals were expected by the main interest groups, but the form of the presentation of some of these policies was of considerable interest and importance.

In particular the diversification of the colleges was presented positively and enthusiastically. It was stated that: 'the quality and experience of their staff and the strength of their physical resources admirably equip a number of colleges to share in the expansion of higher education' and 'some colleges either singly or jointly should develop over the period into major institutions of higher education' and 'if, as most of them earnestly wish, the colleges of education are to find a fuller and firmer place in the higher education family, their staffs must face major changes'.[2] These phrases suggested a dynamic and interesting future for the colleges. Some colleges could seek 'complete integration with the university sector', others would 'be encouraged to combine forces with neighbouring polytechnics or other colleges of further education',[3] and yet others could expect to develop as free-standing diversified institutions of higher education. Certain important constraints were mentioned, and it was pointed out that institutions 'must reach a critical size to obtain full economies of scale'.[4] It was doubted whether 'small or isolated colleges' could develop into 'larger general purpose institutions' offering a viable contribution to diversified higher education provision.[5] This was tempered by the suggestion that 'some of these will continue to be needed exclusively for purposes of teacher training with increasing emphasis on in-service rather than initial training'.[6] Others were promised a future as professional centres. Some were warned that they would have 'to be converted to new purposes'[7] and it was briefly mentioned that 'some may need to close'.[8]

The DES was later criticized for its treatment of certain of these teacher training issues in the White Paper. Brian MacArthur, Editor of the *Times Higher Educational Supplement, inter alia,* alleged that the DES was too secretive about the statistical basis of this part of the Paper, and that, when college reorganization and contraction began, many lecturers were taken completely by surprise.[9] Both William Pile and Toby Weaver denied that there was insufficient consultation and information and pointed out that some target figures were included.[10] There can be little doubt, however, that in the period 1970 to 1972 the DES was less than forthcoming and that the lack of detailed statistical information in the White Paper further fuelled existing suspicions. Pile has argued with complete justification that the cut in initial teacher training announced in December 1972 did not 'burst on an astonished world'[11] and that the reasons for it had been 'clear to at least the leaders of the interested parties for some considerable time before'.[12] Pile felt that it was sad if lecturers had failed to grasp what was happening and commented 'it may well be that the institutional arrangements within the party concerned were not adequate to get the message on its way'.[13] The clear implication of this was that internal communications between ATCDE leaders and members were at fault. ATCDE representatives admitted that there were problems in this area, for Baird, the Acting General Secretary who succeeded Hewett, is on record as saying 'you can take a horse to the water but it is very difficult to make him drink. All the information that was given to the ATCDE was in fact published by Stanley Hewett but having been round colleges recently in the last few months, I have been astounded to discover how few people have taken it in ... there was no secret information which the officers of the ATCDE knew and which they did not pass on'.[14] On the other hand, ATCDE leaders stressed that as a result of the White Paper its members 'genuinely believed that they were in an exercise which involved a curriculum change and a curriculum development within the context of teacher education and diversification via the DipHE into other avenues, and the idea of a mass closure and mass redundancy ... was not part of this'.[15] It was pointed out that 'the whole emphasis was upon diversification and expansion. After all that was the name of the White

Paper'.[16] This was fair comment, for in its desire 'to sell' the White Paper to the major interest groups, the teachers and the public at large, the DES emphasized its positive aspects and chose to employ language which maximized its acceptability. Negative measures, like the possibility of closures, were not given prominence and were not developed. It was understandable that readers gained the impression that colleges were to be involved in an interesting, challenging exercise in curriculum development. The college lecturers expected, even welcomed, these challenges and continued to accept the White Paper at its face value for some time. They felt that, with a few unlucky exceptions, the future existence of their institutions (albeit often in a new guise) was secure. Some years later Pile tended to claim that DES could not be blamed for these false impressions, but the presentation of the issues in the White Paper cannot be so easily exonerated.

There were other respects in which the White Paper was less than frank and forthcoming. It was relatively easy for contemporary readers to gain the impression that individual colleges would be able, to a considerable extent, to determine their own destinies. It was not made explicit at this stage that the providing bodies (for the majority of institutions the LEAs) and not individual colleges would draw up the plans for the future. Section 17 stressed the diversity of the futures open to the colleges, and although certain constraints were mentioned the whole tone suggested that individual preferences of different colleges would normally be respected. At the national level, however, the DES made it abundantly clear in Section 18 that, 'the great majority'[17] of diversified colleges would be assimilated into 'the non-university sector of further and higher education'.[18] It predicted that in the future such colleges would not be 'easily distinguishable by function, from a polytechnic or other further education college'.[19]

The White Paper proposals for teacher training were welcomed by the local authorities without reservation and were commended for their realism by Alexander of the AEC.[20] Polytechnic spokesmen were enthusiastic, for example, at a local level Patrick Nuttgens, Director of Leeds Polytechnic, was very soon arguing for a merger between the Leeds colleges of education and its polytechnic.[21] UCET, if lacking in enthusiasm for certain parts of the White Paper, was certainly not strongly critical. It tended to be self-congratulatory about the defeat of the BA(Ed) and paid rather scant attention to the ground which the universities had lost. The Chairman, Norman Haycocks, often stressed that many options were still wide open[22], but, with hindsight, it is clear that several issues were rather less open-ended than UCET was led to believe by DES rhetoric. Even at this early stage all the interest groups, including UCET, grasped that there were unlikely to be many mergers between universities and colleges of education.

The reactions of the colleges themselves as expressed through the ATCDE were of fundamental importance. In 1971 in its evidence to the James Committee the ATCDE had come out strongly against mergers between advanced further education institutions and colleges of education and still favoured 'the university connection'. By mid-1972 it had tempered this position significantly and accepted that some colleges might wish to move to CNAA for validation of their courses. This position was broadly in line with the DES's seemingly open policy of 'different solutions for different colleges' which was advocated in the post-James era. Stanley Hewett commented that the White paper 'knocks the James Report into a workable shape very much along the lines that ATCDE suggested'.[23] He particularly welcomed the integration of teacher education into higher education, but warned that 'the reorganization together with the reduction in the output of teachers will mean major upheaval in the colleges'.[24] Harry Peake, Chairman of ATCDE and Principal of Sheffield City College, commented that 'the message seems clear — they (the colleges) must "go public" and cease to straddle the binary line'.[25] Peake argued that a necessary consequence of this should be the merging of the Advanced Further Education and Teacher Training Pools which would be advantageous for the colleges as it would put them 'within the growth area of the binary system'.[26] Hewett tended to raise questions about the past before he looked to the future. He wondered whether it had been really necessary to open so many *new* teacher training colleges (instead of expanding existing ones) in the 1960s when it now appeared that amalgamations were necessary to produce viable institutions. He pointed out that the 1960s had seen the opening of between twenty and thirty colleges and predicted that the 1970s could see the closure of a similar number[27], and Hewett was most concerned about those who had made their careers in the colleges during the 1960s. At its December meeting ATCDE Council passed resolutions welcoming much of the White Paper, but asking for further consultations with the Secretary of State about, *inter alia*, the criteria for the various forms of institutional reorganization, staffing the necessary curriculum redevelopment and safeguarding the position of staff affected by reorganization.[28] With regard to the latter, various kinds of safeguards were specified in some detail, and Margaret Thatcher very soon announced that discussions on these issues were beginning.[29]

In her study of the ATCDE Joan Browne makes the important point that ATCDE official policy, as declared by the 1971 Council, was to continue to support 'the university connection', and this policy was never rescinded.[30] On the other hand, the Association, led by Hewett, implicitly accepted the DES initiative to incorporate most of the colleges fully into the local authority sector of higher education. At no point did the ATCDE condemn or oppose the Government's general strategy as set out in the White Paper. Different writers have suggested different reasons for this. David Hencke suggests that Hewett 'could not challenge the whole of the government's policy because the facts of a declining birth rate and a bad economic situation were against him. Instead he decided to negotiate the best redundancy terms for his members'.[31] Hugh Harding argues that in Hencke's interpretation 'there is an implication that they (ATCDE and Hewett) sold their professional souls for a mess of Crombie',[32] and he regards this slur as 'totally undeserved'.[33] Hencke was no doubt correct about the influence of the falling birth rate and the bad economic situation, but other factors needed to be mentioned too. By late 1972 senior civil servants had ministerial agreement for their policies and were in a position to push them very strongly indeed. Local authority support was also in no doubt. The universities were so relieved that the James' notions of the BA(Ed) and 'the third force' had been abandoned, they were not now disposed to oppose the main thrust of the Government's policy for the colleges. The attitude of the universities towards the validation of the awards of DipHE, BA and BSc in the colleges was still not known. If the ATCDE had adopted a policy of outright opposition to the Government, it could easily have found that it was standing alone. It probably foresaw its potential isolation by mid–1972 and so it conceded that some colleges might wish to go to CNAA for validation — a point conceded by UCET even earlier. Browne's view that 'ATCDE seemed to be taking stock of what it was likely to be able to secure, and to be in the process of deciding that the continuance of the Robbins' policy was not among the possibilities'[34] is convincing. These was little point in the ATCDE fighting a battle which it could not win. Hewett could envisage a situation in which ATCDE opposition failed and Government policy was implemented. In these circumstances ATCDE members would find themselves in the unenviable position of carrying out policies which they had consistently opposed and working in institutions which they and their union had tried to discredit. It was not surprising that the ATCDE leaders were reluctant to take the grave risks that outright opposition to Government policy involved, and only the harshest of critics would condemn them for their lack of consistency at this particular juncture. On the other hand, the leadership is more open to the criticism that it should have changed its policy in an overt manner explaining how various pressures and circumstances had forced its hand. By leaving its former policies on the stocks and by pursuing new ones which were, in practice, in conflict with them, it confused some of its membership at a difficult time. The main reason for not highlighting the shift in policy was almost certainly the desire to avoid deep internal divisions within the Association.

The Association's difficulties in responding to the White Paper were exacerbated because the Government had chosen to make three separate, but related, issues highly interdependent. These were: (i) the future demand for teachers; (ii) the diversification of the colleges of education; and (iii) the development of the binary system of higher education. There was little that the ATCDE could do about the demand for teachers and it had been asking for the integration of teacher training into higher education for some time. It stressed that it was 'not in the long-term interests of the teaching profession or the colleges to have more than a minimum of institutions wholly dependent for their existence on the manpower need of a single profession'.[35] There was no inherent reason why the Government and its civil servants needed to link these issues with the development of the binary system, but it suited their purposes to do so. The ATCDE grasped that the White Paper had been written on the assumption that the binary system would be developed, and it felt, not unreasonably, that it had to respond making the same assumption. At the same time it tried to distance itself from this assumption stressing that it did not support the binary principle or regard it as 'immutable'.[36] It claimed that such a system was likely to be 'uneconomic, socially divisive and educationally indefensible'[37] and 'must be regarded as an evolutionary stage towards the creation of a unified system of higher education'.[38] Thus the ATCDE continued to express distant aspirations as it reacted to immediate pressures and realities.

Some of the points made by the DES about planning also caused ATCDE considerable concern. Paragraphs 145 and 146, which dealt with geographical concentrations of students and institutional size respectively, had not been mentioned in prior consultations[39] although they were of critical importance. Paragraph 145 made it clear that the Government would question proposals involving three centres of higher education in one city. Paragraph 146 stressed that institutions must attain 'a critical size to obtain full economies of scale',[40] and it queried whether small or isolated colleges were suitable for diversification. The 'three centres' condition offered 'little hope of independent growth'[41] to colleges near universities and polytechnics, and was opposed by the ATCDE. Browne has pointed out that during the previous ten years the DES pursued policies of building up institutions in large urban areas and 'no adequate explanation was ever given' for how these circumstances had changed.[42] ATCDE questioned whether it was wise 'to develop two massive and possibly unmanageable institutions'[43] where there might be 'three or even four perfectly viable institutions'.[44] Similarly ATCDE was sceptical of the idea of 'critical size'. There was little research evidence about this and it was mentioned that diseconomies as well as economies of scale might be relevant. It was conceded that small, isolated colleges were 'perhaps ill-suited' for 'major development',[45] but it was still felt that they had a role to play. The Association feared that the colleges were being 'ground between the cogs of the various criteria' and predicted 'a bleak outlook if the existing criteria were applied inflexibly'.[46] ATCDE warned that diversification, either singly or jointly, required additional student numbers, which did not appear to be forthcoming.[47] Colleges which remained monotechnic institutions would face severe competition in their attempts to attract students. Mergers with further education colleges were not opposed, but it was stressed that amalgamation with institutions 'carrying a large amount of low level work' or 'catering for 16–19 year olds'[48] was hardly 'a way of joining "the higher education family"'.[49] Mergers between polytechnics and colleges were acceptable to the ATCDE as long as 'due regard was paid to the wishes of both institutions'.[50] The Association declared itself against 'shot-gun marriages'[51] and emphasized that 'the educational advantages to the colleges must be clearly demonstrable otherwise such mergers may appear as devices by which polytechnics can acquire capital resources, in particular residential accommodation'.[52] ATCDE, thus, gave the White Paper its blessing, but only with reservations and misgivings. It is difficult to see any other course of realistic action which was open to it.

The DES moved quickly after the publication of the White Paper, and, according to Hugh Harding, a draft of what later became Circular 7/73 was with ministers almost immediately.[53] Harding explained that 'early decisions were needed if they (the colleges) were to have a reasonable opportunity to share in the expected rapid growth of higher education'.[54] It would have been equally accurate to say that speed was required because the DES now regarded the reduction of teacher supply as an urgent matter. Early in 1973 the draft circular was sent to the main interest groups for their comments. The circular, entitled *Development of Higher Education in the Non-University Sector*, set out the planning procedures for implementing the White Paper. It stressed that the providing bodies (the local authorities or the churches) were to be responsible for producing the plans, but they were required to consult college governing bodies and academic boards, RACs, ATOs and neighbouring authorities. Thus, except for the voluntary colleges, the LEAs became the initiating and dominant partners in the reorganization process. Given that the ownership of the colleges was vested in the LEAs this was not surprising. Some years later a DES spokesman explained: 'we have not attempted to conduct a dialogue with individual colleges, quite deliberately . . . We put the weight of responsibility on the local education authority, because very often there has not been just one but several institutions in the same local education authority area whose needs have had to be weighed up together, and only the local education authority is competent to do that'.[55] This was fair comment, but it was not the whole story. These procedures suited the DES well. Senior civil servants realized that LEAs wanted to preserve their control of the colleges. They knew that some LEA spokesmen had favoured mergers between advanced further education and teacher training institutions over a long period, and that, given projected demographic trends, such mergers became urgent if LEAs were to maximize the utilization of their existing capital assets. Lastly, civil servants must have grasped that if, in the difficult circumstances of contraction, LEAs were given the responsibility of drawing up the plans, they would share in any opprobrium which might result.

Local authorities were urged to consider regional, as well as local, needs and were given some guidance about this. Paragraphs 145–7 of the White Paper were quoted in the circular and it was stressed that these criteria had to be met. The importance of economies of scale was mentioned, but it was acknowledged that 'experience so far suggests that institutions specializing primarily in the arts and social sciences can be considerably smaller than the average size contemplated for the polytechnics. It should be possible to offer a reasonable range of advanced courses in this area in institutions with 1000–2000 full-time and sandwich students'.[56] The DES also made it clear that advanced and non-advanced courses could be provided in the same institutions. Government support for diversification was reiterated, and again it was stressed that 'the potentialities of many (colleges) may best be realized by incorporation in a polytechnic or by merger with other institutions'.[57] On the other hand, the DES expected some, but not many, monotechnic colleges to survive, and it held out particular hopes for those which had or could develop specialist roles. Another possibility was that some small colleges might be retained as professional centres, but, more ominously, closure was also specifically mentioned in this context.

The local authority response to this draft circular is particularly interesting. The AEC welcomed it without detailed comment[58], but several trenchant points were made by LAHEC.[59] The local authorities complained that the proposed timetable was too short and that the basis for regional planning was far from clear. It was pointed out that there were basic conflicts between the different planning criteria. The need for minimum institutional size to obtain economies of scale, for example, did not fit well with the need to avoid large concentrations of students or to make higher education provisions available for students near to their homes. LAHEC did not see why local authorities should initiate college closures and argued that 'the DES ought to indicate to local authorities their view as to colleges which might need to close'. To justify this, it pointed out that 'national, as well as regional considerations, were involved in decisions to close'.[60] The CCA representatives on LAHEC felt that there was 'an apparent lack of interest in the maintenance of genuinely committed teacher training institutions of high standard'.[61] They feared that important assets would be lost if 'good medium-sized colleges were closed or merged'.[62] There was also some feeling that the demand for teachers could be higher than anticipated and the demand for general higher education places lower. These comments were not made public and it was not well known that the local authorities had important misgivings. Circular 7/73 was issued at the end of March with only minor alterations. The DES stuck to its guns.

After the publication of 7/73 Edward Britton of the NUT organized a national inter-association (ATCDE, ATTI, AUT, NUT, NUS, UCET) conference to consider its implication. A resolution was forwarded to Margaret Thatcher expressing concern about future educational expenditure and student numbers, teacher supply and DES consultation procedures[63], but it received little response. Later the participating organizations agreed to concentrate their attention on the cuts in teacher training proposed for September 1974 and asked the local authority associations for consultations.[64] In 1973 the local authorities still found it difficult to believe that the days of teacher shortage were over and tended to query DES projections. The Society of Education Officers felt much the same and were strongly opposed to the disposal of college buildings. It contended that 'the continued existence of small and undiversified institutions would be forgivable: a relapse into teacher supply difficulties would not'.[65] When, however, a deputation from the inter-associations met the AEC early in 1974, Alexander would not accept their arguments concerning staffing standards, teacher supply and educational resources.[66] He pointed out that he shared their aims, but he rejected their statistical premises. Alexander, who was a member of the newly-created ACSTT and in possession of the latest data, suspected that DES projections of teacher demand were more likely to prove too high than too low. The future was to show that Alexander was correct, and un-wittingly the inter-associations had emphasized the weaknesses rather than the strengths of their case. The continued fall in the birth rate and the economic aftermath of the oil crisis made it unlikely that politicians would accept these arguments. Despite the activities of the inter-associations and a short-lived pressure group entitled Campaign for the Advancement of Teacher Education[67], there was no sustained national attack on Circular 7/73. Protests from individual colleges which were unhappy about their proposed futures were common, but little or no attempt was made to direct, coordinate or orchestrate these.

One of the primary aims of the White Paper and the Circular was to merge teacher training colleges with their capital resources into the expanding polytechnics. This had an obvious appeal to urban authorities with both polytechnics and colleges, and also to ambitious polytechnic directors who knew who were likely to emerge as the senior partners. Such schemes were further reinforced by Paragraph 145 of the White Paper which discouraged the development of three centres of higher education in one city. As has been mentioned, ATCDE accepted the principle of mergers between polytechnics and colleges, but strongly opposed 'shot-gun marriages'. UCET feared that too many mergers with polytechnics (or indeed universities) 'might work to the disadvantage of teacher education'.[68] Its Chairman maintained that good colleges, might be 'diversified' out of the teacher training function altogether.[69] Neither ATCDE nor UCET was in a position to bring influence to bear, and in certain instances at the local level marriages in which one of the partners was less than willing were undoubtedly being arranged. During the second half of 1973 ATCDE/UCET misgivings intensified as major colleges announced that they were moving to CNAA for validation.[70] In cases of mergers between polytechnics and colleges CNAA validation was a probable corollary. Margaret Thatcher argued that a change from university to CNAA validation was likely to contribute to the 'real integration' of the new institution.[71] Patrick Nuttgens, Director of Leeds Polytechnic, put the case in stronger terms maintaining that part of a merged polytechnic could not come 'under the tutelage of an outside body (a university) for which it is no way responsible', as this would 'relinquish the freedom and responsibility' achieved under CNAA.[72] ATCDE/UCET were particularly concerned when the ILEA 'implicitly expressed a preference for CNAA'.[73] ATCDE reacted sharply to this pressure as did Richard Peters of the London Institute of Education.[74] The Association firmly reminded local authorities that 'the determination of academic policy is the responsibility of academic boards of colleges working through their governing bodies'.[75] In this context it is interesting to note the views of the Society of Education Officers. It felt that the powers of governing bodies and academic boards of colleges created problems for LEAs as they tried to plan following Circular 7/73.[76] It urged that these powers should be reduced. The long-standing tensions in the system were running as high as ever.

After considerable deliberation ATCDE produced a considered reaction to Circular 7/73.[77] It reiterated its long-term commitment to the abolition of the binary system, but it was mainly concerned with the role of the colleges in the non-university sector in the immediate future. Rationalization and specialization in further and higher education were advocated, and it was hoped that, in general, designated institutions of higher education would be set up separate from further education colleges. Eric Robinson's comprehensive post-school colleges' found no favour with the ATCDE. The Association maintained that higher education in the non-university sector should be planned as a whole without distinction between polytechnic and non-polytechnic institutions. It pointed out that in 1971–72 56 per cent of higher education places in this sector were provided by the colleges of education, 32 per cent by the polytechnics and 12 per cent by the colleges of further education.[78] The wisdom of concentrating expansion so heavily in the polytechnics was questioned and a more even distribution within the sector was called for. ATCDE stressed that a small group of institutions would grow very quickly and a much larger group very slowly 'possibly failing to reach a size where economic provision of a range of higher education would be possible'.[79] Attention was drawn to the DES's notion of 'critical size' which was regarded as unsatisfactory and based on insufficient evidence. In an early draft circulated to the local authority associations, ATCDE maintained there was a strong case for developing 100 designated institutions of higher education with student populations in the range 2000–3000.[80] These figures were dropped from the later published version, and the Association was reduced, probably to avoid offending members who now found themselves in many very different situations, to calling for 'a flexible' variety of institutions'.[81]

Even before the end of 1973 some of the ATCDE's worst fears were being realized. DES officials realized that LEA responses to 7/73 were producing too many higher education places.[82] Over-provision was greatest in the very areas where the colleges were strongest — teacher training and liberal arts courses. This soon led to pressures for amalgamations between colleges of education and non-advanced further education institutions. Norman St. John-Stevas, the Minister of State, suggested that colleges of education needed to offer a wide range of courses 'at several levels',[83] and added that proposals for liberal arts courses were 'far in excess of student demand'.[84] Margaret Thatcher confirmed that projections of student numbers in higher education were to be reduced, and encouraged diversification above and below the 'A' level divide.[85] Tom Driver of the ATTI welcomed such developments, and a senior education officer, C P Milroy, who had served on the James Committee, thought that they were inevitable.[86] The change in Government in February 1974 made little difference in this respect. The new Minister of State, Gerry Fowler, soon told ATCDE that he had no objection to under and over 18s being taught in the same institution[87], and argued that there might be positive gains in such arrangements. He maintained that would-be teachers could hardly object to 'rubbing shoulders' with the under 18 'as they would spend the rest of their lives teaching them'.[88] Edward Simpson, a Deputy Secretary at the DES, pointed out that less than half of the students at polytechnics and colleges had two 'A' levels, and strongly supported Fowler's arguments. This approach was underlined in June when the DES responded to the ILEA's proposals under 7/73. Eric Briault, the CEO, was warned that too many schemes for liberal arts courses were being submitted, and that 'there was considerable reluctance to (colleges of education) undertaking less advanced work'.[89] Hugh Harding stressed that because of the changed economic situation capital developments were being curtailed, and in these circumstances DES urged that the colleges' capital assets should be utilized fully.[90] The clear implication was that some of this utilization needed to be in the non-advanced further education sector. Meanwhile, behind the scenes, UCET gave ATCDE a little support[91], but, in general, the latter fought this battle alone. Throughout 1974 ATCDE stressed that such developments were incompatible with the White Paper's statement that the colleges would be 'wholeheartedly accepted into the family of higher education institutions'. The Association argued that institutions which straddled advanced and non-advanced work would have difficulty in recruiting able school leavers who wanted to move into unequivocal higher education institutions catering exclusively for the post-18 age group on post-'A' level courses. In a similar way high calibre staff were unlikely to be attracted to institutions 'where a relatively small amount of teacher training was overlaid by substantial amounts of non-advanced work'.[92] ATCDE was convinced that such schemes would reduce the quality and status of teacher training. Harding estimated that there were likely to be about fifteen such combinations[93] (later, in 1977, the DES put this figure at twenty).[94] Despite the protests DES retained this policy, but it, at least, ceased to attempt to justify it in educational terms. Harding acknowledged in the autumn of 1974 that 'shortage of resources and the slowing up of the expansion of higher education would prevent the Government's aim (of incorporating the colleges of education fully into the family of higher education) being achieved immediately'.[95]

LEA interim responses to 7/73 showed that they 'were unable to plan collectively for contraction themselves'.[96] Too many teacher training places remained. DES knew that more drastic cuts were necessary, but, initially, to avoid the problems of college closures, tried to preserve teacher training in as many institutions as possible. Although UCET and ATCDE hated the prospect of college closures, they were convinced that small teacher training units spread thinly throughout the higher education system would threaten academic and professional standards. Consequently Hugh Harding's proposals for teacher training units containing 400 students were strongly opposed by both associations[97], and DES amended this figure. Harding told ACSTT that 'the average institution would have 600 to 700 teacher training students (including in-service)',[98] and this was in line with the Inspectorate's advice.[99] UCET and ATCDE welcomed this increase, but ATCDE still held the view that too many colleges were retained in the contracting situation.[100] In the longer term, of course, the DES pursued policies which led to more college closures, but it is interesting that at this early stage it found it easier to countenance small units than closures and that the professional associations and perhaps the Inspectorate pushed for changed priorities.

By the autumn of 1974 Harding was speaking to interested parties about the likely institutional patterns in the future.[101] He predicted that about twenty-five or twenty-six polytechnics would be involved in teacher training after mergers with colleges of education, and about forty institutions would be formed by combinations between further education colleges and colleges of education (twenty-five of these would be largely concerned with advanced further education courses, but fifteen involved substantial levels of non-advanced work). He suggested that there would be about forty free-standing colleges (or combinations of colleges) with about twenty-five of these developing diversified courses and fifteen remaining monotechnic. It was also clear that five or six colleges would be incorporated into the universities. Harding claimed that this 'diversity of institutions' was a 'source of strength'[102], and it was very much in line with the DES policy promulgated in the immediate post-James period. Others were concerned about how this 'diversity' would work out in practice. UCET argued that large urban colleges should be retained as free-standing institutions which could 'set the pace and establish standards',[103] and was frustrated when these 'potential pace-setters' were often the very colleges to be merged into other institutions. At the same time small and remote colleges were sometimes retained as independent, monotechnic institutions. In general, ATCDE kept a low profile concerning the emerging institutional arrangements at local level. In September 1974 a NUT deputation to Minister of State, Gerald Fowler, questioned the wisdom of some of the proposed mergers.[104] According to the educational press, Fowler offered to consider more university-college combinations, to discuss proposals that more colleges should remain independent and to explore the possibility of academic association between institutions which fell short of total amalgamation.[105] The ATCDE's Principals' Panel immediately resolved that Fowler's offers, as reported, should be taken up.[106] Stanley Hewett reacted differently, and 'warned members not to believe press reports based on secondhand evidence'.[107] It was evident that Hewett did not detect a change of heart at the DES, and that he did not want his members to build up false hopes.

Although post-James DES policy was not rigid and allowed for diversity, this did not imply that it was open-ended in terms of the expected national outcome. According to one report, when Harding stressed DES flexibility to the Principals' Panel he added that he was 'an unrepentant amalgamationist'.[108] The DES wanted it both ways, and at times, with skilful and ambiguous public presentation, it was successful. The White Paper referred to 'much closer assimilation into the rest of the non-university sector of further and higher education'[109] and this was the Department's primary objective. In practice, if not in theory, this reduced the scope for flexibility.

From 1974 a new type of institution emerged in English higher education. The hotchpotch of solutions in response to Circular 7/73 led to the development of institutions with a variety of titles including 'college of higher education', 'institute of higher education', 'college of education' and sometimes just 'college'. The principals of these institutions soon formed their own association called the Standing Conference of Directors and Principals of Colleges and Institutes in Higher Education. In contrast with the polytechnics with their emphasis on science and technology, these new institutions concentrated largely on arts and social science subjects, but, like the enlarged and reconstituted polytechnics, they normally contained teacher training units. In general, they were considerably smaller than the polytechnics, and the questions of relative size and concentration of resources soon became bones of contention. The DES and many (but not all)[110] LEAs favoured the creation of large institutions[111] through college of education mergers with polytechnics or substantial further education colleges. Fowler has argued that such mergers 'permitted diversification and flexibility in the use of places while maintaining quality and quantity of subject teachers'.[112] On the other hand, a few very small colleges survived, and it must be remembered that 7/73 recognized that colleges and institutes of higher education, on average, would be considerably smaller than polytechnics. The CDP was sceptical about these new developments. It claimed that 'without advancing any justification the DES has apparently abandoned the former theses of economies of scale and merits of concentration'.[113] It wondered why the case for the designation of further polytechnics had not been considered and tended to question the wisdom of creating 'a multiplicity of merged or diversified colleges'.[114] CDP was convinced that the latter policy was pursued 'to make the fullest use of the considerable release of building resources'[115] rather than for educational reasons. This view can be contrasted with that of the ATCDE which wanted to see student numbers transferred from the projected expansion of the polytechnics to the higher education colleges so that they could be built up on firmer foundations. The DES ignored both these pressures retaining its commitment to the growth of the polytechnics, but also showing its determination to utilize the substantial capital assets of the former teacher training colleges.

The institutional arrangements which emerged in the mid and late 1970s as a result of the White Paper and 7/73 were influenced by a number of factors. By 1969–70 DES fully expected a fall in the demand for teachers, but it was surprised again and again by the *extent* of the demographic shifts in the 1970s. The 1972 projections were too high, and it soon proved impossible to plan on the basis of these unrealistic figures. After 1973 LEAs regularly complained that they did not know where they stood in this respect, and the evidence from several studies suggests that the DES was in no better position itself. In addition, when the Department undertook its crucial planning in the period 1970 to 1972, it was not able to foresee the real extent of the declining economic fortunes of the nation. The oil crisis of 1973 and the subsequent cuts in public expenditure made matters considerably more difficult, and Labour's new Secretary of State, Reg Prentice, emphasized that education would have to share in the retrenchment which was to be part of the Government's anti-inflation programme.[116] Party politics played little part in these proceedings. The policies being pursued in this area of education were unaffected by the change of Government in 1974 and this was, unusually, acknowledged in a DES document.[117] As had been indicated, ATCDE, the main professional association involved, put its case but had little influence. It had a limited power base and few allies. Its leadership has been criticized for failing to organize more widespread support, but this was more easily said than done and the likely effectiveness of such support should not be overestimated. It must also be remembered that by 1972 the ATCDE had accepted the DES's overall strategy, and its leaders were encouraging members to try to come to terms with the new situation. As Brian MacArthur has pointed out they resisted the temptation 'to beat up a sort of opposition drum to what was happening to cater for the feelings of despair by their members'.[118] Hugh Harding praised this responsible attitude, but it hardly led to strong opposition.

Circular 7/73 made it clear that the responsibility for planning at the local level rested with the providing bodies (in the context of this study the LEAs). The DES stressed this again and again in 1973–74 and insisted, quite correctly, that it did not issue closure or reorganization proposals. On the other hand, it did not accept LEA plans automatically and several interim proposals were referred back by the DES for further local consideration. If an LEA held its ground, as happened in the case of East Sussex and Brighton College of Education[119], the LEA was allowed to have its own way as it, and not the DES, was the property owner. Nonetheless, East Sussex was an exceptional case, and in many instances DES influence was clearly much greater than the formal position suggested.[120] The role of the DES in these proceedings has been discussed in previous books and different interpretations offered. It is not intended here to go over this ground again in detail. David Hencke came close to suggesting that DES civil servants were working to a master plan and were conspiratorial in their methods. It is doubtful whether even DES civil servants were able to control events as successfully as this suggests. At times DES itself was surprised by, and had to react quickly to, unexpected economic and demographic changes. Moreover, some of the policies it pursued in the early months of reorganization were later abandoned, for example, initially, because of the political difficulties involved, it showed a marked reluctance to contemplate college closures. On the other hand, even Harding has acknowledged that the DES was secretive and authoritarian in its style of leadership.[121] The Department certainly made no effort to explain the criteria it employed in determining the future of the various institutions in the public sector of higher education. This lack of public information strengthened the hand of the DES in negotiations, but encouraged its critics to believe that the main criterion was expediency. There was, nevertheless, one overriding and consistent aim in DES strategy, and this was to incorporate the bulk of teacher training into a less differentiated local authority sector of higher education. Toby Weaver had pushed this policy from the mid-1960s and he had a major responsibility for planning in the crucial period from 1970 to his retirement in May 1973. Although Harding looked after the detailed implementation of these policies, the strategy remained Weaver's. If there was a lack of coherence in the DES policy for teacher training, it must be remembered that this was a secondary consideration. The primary aim remained to build up a larger and more unified sector of local authority higher education. Demographic and economic trends frequently and considerably impinged on this policy, but they were not the originators of the basic strategy.

Notes

1   DES, *Education: A Framework for Expansion*, (December 1972), p. 44.
2   *Ibid.*, pp. 44–5.
3   *Ibid.*, p. 44.
4   *Ibid.*, p. 42.
5   *Ibid.*, p. 44.
6   *Ibid.*
7   *Ibid.*
8   *Ibid.*
9   House of Commons, Expenditure Committee, Tenth Report, *Policy Making*

in the DES, (1975–6), p. 36.

10 *Ibid.*, pp. 111–2 and 385.

11 *Ibid.*, p. 113.

12 *Ibid.*

13 *Ibid.* p. 114.

14 *Ibid.*, p. 253.

15 *Ibid.*

16 *Ibid.*, p. 251.

17 DES, (December 1972), *op. cit.*, p. 46.

18 *Ibid.*

19 *Ibid.*

20 *Education*, 15 December 1972.

21 LUIE, File 3757, Conference, City of Leeds and Carnegie College Branch ATCDE, 31 January 1973.

22 *Ibid.*, UCET Executive Committee Minutes, 8 December 1972 and Haycocks to UCET members, 2 February 1973.

23 *Education*, 15 December 1972.

24 *Ibid.*

25 *Ibid.*, and 22 December 1972.

26 *Ibid.*

27 *Ibid.*

28 AEC, File A1138, ATCDE, Resolutions passed by Council 1972, (19–20 December 1972).

29 *Education*, 12 January 1973; and *THES*, 12 January 1973.

30 J D Browne, *Teachers of Teachers*, (1979), p. 224.

31 D Hencke, *Colleges in Crisis*, (1978), pp, 120–1.

32 *Education*, 5 January 1979.

33 *Ibid.*

34 J D Browne, (1979), *op. cit.*, p. 225.

35 ATCDE, Executive Committee, *Education: A Framework for Expansion. A Commentary*, (1973), p. 20.

36 *Ibid.*, p. 24.

37 *Ibid.*

38 *Ibid.*

39 House of Commons, Expenditure Committee, Tenth Report, *Policy Making in the DES*, (1975–6), p. 243.

40 DES, (December 1972), *op. cit.*, p. 42.

41 ATCDE, Executive Committee, (1973), *op. cit.*, p. 18.

42 J D Browne, (1979), *op. cit.*, p. 222.

43 ATCDE, Executive Committee, (1973), *op. cit.*, p. 18.

44 *Ibid.*

45 *Ibid.*, p. 17.

46 *Ibid.*, p. 18.

47 *Ibid.*, p. 19.

48 *Ibid.*

49 *Ibid.*

50 *Ibid.*, p. 18.

51 *Ibid.*

52 *Ibid.*
53 *Education*, 29 December 1978.
54 *Ibid.*
55 House of Commons, Expenditure Committee, Tenth Report, *Policy Making in the DES*, (1975–6), p. 112.
56 DES, *Circular 7/73*, (March 1973), p. 3.
57 *Ibid.*, p. 7.
58 AEC, File E41, Alexander to Harding, 26 February 1973.
59 AEC, Files A1039–40, McCall to Harding, 1 March 1973.
60 *Ibid.*
61 *Ibid.*, LAHEC, Working Group, Comments by CCA Advisers, 27 February 1973 and McCall to Harding, 1 March 1973.
62 *Ibid.*
63 AEC, File E86, Morris and Hewett to Thatcher, 12 October 1973.
64 *Ibid.*, Jarvis to Alexander, 22 November 1973.
65 *Education*, 24 August 1973.
66 AEC, File E86, Alexander's private notes, 5 February 1974.
67 *THES*, 6 July 1973.
68 LUIE, File 3757, UCET, N Haycocks' comments on Circular 7/73, 9 April 1973.
69 *Ibid.*
70 Berkshire and Didsbury Colleges were the earliest to make such announcements.
71 LUIE, File 3757, Thatcher to Boyle, 23 February 1973.
72 *THES*, 30 March 1973.
73 *THES*, 23 November 1973.
74 *THES*, 16 November 1973.
75 AEC, File A1138, ATCDE, Resolutions of Council, December 1973.
76 *Education*, 24 August 1973.
77 AEC, File A1138, ATCDE, *A Policy for the Development of Higher Education in the Non-University Sector*, (November 1973).
78 *Ibid.*, p. 3.
79 *Ibid.*, p. 8.
80 AEC, Files A1039/40, ATCDE, A Discussion Paper, June 1973.
81 AEC, File A1138, ATCDE, (1973), *op. cit.*, p. 9.
82 D HENCKE, (1978), *op. cit.*, pp. 56–7; LUIE, File 3916, *UCET Conference Summary Report*, (16–18 November 1973), p. 2.
83 *THES*, 11 January 1974.
84 *Ibid.*
85 J D BROWNE, (1979), *op. cit.*, p. 226.
86 *Education*, 1 March 1974.
87 *THES*, 12 April 1974.
88 *Ibid.*
89 D HENCKE, (1978), *op. cit.*, p. 58.
90 *Ibid.*
91 LUIE, File 3916, Haycocks to Harding, 14 January 1974.
92 AEC, File A971, ACSTT (74) 10, *The Reorganisation of Initial Training*, (ATCDE submission), p. 5.

93   *Ibid.*, ACSTT, Minutes, 25 September 1974.

94   DES, Report on Education 90, *The Management of Non-University Higher Education*, (May 1977), p. 2.

95   AEC, File A971, ACSTT, Minutes, 25 September 1974.

96   G Fowler 'Policy formulation and administration: A critique' in R J Alexander, M Craft and J Lynch, *Change in Teacher Education*, (1984), p. 274.

97   LUIE, File 3916, Haycocks to Harding, 14 January 1974, J Browne (1979) *op. cit.*, p. 227.

98   AEC, File A971, ACSTT, Minutes, 25 September 1974.

99   AEC, File G25, ACSTT, Criteria for restructuring the teacher training system, 1977.

100 House of Commons, Expenditure Committee, Tenth Report, *Policy Making in the DES*, (1975–6), Evidence of ATCDE, p. 243.

101 AEC, File A971, ACSTT, Minutes, 25 September 1974 and File E51, CLEA, Minutes, 31 October 1974.

102 *Education*, 5 January 1979.

103 LUIE, File 3916, Haycocks to Harding, 14 January 1974.

104 *THES*, 20 September 1974.

105 *Ibid.*, and *THES*, 11 October 1974.

106 J D Browne, (1979), *op. cit.*, p. 232.

107 *Ibid.*, p. 231.

108 *THES*, 8 November 1974.

109 DES, (1972), *op. cit.*, p. 46.

110 *THES*, 15 November 1974.

111 K 'Fenwick. 'Change in the public sector and the role of LEAs', in R J Alexander, J M Craft and J Lynch, (1984), *op. cit.*, p. 62.

112 G Fowler, (1984), *op. cit.*, p. 275.

113 House of Commons, Expenditure Committee, Tenth Report, *Policy Making in the DES*, (1975–6), p. 311.

114 *Ibid.*

115 *Ibid.*

116 AEC, File A971, DES Press Notice, 8 November 1974.

117 House of Commons, Expenditure Committee, Tenth Report, *Policy Making in the DES*, (1975–6), DES Memorandum p. 4.

118 *Ibid.*, Evidence of B MacArthur, p. 40.

119 G Fowler, (1984), *op. cit.*, p. 270.

120 D Hencke, (1978), *op. cit.*, pp. 56–73.

121 *Education*, 5 January 1979.

Chapter 9

Continued Tensions in the New Sector: Who is to Control Local Authority Higher Education?

Sir Norman Lindop claimed with justification that the White Paper of 1972 was 'the high water mark of declared support for the polytechnics'.[1] It predicted that by 1981 there would be 335,000 full-time students in the non-university sector in England and Wales of whom 180,000 would be in the polytechnics. This represented a phenomenal increase as the White Paper figures indicated that there were 66,000 full-time students there in 1971–72.[2] The Government praised LEAs, governing bodies and polytechnic staff for 'the speed and vigour with which these new institutions have assumed and pursued their innovative task'[3] and it hoped that they would be able to reach these high target figures. Alexander of the AEC, who was enthusiastic about much of the White Paper[4], argued that it brought the university and local authority sectors into 'broad parallelism'[5] correcting an existing inbalance. There can be no doubt that *Education: A Framework for Expansion* gave the polytechnics an important fillip and increased the confidence of their leaders considerably. Of the major institutions of higher education the polytechnics clearly gained by far the most from the commitments in the White Paper, and their leadership of the local authority sector was confirmed. Lindop, Chairman of the CDP, acknowledged that he saw the situation in this way describing the polytechnics as the 'spearhead' of the advanced further education sector.[6] Some years later in 1977, the then Secretary of State, Shirley Williams, reaffirmed this view choosing exactly the same expression as Lindop.[7]

During 1973 the CDP pressed the Government to provide the capital resources necessary to implement the polytechnic expansion programme. Similar pressure was applied by the ATTI and the newly-created APT (Association of Polytechnic Teachers). Although capital projects were sanctioned, expansion plans were soon considerably affected by the oil crisis and the consequent cuts in public expenditure. In June 1974 Lindop felt that the White Paper was a 'dead letter'[8] as more and more emphasis was being placed on the need for economy. The target figures for student numbers in higher education were revised downwards, and CLEA (Council for Local Education Authorities) invited 'LEAs maintaining polytechnics to have special regard to the requirement of "no growth in real terms" being applied equally to pooled expenditure as to expenditure borne on their own rates'.[9] It also asked CNAA to consider these financial constraints when it laid down conditions for the recognition of new courses. Thus, the optimistic outlook for the polytechnics ushered in by the White Paper proved shortlived. Their spokesmen, particularly CDP and APT, put increasing emphasis on the need for parity of financial support with the universities, and it was regularly claimed that the latter were more generously treated over salaries, levels of senior staffing, ancillary help, student accommodation and capital developments. At the same time doubts were expressed about the policy of developing arts based colleges and institutes of higher education. Both CDP and APT saw these as a threat[10] and considered that their emergence undermined the DES policy of concentrating resources within selected institutions in the local authority sector of higher education. Some would have preferred the designation of additional polytechnics, and felt that the polytechnics needed to be more clearly differentiated from further education so that they could more easily stand comparison with the universities. Old issues of status remained.

The administrative machinery required for planning and coordinating the expansion of the local authority sector of higher education was considered briefly in the White Paper. It welcomed the local authority associations' recent decision to set up LAHEC and hoped that discussions between the DES and the local authorities would soon be resumed. In response the local authorities arranged a meeting of LAHEC, and Alexander, who 'was personally delighted with the White Paper',[11] predicted that both LAHEC and his own proposals for regional councils for higher education would have important parts to play in the new situation.[12] He strongly supported the policy for more home-based students in higher education, which he regarded as essential when financial resources were so limited, and this, of course, fitted in well with his ideas for greater regional control.

LAHEC met in February 1973 and considered the recently completed Report *LAHEC — Its Functions, Structure and Procedures* by Sir Eric Richardson. In preparing his Report Richardson had consulted widely, but felt that it had been 'somewhat unfortunate that conversations with the DES and with the Pooling Committee failed to happen'.[13] Richardson's main piece of advice to LAHEC was to appoint a chief officer with a small supporting administrative team as soon as possible. He argued that such an appointment was essential to LAHEC's credibility.[14] The Report also proposed that LAHEC's main committee should continue to be composed entirely of local authority representatives, but a new advisory board, a new financial resources committee and new academic boards would contain substantial representation from other interest groups.[15] It was envisaged that LAHEC would make full use of the RACs as a regional support structure. LAHEC with its administration support unit would undertake work on manpower planning and statistical analysis, and it would coordinate development plans submitted by the RACs and negotiate with the DES over the allocation of resources. LAHEC accepted the central recommendation to appoint a chief officer and set up a working group to deal with the matter.[16] It was also resolved to examine the detailed aspects of the Report at a later meeting. The local authority associations were clearly impressed by the Richardson Report, and Alexander quickly drafted a statement for publication about LAHEC's latest initiatives.[17] Robin McCall, Secretary of the AMC, sent William Pile at the DES a copy of the Richardson Report and mentioned LAHEC's proposals. He expressed the hope that the DES would meet representatives of LAHEC to discuss its future role in the context of the White Paper.

The Richardson Report caused immediate consternation at the DES, and McCall and Berry of the AMC were quickly summoned to discuss it with Pile, Weaver and Simpson. Pile described it as 'a wholly impracticable and theoretical basis for action'.[18] The DES spokesmen claimed that the proposed administrative unit would be very costly and would take at least three years to get off the ground. Pile thought that 'it contemplated a substantial incursion into the Ministry's functions'[19] and wondered whether 'the LAHEC unit would be taking over negotiating in detail with the Department on behalf of the authorities'.[20] He stressed that there were 'no statutory powers for these proposals'.[21] When McCall mentioned that there had been DES encouragement for some form of local authority higher education coordinating committee and for the kind of approach adopted in the Report, Pile replied that 'the Department had had in mind something limited to the polytechnics on a very limited scale compared with the 500 units of organization due to be coordinated under the Richardson report'.[22] This was a crucial issue as the DES saw 'the enormous span of work outlined by Sir Eric Richardson as a recipe for disaster'.[23] but it is likely that there was an additional reason for such strong opposition. It was implicit in the Richardson Report that LAHEC would remain firmly under local authority control, and other bodies, including the DES, although consulted, would have little ultimate influence. This was unacceptable to the Department. Pile made it clear that he did not wish LAHEC to appoint a full-time administrative team and that he was against the publication of LAHEC's initiatives on the Richardson Report before much further discussion had taken place.

McCall admitted that he was 'somewhat taken aback by the strength of the Department's reaction against the Report',[24] but it was recognized in the LAHEC working group that the local authorities could not go ahead against DES opposition. McCall told Pile that he felt that the DES civil servants had misinterpreted the Report because they had seen it out of context. He denied that it was a recommendation 'for a form of UGC', and LAHEC saw itself as filling 'a coordinating role essentially advisory in character'. It was stressed that the proposals were not intended to 'alter the basic relationship between the Department, LEAs and their institutions'.[25] On the other hand, he pressed the point that 'LAHEC will be an empty shell if it cannot be staffed',[26] and asked for further discussions with the Department. These took place in March and were much more amicable with Carlton Hetherington of the CCA feeling that 'Pile was beginning to grasp our general approach'.[27] After this meeting the DES removed its opposition to LAHEC appointing a chief officer on the understanding that this did not imply that full implementation of the Richardson Report would follow. Alexander thought that the local authorities needed 'to clear the air in terms of power as distinct from advice and to establish the significance of regional advice and coordination as distinct from national, direct control in higher education as a whole',[28] and he prepared some notes on regional machinery[29] with this end in mind.

Alexander's proposals assumed that the existing ATOs and RACs would be abolished. He wanted them replaced by ten regional councils for higher education containing representatives from the local education author- ities, universities, polytechnics and colleges in the region, and people from industry and commerce. Their functions were to be to coordinate and advise on the planning of overall provisions for higher education (including teacher training) and to approve the establishment of new courses. At the national level LAHEC would advise and consult with the DES in the same way as the local authority associations did before LAHEC was instituted. It was not suggested that any of the Secretary of State's powers would be vested in LAHEC, and it was assumed that the two levels where statutory powers existed — the Secretary of State and the local education authorities — would not be changed. Alexander made his notes available to Pile[30] at the DES without informing his local authority colleagues that he had done this. Evenually towards the end of May Alexander's paper, slightly amended, was submitted formally to the DES for consideration.[31]

The local authority associations were soon asking the DES for a meeting to discuss LAHEC's proposals, but it was clear that the DES intended to take its time.[32] In December Pile contacted McCall proposing a further meeting. He emphasized, however, that the DES found it difficult 'to make any very precise response to your paper until we can see our way ahead more clearly',[33] and he asked for discussion of specific issues rather than consideration of questions of future organisation. The local authority representatives, particularly Alexander[34], found this frustrating, but they agreed to a meeting on these terms. No progress was made as the DES pointed out that it could not commit itself on any regional structure when a general election was pending.[35] It stressed that policy decisions would have to be made by a new government. At about this time Alexander spoke about his ideas on regional structure. D E Lloyd Jones of the DES was sceptical about how the proposed regional machinery could cope with institutions which combined advanced work with more elementary studies.[36] Sir Norman Lindop, former Chairman of the CDP, was even less enthusiastic. He argued that a national plan was not simply an agglomeration of regional plans[37], and stressed that Alexander's proposal to include the universities, which guarded their autonomy jealously, was completely unrealistic. Lindop felt that, if the universities remained outside, there would be a national sector of university education but a localized, regionalized public sector. He was totally opposed to giving local authority sector institutions regional catchment areas, but allowing the universities to recruit as before. In his view this would 'result in deterioration in the institutions themselves and would perpetuate and exacerbate the split between the components of the binary system'.[38] There was little prospect of early agreement on this issue.

Local government reorganization and the reconstitution of the local authority associations led quickly to the demise of LAHEC. During 1974 the newly-created Association of Metropolitan Authorities (AMA) and Association of County Councils (ACC) swiftly eroded the AEC's power base, and these new associations set up the Council of Local Education Authorities (CLEA) to act as their own joint educational forum. In September 1974 it was agreed that 'CLEA itself should supersede LAHEC'[39] and this, in practice, excluded the AEC from future proceedings. The AEC, and particularly Alexander, was not surprised by this development as it had received similar treatment over a wide range of issues during 1974. Alexander commented that LAHEC had not met since February 1973 and was probably dead already. He predicted that higher education would soon be taken out of the hands of local authorities altogether.[40]

During 1974 the DES and ACSTT became increasingly concerned to replace the ATOs with new regional machinery to control the in-service training of teachers, induction and teaching practice. CLEA soon realized that the DES intended to go ahead in this area although it did not have immediate plans for establishing regional machinery to control the distribution of initial teacher training courses and advanced further education. In September Eric Briault, speaking on behalf of local authorities, told ACSTT that the creation of unitary regional bodies for these latter functions was no less urgent.[41] Hugh Harding replied that in view of the impending election the DES could not discuss this matter. He did not think that it would be realistic to expect new ministers to give an early indication of their views, and he felt that this issue would have to await government policy decisions on devolution and local government finance where enquiries were in progress.[42] DES and ACSTT pressed ahead with their original proposals, but left the larger question in abeyance. CLEA found this unsatisfactory and continued to press its views on the DES. A CLEA deputation met Lord Crowther Hunt, the Minister of State, in February 1975, and CLEA was invited to submit a paper on the subject. At a further meeting Crowther Hunt expressed 'general sympathy'[43] with CLEA's paper which was issued by the DES to interested groups as a basis for consultation.

Alexander claimed that CLEA's proposals were 'essentially the same as those which were submitted to the Department by LAHEC some two or three years ago and for which, frankly, I was personally responsible for drafting'.[44] Although Alexander's assertion was broadly true, there were some important differences between LAHEC's submission in 1973 and CLEA's in 1975. Alexander wanted to involve the universities in the regional machinery, but CLEA excluded them. On the other hand, CLEA wished the new regional bodies to consider both advanced and non-advanced further education as it felt that 'it would be wrong to operate on the basis of any dichotomy between the two parts'.[45] CLEA expected that a national standing conference of its regional councils would be set up, but it did not propose that this body would negotiate with the DES and its role was clearly to be much more limited than that envisaged for LAHEC in 1973.

When Crowther Hunt recommended CLEA's paper to ACSTT, he was asked why the DES had changed its attitude. It was stressed that two years earlier the Department had rejected similar proposals on the grounds that enquiries into devolution and local government finance 'precluded anything but interim arrangements'.[46] Crowther Hunt and the local authority spokesmen replied that the machinery now proposed could 'accommodate itself to the longer term developments'.[47] Some members of ACSTT, representing the interests from school teaching and teacher training, were disturbed that the CLEA proposals involved a basic change from the recently agreed principles for the establishment of regional committees for in-service teacher training. They felt that the voice of the (school) teaching profession, and additionally the university interest in teacher training, would be submerged in the suggested arrangements by further education issues.[48] Edwin Kerr of CNAA also expressed the need for 'a strong national coordinating body' and regarded the proposals as inadequate in that respect.[49]

In many ways these early reactions to the CLEA proposals in ACSTT presaged the future. CDP and CNAA took the opportunity to press the case for a new national body, and CDP urged that this body should not be 'an afterthought to regional machinery'.[50] CDP, which was scathing about several aspects of the proposals, contrasted the confidence that the universities place in the UGC with the lack of confidence that local authority colleges place in the RACs.[51] The ATTI gave 'guarded support' to the proposals but expressed specific reservations.[52] The APT, the APC and ACFHE all came out strongly against CLEA, and the CVCP and UCET, although not concerned with all aspects, expressed opposition to the proposed arrangements for the regional control of teacher training. There was clearly no consensus on the basis of the CLEA proposals, and the DES was again left with the problem. In July 1976, following the publication of the Layfield Report on local government finance, the DES decided that a further attempt had to be made to deal with these difficult and now long-standing issues. The new Secretary of State, Fred Mulley, told CLEA that its memorandum gave 'insufficient recognition to the national as distinct from the regional character of higher education'.[53] The DES also felt that it did not address explicitly 'the problems of management',[54] and that it assumed the continuation of the 'divorce in financial and academic control of institutional development'[55] thus offering no solution to problems of accountability. Mulley proposed to set up a group under the chairmanship of the Minister of State with the following terms of reference:

> To consider measures to improve the system of management and control of higher education in the maintained sector and its better coordination with higher education in the universities, and, in the light of developments in relation to devolution and local authority finance, what regional and national machinery might be established for this purpose.[56]

The tensions surrounding the creation and early work of LAHEC showed that even at its inception there was no agreement about how the local authority sector of higher education should be controlled and administered. Decisions to develop this sector were made before these crucially important questions of principle were addressed. It soon became apparent that the DES and the local authorities made different assumptions and had different conceptions of these basic issues. DES civil servants felt strongly that mainstream local authority higher education should be concentrated in a limited number of institutions and that new machinery should be developed to deal only with those institutions where advanced further education courses predominated. They had little time for more open-ended structures which would control a wide range of further education institutions. The DES was quite prepared to support the creation of a national committee which had decision-making and executive functions as long as a broad range of interested groups, including itself, were represented. Civil servants, however, would not countenance a national committee with executive functions which was built up from regional machinery and dominated by local authority representatives. On the other hand, the local authorities, leaving aside the AMC's initial scheme which was rejected by the other associations but supported and possibly inspired by Weaver, insisted on making extensive use of regional bodies and on constructing national structures and policies from regional inputs. In this way they hoped that they would protect their own interests and, indeed, their own power base from central government interference. They also insisted that new machinery covered *all advanced* further education (later *all* further education) and not selected institutions. The local authorities always stressed that this was necessary to avoid divisiveness in the further education sector, but this policy was also used as a protective measure. The local authorities were suspicious that if new national machinery embraced only selected higher education institutions (for example, the polytechnics), it could be used by the DES, with the support of certain groups, as a means to remove these institutions from local authority control altogether. It was not surprising that with these entrenched positions it proved impossible to find a compromise solution. Even in 1975 when the Minister of State, Crowther Hunt, was prepared to give some backing to the local authority position and thus pursued a very different line from that taken by DES civil servants from the early 1970s, no progress was made. Those directly involved in the polytechnics and the colleges came out so firmly against the strengthening of regional and local authority control that the proposals had to be dropped.

Notes

1   *THES*, 21 June 1974.
2   DES, *Education: A Framework for Expansion*, (1972), p. 41.

3   *Ibid.*
4   AEC, Files A1039/40, Alexander to Swaffield, 7 December 1972.
5   *Education*, 15 December 1972.
6   *THES*, 21 June 1976.
7   AEC, File E39(a), DES Press Notice, 2 March 1977.
8   *THES*, 21 June 1974.
9   AEC, File E51, CLEA Minutes, 31 October 1974.
10 House of Commons, Expenditure Committee, Tenth Report, *Policy Making in the DES* (1975–6), Evidence of CDP and Memorandum from APT.
11 AEC, Files A1039–40, Alexander to Swaffield, 7 December 1972.
12 *Ibid.,* and *Education* 15 and 29 December 1972.
13 *Ibid.,* Richardson to Hatton, 31 January 1973.
14 *Ibid.*
15 *Ibid.,* E RICHARDSON, *LAHEC — Its Functions, Structure and Procedures*, (1973).
16 *Ibid.,* LAHEC, Minutes, 8 February 1973.
17 *Ibid.,* Alexander to McCall, 9 February 1973.
18 *Ibid.,* Notes of meeting at the DES, 26 February 1973.
19 *Ibid.*
20 *Ibid.*
21 *Ibid.*
22 *Ibid.*
23 *Ibid.*
24 *Ibid.,* McCall to Pile, 27 February 1973.
25 *Ibid.*
26 *Ibid.*
27 *Ibid.,* Hetherington to Alexander, 23 March 1973.
28 *Ibid.,* Alexander to Hetherington, 19 March 1973.
29 *Ibid.,* Notes on the Proposals for Regional Machinery in Higher Education, undated but March 1973.
30 *Ibid.,* Alexander to Pile, 3 April 1973.
31 *Ibid.,* McCall to Pile, 23 May 1973.
32 *Ibid.,* McCall to Alexander, 30 July 1973.
33 *Ibid.,* Pile to McCall, 7 December 1973.
34 *Ibid.,* Alexander to McCall, 17 December 1973.
35 *Ibid.,* McCall to Jamieson, 20 February 1974.
36 AEC, File E27, Notes of speeches at ACFHE Conference, 21–22 February 1974.
37 *Ibid.*
38 *Ibid.*
39 AEC, Files A1039–40, Hetherington and McCall to Alexander, 15 October 1974.
40 *Ibid.,* Alexander to Hetherington, 21 October 1974.
41 AEC, File A971, ACSTT, Minutes, 25 September 1974.
42 *Ibid.*
43 AEC, File E51, CLEA, Report of Work 1974–5, p. 5.
44 AEC, File E66, Alexander to Simpson, 29 September 1975.
45 *Ibid.,* CLEA, *Regional Machinery in England beyond School Level*, (1975).
46 AEC, File A971, ACSTT, Minutes, 1 July 1975.
47 *Ibid.*

48 *Ibid.*
49 *Ibid.*
50 *THES*, 21 November 1975.
51 *Ibid.*
52 *Ibid.*, 21 December 1975.
53 AEC, File E39(a), DES Press Notices, 14 July 1976.
54 *Ibid.*
55 *Ibid.*
56 AEC, File E66, Simpson to Alexander, 14 July 1976.

Chapter 10

The Party Politicians Look for Solutions

By the late 1970s the outlines of the reconstructed local authority sector of higher education had been clearly drawn although its dimensions continued to change because of the decline in the demand for teachers. On the other hand, the machinery to control this new sector still had to be developed. In 1976 the Labour Government promised an enquiry into this matter, and by February 1977 a working group under the chairmanship of the Minister of State, Gordon Oakes, had been appointed. Members of this Group were either nominated by the main interested parties or appointed by the Secretary of State. The associations, notably CLEA, CDP and NATFHE, took great care to brief their representatives on the Oakes Committee, and predictable stances, reflecting the views and policies of the various nominating bodies, were taken up from the outset. Leaks from the Oakes Committee became a regular feature of the educational press during late 1977 and early 1978, and the positions taken up by the interest groups were very much in line with those which had been held since the early 1970s. There were differences over the desirability of creating a new national body, the range of institutions which would come under the jurisdiction of any such body and the question of national or local funding. By the end of October 1977 it was clear that, despite initial AMA misgivings and opposition, Oakes was going to recommend the setting up of a national body, but doubts about its scope, membership and funding remained.[1] Membership proved a particularly intractable issue with the local authority associations, especially the AMA, pressing for increased representation. Eventually the associations' representatives agreed to sign the report, which gave them only a minority voice on the proposed national body, but they made it plain that this did not commit them to the report in any way in further consultations.[2]

When the Oakes Report was published it received an unenthusiastic reception. NATFHE gave it a general welcome, but the CDP expressed 'the gravest misgivings'.[3] The local authority associations were guarded and reserved their positions. Conservative spokesmen were sceptical, and Keith Hampson, Vice-Chairman of the Conservative Education Committee, had indicated his opposition to the Oakes line as early as December 1977.[4] Hampson preferred the idea of a Polytechnic Grants Committee on UGC lines, and he also argued that the suggestion to transfer a proportion (15 per cent) of the costs of advanced further education from the pool to the providing local education authority would impose an unmanageable burden in certain localities. Former Labour Minister of State, Gerald Fowler, supported Hampson on the latter point, although Sir Ashley Bramall, Labour leader of the ILEA and a member of the Oakes Committee, maintained that the consequent rate increases predicted by the Conservatives for certain authorities were alarmist.[5] Party political factors were now (and in many ways for the first time) becoming crucial in the debate about the future of the local authority sector of higher education. The situation was complicated further by the Conservative victories in the May 1978 local elections as the control of the AMA moved from Labour to Conservative. By the end of June the Conservative ACC Education Committee had accepted the Oakes Report largely because it feared the alternative recoupment scheme favoured by some metropolitan authorities would be detrimental to its members' financial interests. On the other hand, the now Conservative-controlled Education Committee of the AMA rejected Oakes partly because it was concerned about the funding arrangements but mainly because it felt that local authority autonomy was threatened by the proposed national body. Meanwhile, in Parliament some Tories, led by Keith Hampson, continued to oppose Oakes but on very different grounds from what was by this time the AMA's main stance.

It was against this background that the Labour Government had to decide its policy. By early July there were strong rumours that a bill was being prepared to implement the major recommendations of the Oakes Report.[6] This led to further party political manoeuvres. The ACC referred back its Education Committee's approval of Oakes with almost no explanation[7], and there were 'rumours that instructions were received from the Conservative hierarchy (some say Mrs. Thatcher herself) to LEA party faithfuls to block the Oakes proposals being implemented before the general election'.[8] There was, with little doubt, a Conservative desire to create as much difficulty as possible for the Government in the pre-election period, and there was also genuine opposition to the Oakes proposals.

When the Government published its Education Bill later in the year, it included clauses to set up advanced further education councils in England

and Wales on Oakes lines. Detail in the Bill was kept to a minimum, and contentious issues such as membership and constitution were left for the Secretary of State to settle later. Conservatives in the Commons continued to attack the Government's proposals vigorously and claimed that the new bodies would lead to 'time-wasting, bureaucracy and inefficiency',[9] but the local authority associations tempered their opposition considerably as certain concessions were made by the Government to their viewpoints.[10] When the clause in the Education Bill relating to the advanced further education councils was debated by a Standing Committee of the House of Commons the discussion, if not the voting, cut across party lines. Keith Hampson persisted in his opposition to Oakes and continued to advocate a national body which took responsibility from the local education authorities for a relatively small number (about thirty) of selected institutions of higher education. In contrast, William Van Straubenzee, the former Conservative Minister of State, expressed some support for the Oakes Report and argued that a future Tory government would have to think very carefully before it weakened local authority involvement in higher education. Labour members generally supported the clause but Gerald Fowler admitted that he had considerable sympathy for Hampson's idea but would prefer the new national body to control ninety, rather than thirty, institutions. Voting on the clause was on party lines with the Liberal member supporting the Conservatives. This led to a tie, but the Labour Chairwoman cast her vote in favour of the Government. All this was to no avail, however, as a few days later the Education Bill was dropped because of the 1979 general election.

The return of the Thatcher Government in May 1979 led to changes in policy. The plans to implement the Oakes Report were suspended, although the new Secretary of State, Mark Carlisle, indicated that the concept of creating a national body had not been totally abandoned.[11] For the moment, in line with the new Government's general attempt to exert greater control over public expenditure, efforts were concentrated on 'capping' the advanced further education pool. This was implemented in the Education Act of 1980. Each LEA remained free to spend what it wished on higher education, but from 1980–81 the amount of its poolable expenditure was no longer open-ended, but controlled and pre-determined.[12] This important change was not opposed by the major interest groups, but the local authorities, the Society of Education Officers and NATFHE, *inter alia*, maintained that this should be regarded as an interim measure and should be seen as the precursor of more radical changes in the control and funding of local authority higher education.

In October 1980 a Commons Select Committee chaired by Labour member, Christopher Price, reported on *The Funding and Organisation of Courses in Higher Education*.[13] The Committee was critical of the DES in several respects, and, moreover, recommended the setting up of a new national Committee for Colleges and Polytechnics which was to advise the Government about the finance, administration and planning of maintained advanced further education. It proposed that this new Committee and the UGC should have a joint secretariat. At about the same time there was major reorganization within the DES and the responsibilities of senior civil servants were changed. Richard Bird took over as the Deputy Secretary for Higher Education, and the local authority sector of higher education became the particular responsibility of Assistant Secretary Stephen Jones who worked in John Thompson's Further and Higher Education Branch 1. With hindsight it is clear that Stephen Jones set out almost immediately to devise a plan for a new national body for the polytechnics and colleges.

In the Jones scheme, unlike Oakes, the proposed national body was to oversee institutions rather than courses. Jones envisaged that ninety-eight institutions, including sixty-seven currently controlled by LEAs, would come under its auspices. There were also radical proposals that funding should flow from central government via the national body to the polytechnics and colleges, and that local government ownership and control of these institutions should cease. Rumours of this scheme were leaked in late January 1981, and then in early February a detailed memorandum on the subject from Mark Carlisle to fellow ministers was printed in *The Times Higher Educational Supplement*. This confirmed the rumours and also under-lined that the scheme was seen as a means to contract and rationalize the non-university sector in the 1980s. Carlisle claimed that there was so much mutual disenchantment between LEAs and their major institutions that the effectiveness of the system was being seriously undermined, and he was also convinced that LEAs could not manage the required contraction efficiently.[14]

The local authority associations, which had not been consulted about these DES proposals, reacted forcefully to these disclosures. Strong opposition from the now Labour controlled AMA was predictable[15], but the Conservative ACC's response was only marginally less hostile.[16] Behind the scenes the proposals began to run into difficulties. It was reported that, although the Treasury was in favour, other departments were sceptical about the scheme's potential cost-effcctiveness.[17] Eventually Cabinet Committe H, chaired by William Whitelaw, failed to reach agreement about the scheme, and Mark Carlisle was only given permission to prepare a consultative document on the subject.[18] It is likely that the opposition of the Conservative local authorities influenced the Cabinet Committee's deliberations. For a short time the local authority associations were so incensed with the DES that further discussions were suspended, but at a private meeting between Carlisle and Conservative local education authority leaders it was agreed that

CLEA could put forward its own proposals.[19] CLEA moved quickly and soon came up with proposals which were similar to those submitted in 1975. The local authority stake in higher education was to be preserved, and, although principals, teachers, industry and commerce were to be represented on a new national body, the majority of the membership was to be drawn from the local authorities. The national body was to cover all non-university higher education and was not to be restricted to selected institutions as in the Jones scheme. On numerous occasions in the 1970s the DES and the local authorities had squared up it this way, and the two parties seemed set for yet another stalemate.

By May Carlisle was under conflicting pressures with the Conservative Party's National Advisory Committee on Education strongly supporting the local authority associations and his senior civil servants still advising him to proceed with their plans to take higher education institutions out of local authority control. DES civil servants doubted whether the local authorities would be able to implement the necessary rationalization and contraction. On the other hand, it was becoming increasingly clear that it would be difficult to remove the legal ownership of local government premises if the local authorities resisted. Private meetings between the DES and CLEA in May and early June 1981 seemed to be making progress and compromise looked more likely, but hopes were dashed in July when CLEA argued that the discussion in the DES's consultative document[20] did not do justice to the local authorities' case.[21] The consultative document set out two alternative models for a national body. Model A was based on the CLEA proposals, and was soon supported by NATFHE. Model B was a restatement of the DES scheme leaked in January, and this received support from the CDP and the APT. No intermediate positions were offered or considered in the document, and the situation remained polarized.

During September a new team of ministers took over at the DES. Sir Keith Joseph succeeded Mark Carlisle as Secretary of State, and William Waldergrave became the Under-Secretary in charge of Higher Education. Waldergrave has acknowledged that the new ministers saw the question of a new national body for local authority higher education as urgent and that they wanted 'to move very fast towards the construction of an interim planning structure'.[22] The Conservative Party, eager to avoid 'the spectre of further in-fighting between Conservative ministers and councillors'[23] also took the issue seriously. A high-powered working party of the Conservative National Advisory Committee on Education, which included Sir William Van Straubenzee (a former Minister of State), Keith Hampson (a former shadow minister) and two former leaders of CLEA, Angela Rumbold and John Morrell, set about trying to find a compromise solution. Of these important figures only Hampson had much sympathy for Model B, and by October the DES had abandoned its earlier leaked proposals and was embracing interim arrangements which were much closer to CLEA's Model A scheme.[24] The local authorities were jubilant, and Christopher Price, the former Labour Chairman of the Select Committee, interpreted this outcome as a victory for a CLEA alliance of cities and countryside over DES civil servants.[25] This was certainly a valid explanation, but it could have been expressed rather more starkly. In many ways the need to preserve Conservative Party unity had prevailed over a scheme which, albeit in different guises, senior DES civil servants had been pushing for over a decade.

The deal negotiated between ministers and leaders of CLEA has in practice proved longer lasting than the interim arrangements at first envisaged. It should be seen in the context of 'current resource constraints and movements of student numbers',[26] and coping with such problems was acknowledged to be one of the primary purposes of the new machinery. A three-tier structure was created consisting of (a) A Committee for Local Authority Higher Education; (b) A Board for Local Authority Higher Education; and (c) *Ad hoc* groups of appropriate interests to examine particular academic areas and subjects and to report to the Board. The Committee was to be composed of the Under-Secretary of State, William Waldergrave, the independent Chairman of the Board — later Christopher Ball was appointed to this office by the Secretary of State — and three representatives each from the ACC and the AMA. The Board consisted of its independent Chairman, six representatives from the DES, three each from the ACC and the AMA, two each from CDP and NATFHE, one each from the Association of Principals of Colleges, the Standing Conference of Principals and Directors of Colleges and Institutes of Higher Education, CNAA, the Business/Technician Education Council and the Trades Union Congress. One observer from each of the UGC, the CBI and the Welsh Joint Education Committee were also to attend. A small secretariat was to be appointed to serve both the Committee and the Board. It was envisaged that the new machinery would consider different subject areas in turn commencing with fields which required the most urgent attention. The CDP and the college principals were concerned about the new structure, and they argued that, with twelve out of the twenty-one representatives from the DES and local authorities, the Board lacked academic credibility.[27] Some support for this view was gained from CNAA, CVCP and other groups, and even Christopher Ball expressed some sympathy for it.[28] Despite their reservations, the directors and principals eventually agreed to participate, and the National Advisory Body, as the new machinery was soon rechristened, held its first meeting early in 1982. At last new national machinery to monitor, control and develop the local authority sector of higher education had emerged.

The problems which have faced NAB in the 1980s have been those which have dogged the English educational system generally. Existing and projected demographic trends have caused difficulties as has the continued economic decline of the nation. These factors have been exacerbated by the political and ideological commitment of the elected government to reduce real levels of public expenditure. Between 1972 and 1980 there was a small decline in full-time course enrolments to public sector institutions. This general trend masked a sharp fall in initial teacher training courses and increases in other areas. During the same period enrolments to part-time courses increased by fifty per cent. Since 1980 important changes have taken place and annual full-time enrolments have increased considerably and at a faster rate than their part-time counterparts. During the 1980s this much increased full-time recruitment has taken place against a background of dwindling real resources for the institutions providing the places. In its 1984–5 planning exercise, NAB, led by Christopher Ball, was not prepared to rule out lowering the unit of resource so that more students could be accommodated and access to higher education preserved. NATFHE and CDP were opposed to this and argued forcefully that the standards of education provided would suffer. NAB continued to put pressure on the Secretary of State, Sir Keith Joseph, to provide funds to top up the AFE pool and eventually was successful in obtaining most, but not all, it had requested. The threatened crisis for 1984–5 was averted, but the basic tension between available funding and potential student numbers remained.

NAB considered a number of ways in which money could be saved in the longer term. As early as 1982 Christopher Ball came out strongly in favour of new two year vocationally orientated sub-degree courses.[29] This notion disturbed some members of NAB, particularly those who represented the AMA and the teachers. Ball indicated that 'there might be a case for replacing a large number of three year degree courses with two year diplomas'.[30] This brought swift negative reactions from CDP, NATFHE and individual institutions, principals and teachers. NATFHE and the local authority associations were also firmly opposed to related proposals for two year degree courses particularly if such awards were confined to only one side of the binary line. CNAA was prepared to contemplate two year degrees as long as they received proper financial support, were related to existing qualifications and, above all, were available on both sides of the binary line. Sir Keith Joseph was much more sympathetic, and he encouraged NAB to question 'traditional assumptions'.[31] Ball retained his interests in changes on these lines, but in its 1984 publication, *A Strategy for Higher Education in the late 1980s and Beyond*, NAB set out the cases both for and against these kinds of development. In general NAB accepted 'the arguments against a general move to a two year degree pattern',[32] but claimed 'at the margin there are students on first degree courses in both universities and public sector institutions who would have been better suited to higher national diploma courses'.[33] It concluded that 'a small shift in the balance of provision between first degree and higher national diploma courses in the system as a whole may be warranted.'[34] These were modest proposals compared with those mooted two years earlier, and it is clear that NAB, as a whole, took a less radical line on this issue than the chairman of its Board. More recently, Ball has produced a personal paper on student support which would encourage 'dramatic growth in two year diploma courses at the expense of degrees'.[35] Under this scheme students would receive a full grant for two years to follow diploma courses, but those who wanted to continue for a further year to complete a degree would have to look elsewhere for the necessary financial assistance. Although this paper was produced independently of NAB, it has been submitted to the DES. This issue remains a live one, and, on past evidence over a considerable period, there are those in the DES who will welcome Ball's ideas.

The major way in which NAB has sought to make savings has been through the shedding of 'uneconomic' units and through the further concentration of advanced work. Isolated advanced courses in predominantly non-advanced further education institutions have come under particular pressure, and whole higher education institutions (as well as courses and departments) have been threatened with closure. During NAB's 1984–5 planning exercise, for example, six colleges were mentioned as likely candidates for closure or amalgamation. As soon as plans for individual institutions under threat are made known, vigorous local and national campaigns are normally conducted by the colleges concerned to justify their continued existence. Such campaigns form part of a period of uncertainty in which the various interest groups try to arouse public support for their cause and at the same time engage in relatively private 'horse-trading' with the other groups involved including NAB and the DES. In practice, some schemes are dropped, some are amended and others are implemented relatively unscathed. It would take much too long to catalogue the complexities of individual case histories here, but there are already a number of interesting accounts of power struggles and policy-making in education to be written from this area. As DES and NAB continue to attach considerable importance to 'economies of scale', it seems certain that further concentration of advanced work will take place and that the fears of closure which have troubled institutions, particularly smaller ones, in the 1970s and 1980s will not be removed in the foreseeable future.

In 1984 NAB came out strongly in favour of at least steady funding for its sector of higher education. It stressed that reductions in the unit of resource in the 1980s had led to 'serious misgivings about the maintenance of standards'[36], and it firmly rejected government suggestions that further reductions could be made. NAB claimed that there was 'a significant gap in unit costs for teaching purposes between the universities and the public sector'.[37] It concluded, 'Our concern must be adequate funding for our sector: adequacy and equity, not equivalence for its own sake. But we can see no good reason for the discrepancy in the inter-sectoral allocation of public funds, and believe that the principle of similar funding for similar work should be applied across the binary line.'[38] It was reported that DES representatives on NAB's Board did not want these claims for parity included in the report, and that they questioned 'why it was wrong if the public sector was cheaper'.[39] NAB, however, was soon under pressure to allow the unit of resource to fall again so that student access to higher education could be preserved. Eventually, led by Minister Peter Brooke and Chairman Christopher Ball, NAB voted by a slim majority to keep student numbers at their existing level and sacrifice the unit of resource.[40] This decision infuriated the CDP representative and caused consternation amongst several other members. NAB had asked the Government for extra funds to be allocated to the pool for 1986–7 but received no response. NAB's secretary, John Bevan, warned that if nothing was done for 1987–8 12,000 students could be left without places.[41] This brought a response from Sir Keith Joseph who offered some extra funds but insufficient (in NAB's view) to preserve the unit of resource and meet projected student demand. The Secretary of State blamed the difficult situation on the level of pay rises which lecturers had received.[42] NAB has agreed that it will protect the unit of resource in 1987–8, but it will come under increasing pressure to accommodate more students. As an election approaches the Government, with its new Secretary of State Kenneth Baker, may also be persuaded to allocate more money. These questions remain unresolved, but seem to form part of a never-ending saga.

The origins, functions and composition of NAB have inevitably made it one of the focal points for the many tensions in contemporary higher education. Its relations with the DES have proved of considerable interest and importance. The running battles over student numbers and funding which have repeatedly put NAB into 'an impossible dilemma of having to choose between quality and access'[13] have been the major sources of tension, but they have not been the only ones. When NAB's Committee decided to distribute its small new allocation of research money thinly between thirty-six institutions, Sir Keith Joseph told it to think again and, in effcct, insisted that NAB's Board's recommendation that the funds should be more selectively concentrated on twenty-one institutions (all but one polytechnics) was implemented. There have also been several sharp differences of view over the fate of individual institutions and departments. Finally, when NAB failed to produce a review of teacher training places as quickly as Sir Keith Joseph required, this task was immediately transferred to the DES itself. By the end of 1985 NAB's dealings with Sir Keith were decidedly frosty. NAB's secretary, John Bevan, was open about the rift and its nature: 'The issue is not just one thing or even a list of things it is our relationship with the Secretary of State in offering advice on how most effectively to plan higher education.'[44] NAB knew that on several crucial issues its advice went unheeded. Soon Sir Keith attended a meeting of the NAB Committee taking the opportunity to reassure 'its membership of local politicians of its value to him'.[45] NAB remained far from mollified, and the stresses were hardly lessened by unconfirmed press reports[46] that the DES was yet again considering plans to take over direct control of the funding of polytechnics and colleges. Historical forces put considerable strains on the relations between NAB and DES from the outset, but the degree of hostility registered during the mid 1980s threatened the stability of existing arrangements. Kenneth Baker and his civil servants have to decide urgently between mending fences and resurrecting the DES's old but favoured schemes for funding this sector of education.

Notes

1   *THES*, 28 October 1977.
2   *Education*, 3 March 1978.
3   *Ibid.*, 24 March 1978.
4   *THES*, 23 December 1977.
5   *Education*, 21 April 1978.
6   *THES*, 7 July 1978.
7   *Education*, 4 August 1978.
8   *Ibid.*
9   *THES*, 10 and 17 November 1978.
10   *THES*, 17 November 1978.
11   House of Commons, Education, Science and Arts Committee, *The Funding and Organisation of Courses in Higher Education*, Volume II, (September 1980), Evidence of M CARLISLE, Q 1212.
12   *Ibid.*, Memorandum by DES, p. 2.
13   *Ibid.*, Volume 1.
14   *THES*, 6 February 1981.
15   *The Guardian*, 13 February 1981.
16   *THES*, 20 February 1981.
17   *THES*, 13 February 1981.
18   *THES*, 20 February 1981.
19   *The Guardian*, 19 March 1981.

20 DES, *Higher Education in England outside the Universities: Policy, Funding and Management*, (July 1981).
21 *THES*, 10 July 1981.
22 *Education*, 18–25 December 1981.
23 *THES*, 25 September 1981.
24 *THES*, 16 October 1981, *Education*, 16 October 1981.
25 *Education*, 16 October 1981.
26 DES, *Arrangements for the Management of Local Authority Higher Education in England*, 20 November 1981.
27 *THES*, 18 December 1981.
28 *Ibid.*
29 *The Guardian*, 29, 30 October and 11 November 1982.
30 *Education*, 24/31 December 1982.
31 *Education*, 21 January 1983.
32 NAB, *A Strategy for Higher Education in the late 1980s and Beyond*, (September 1984), p. 16.
33 *Ibid.*
34 *Ibid.*
35 *THES*, 6 June 1986.
36 NAB, *op. cit.*, p. 30.
37 *Ibid.*, p. 38.
38 *Ibid.*
39 *Education*, 27 July 1984.
40 *Ibid.*, 15 November 1985.
41 *Ibid.*, 6 December 1985.
42 *Ibid.*, 18 April 1986.
43 *Ibid.*, 13 December 1985.
44 *Ibid.*
45 *Ibid.*, 7 March 1986.
46 *The Guardian*, 15 April 1986.

Conclusions

The creation of the local authority sector of higher education owed little to the political parties or to individual ministers. The one minor exception to this was Shirley Williams, who as Minister of State in the late 1960s, fought a successful battle for the radical reform of governing bodies. This was achieved in spite of local authority opposition and civil service scepticism, but Williams was aided in this matter by almost consistent support from Edward Boyle on the Conservative benches. In general, however, the major initiatives were made by senior civil servants at the DES. Of paramount importance were the ideas and efforts of Toby Weaver who was the Deputy Secretary in charge of further and higher education from 1963 until his retirement ten years later. Weaver was sceptical of the universities' abilities to adapt to the economic needs of the country. His experience, largely of the ancient universities, had persuaded him that these institutions were too remote from, and insufficiently geared to, future technological and business requirements. On the other hand, Weaver had genuine respect for the technical college traditions of part-time education and of courses overtly applied to industrial needs. In some respects he exaggerated the contrasts between the universities and the leading technical colleges, but it was Weaver's perceptions, rather than their more debatable accuracy, which proved of lasting importance. In the immediate post-Robbins era Weaver was increasingly concerned by what he termed the 'rat race' for university status amongst the leading technical colleges. He was convinced of the need to end this and to create a sector of higher education separate from the universities. From the outset Weaver saw advantages in a merger between the two strands (the technical and teacher training colleges) in local authority higher education. Despite considerable efforts in the 1960s he was thwarted in this aim by his Permanent Secretary, Herbert Andrew, who saw no reason to disrupt the existing arrangements in teacher training. Andrew's successor,

William Pile, was much more sympathetic, and Weaver's plans for a merger figured prominently in the 1972 White Paper.

The local education authorities, particularly through the AEC led by William Alexander, were determined to resist the Robbins plans for higher education. Above all the AEC sought to preserve the local authority stake in higher education, and, as early as 1962, even before Weaver had succeeded Anthony Part, Alexander had put forward firm proposals for an integrated local authority sector of higher education. Weaver could have had no doubts about where the influential Alexander stood on this issue, and, although it would be wrong to imply that the two men worked closely together, they adopted similar stances and worked towards the same goals. Weaver was in the key position to arrange for the major initiatives to be taken, but Alexander ably and consistently provided strong support normally taking the vast majority of AEC members with him. It is unlikely that Weaver's plans would have succeeded without the local authority support which Alexander carefully orchestrated.

It has been claimed that the main drive for the local authority sector of higher education came from the technical college teachers' union, the ATTI. This is an exaggeration. The ATTI was certainly dissatisfied with the Robbins proposals, but there were divisions in the Association about what should be done. It developed its own plans for further and higher education, but these post-dated much of the early thinking which had already taken place within the DES. In a matter of months the differences between Weaver's conceptions and those of the ATTI became glaringly obvious. The latter argued for a continuous spectrum of further and higher educational institutions, but the DES was determined as far as possible, to rationalize advanced courses into selected institutions. In the long term the DES largely had its way. The other teachers' union involved in this area of education was the ATCDE. From the outset it found itself ranged against the united forces of the DES and the LEAs. At times it received some support from the universities, but this tended to be lukewarm and somewhat unreliable. By the early 1970s demographic trends and the declining economic fortunes of the nation which put a stop to educational expansion were also stacked against it. It is not easy to see what its leaders could have done to have stemmed the tide as their power base was so much more limited than those of Weaver and Alexander. In many ways it was the creation of the local authority sector of higher education which led to the demise of the ATCDE. It is difficult to avoid the conclusion that the teachers' unions played only a minor part in the evolution of the new sector.

In the early 1960s higher education was often equated with the universities, and their attitude towards the emergence of a new sector of higher education was a considerable importance. At first many universities failed to appreciate the real significance of the setting up of CNAA, but the initiatives of 1965 and early 1966 made the position clearer. Some university people saw the polytechnics as a potential threat, but others felt that these new institutions had much to offer. They could cope with the increasing demand for higher education places and they could attend to the fluctuating educational requirements of a changing economy. Some, including John Wolfenden, Chairman of the UGC, believed that the development of the polytechnics could offer the universities some protection from pressing national needs and would allow them to perform their established roles in their traditional ways without too many changes. They took the view that the polytechnics would offer first, probably ordinary, degree courses alongside non-advanced work, and would, thus, permit the universities to concentrate on honours, postgraduate and research work. Within the universities, the institutes of education perceived correctly that they were in the most immediate danger. The demise of the institutes, although irritating to some universities, hardly posed a threat to the system as a whole. The universities were originally divided in their attitudes to the new sector, and, although some doubts were expressed in 1966 about the nature of local authority higher education, counter-proposals were never put forward. University leaders realized that it was unrealistic to oppose schemes advocated strongly by the DES when it had support from both the major political parties and the LEAs. In addition, there were those in the universities who believed that this development could save the universities from further, and to some minds unwanted, expansion and disruption. On the other hand, some universities put up a considerable struggle to keep their stake in teacher training, and, although some important concessions were gained in the early 1970s, Weaver largely succeeded in merging the local authority colleges of education into the new sector of higher education.

Devising machinery to control, manage and fund local authority higher education proved an almost intractable problem. The issue consistently opened up broader questions of educational finance and local government autonomy. Local authorities with their own institutions of higher education have almost always taken considerable pride in them and they have fought to retain control of them. As early as the 1960s, however, the local authority associations, on this issue led by Kathleen Ollerenshaw, became more and more concerned about the increasing costs of this expanding sector which, through the pooling system, was taking an ever-growing proportion of local authority education budgets. DES civil servants shared these misgivings, and had no doubt that the answer to controlling expenditure lay in better national coordination and the rationalization of provisions. From the early

1970s the DES urged the local authorities to cooperate in the setting up of a national committee to control the polytechnics, but the local authorities were convinced that such a scheme would lead sooner or later to the replacement of local authority higher education by a new sector under central control. They countered the DES by producing proposals of their own which ensured local authority predominance in new structures. This stalemate continued for about a decade, and polarized conflicts, with considerable feeling on either side, were played out in 1970–1, 1973 and 1981. Although DES mandarins and local authority association leaders had worked in harmony to create the local authority sector of higher education, they could not agree about who should run it or on what principles it should be operated. The basic interests of the two parties and their fundamental differences were exposed again and again during this struggle. The local authorities had always and inevitably regarded local influence and control of paramount importance, but the DES, especially Toby Weaver, had been primarily interested in developing a viable alternative sector of higher education to the universities. The local authorities often wanted to find common ground between their higher and further education provisions, but the DES normally maintained that concentration of scarce resources demanded the selection and development of specialist higher educational institutions. There can be little doubt that the DES increasingly saw local authority control itself as an important barrier to effective coordination and greater rationalization, and the evidence of the 1970s and the leaks of 1981 clearly show that senior civil servants were prepared to contemplate the abolition of the local authority sector.

When in the early 1980s DES civil servants and local authority administrators failed yet again to find agreement about their respective roles in local authority higher education, Conservative politicians, both national and local, became involved in finding a solution. The press leaks of 1981 forced the pace as one of their most immediate consequences was to show that some leading Conservatives supported DES civil servants and others the local authorities. Party unity was reestablished by the decision to set up the National Advisory Body. This solution preserved the local authority stake in higher education and gave them what they wanted. It is too early yet to attempt to assess NAB's work. In some respects it was surprising that the local authorities won a victory in 1981. Despite its non-interventionist ideology, the Thatcher Government has been no friend to local autonomy as its changes in local government finance have clearly illustrated. NAB, however, must be acutely aware of the climate in which it operates, and, if it fails to deliver sufficient 'rationalization' it can expect the civil servants' long-lasting plans for local authority higher education to be resurrected. In the

1960s and early 1970s DES mandarins largely created the local authority sector of higher education. Will they eventually take it over and run it themselves? In the context of the 1980s and 1990s will the party politicians let them? These remain open questions.

Index